NUCLEAR NON-PROLIFERATION AND GLOBAL SECURITY

Nuclear Non-Proliferation and Global Security

Edited by
DAVID B. DEWITT

ST. MARTIN'S PRESS
New York

Library of Congress Cataloging-in-Publication Data

Nuclear non-proliferation and global security.
   Original drafts of chapters were presented at the
Conference on Global Security and the Future of the
Non-Proliferation Treaty, York University, May 1985.
   Bibliography: p.
   Includes index.
   1. Nuclear nonproliferation. 2. Security, International.
1. Dewitt, David B. (David Brian), 1948-
II. Conference on Global Security and the Future of the
Non-Proliferation Treaty (1985: York University)
JX1974.73.N77 1987   327.1'74   86-21004
ISBN 0-312-00367-6

CONTENTS

PREFACE

David B. Dewitt
York University

Article VIII (3) of the Treaty on the Non-Proliferation of Nuclear Weapons establishes the principle of convening, at five-year intervals, 'a conference of Parties to the Treaty . . . in order to review the operation of this Treaty with a view to assuring that the purposes of the Preamble and the provisions of the Treaty are being realized'. The Third Review Conference was held in Geneva in the fall of 1985, a culmination of three sets of preparatory meetings convened during the preceding months. The continued frustrations over the perceived lack of movement on Article VI, the recurring uncertainties regarding aspects of Article IV, and the less than satisfactory conclusion to the Second Review Conference did not augur well for the 1985 review. Yet the intensive preparation by states party to the treaty was in itself evidence of their commitment to the principles and process embodied in the treaty and of the concern over the continued pursuit of its objectives.

The underlying theme of the NPT must be viewed in the context of the changing global environment and, in particular, the issue of global security. Although the early years of the United Nations heard expressions of hope that nationalism would give way to internationalism and a global society, the ensuing 40 years has witnessed the tripling of the number of sovereign states and a concomitant collision of state interests. This proliferation of actors has brought with it the need to regulate the complex network of state interactions, confirming the importance of international organisations and institutions. Yet the dilemma of state security in the face of competition and conflict continues to undermine the viability of a working system of co-operative global management. Nuclear technology, because of its double-edged capability, exacerbates this security dilemma and, at the same time, makes security a global rather than merely a state problem.

The acquiring of nuclear technology occurs for a wide range of socio-economic, political and security reasons, and has repercussions

well beyond any country's borders. Given the difficulties associated
with controlling the impact of nuclear technologies, the most benign
act may have counter-intuitive or unintended consequences, from
environmental degradation due to nuclear waste management difficulties to economic dislocations due to altered energy costs to border tensions as a result of perceived potential military threat. It is in
the intrinsic quality of nuclear technology that uncertainty accom-
panies any and every development. The critical question is the
resilience of the system; that is, the extent to which a change in the
environment is perceived to threaten the viability, continuity and
internal integrity of the system. For example, another nuclear reactor brought on-line in the United States would not be seen by leaders
in a contiguous country as threatening to either their security or ecology; nor would the deployment of another nuclear missile. However,
the introduction of new or additional nuclear technologies to any
region of the world save North America and Europe would be suspect, if not perceived as overtly threatening. The majority of states
have a rather low tolerance for ambiguity and the ensuing uncertainty breeds fear, mistrust and insecurity. The irony is that until recently
such countries had little capacity for responding to this situation,
yet as this capacity emerges the envelope of uncertainty widens.

The spread of nuclear technology in a state-centric world of
inequality will necessarily foster competition and threaten security.
It is not simply the horizontal proliferation of nuclear weapons
which may be destabilising, but a combination of the ambiguity of
technological capacity coupled with the rate of growth. Studies in
ecology and general systems suggest that there exist stable plateaus
in growth curves and that it is during the process of transition from
one plateau to another that controlled change is most difficult and
dangerous. Hence, the argument for or against proliferation may
miss the point. Rather, given the likely continued transfer of technology,
under what conditions can peaks of instability be avoided or their
effects contained?

This question has at least two parts. First, and most distressing, is
the unresolved issue of nuclear weapons stability. Not unlike the
classic post-1945 debate over whether bipolarity or multipolarity
was more likely to ensure peace (that is, stability as it is used here),
the preferred position of many, and certainly of the five nuclear-
weapon states, is fewer (nuclear-weapon states, not nuclear weapons)
is better. The conservative bias in this is obvious, but so too is the
genuine belief that more independent nuclear arsenals increase the

chances for both purposeful and accidental use. On the other hand, sound albeit hypothetical arguments exist which support the stabilising effect of controlled horizontal proliferation among regional powers, for the same regionally focused logic that exists between NATO and the Warsaw Treaty Organisation. Once established, this too would become a conservative, status-quo position, not only enhancing the established powers but conserving the integrity of the intra-regional structure. In this scenario, the danger is both getting there and, once having arrived, re-establishing a new non-proliferation 'regime' which effectively reintroduces the fundamental bargain between eschewing nuclear weapons and getting access to nuclear materials and technologies for peaceful purposes.

The second part of the question focuses on the ambiguity and ensuing uncertainty of non-weapon nuclear capability. This is more difficult because it is less easily defined than weapons development, accumulation and deployment, it is more diffuse in its socio-economic and political impact, and it is extraordinarily difficult to control and monitor throughout the cycles of materials and technology supply, development, production, output and waste management. Declared or implied intent, along with the internal integrity and longevity of the regime, becomes an underlying factor in threat assessment. Given the socio-economic and political imperatives for development, enhanced economic capabilities and political stature, and state security from both internal and external threat, non-weapon nuclear transfers and developments are both more likely to occur and to be inherently unsettling. While overt nuclear weapons proliferation may be dangerous, if it occurs it is more likely to be controlled and constrained. The greater difficulty lies with the non-verifiable products which can emerge from the more diffuse pattern of general nuclear technology transfers and development, exacerbated by the competition, conflict and enmity which exists between unequal actors in the global community. The Treaty on the Non-Proliferation of Nuclear Weapons is a major effort to facilitate progress in reducing ambiguity, alleviating the fears inherent in uncertainty and establishing a practical system of regulation which, over time, is meant to engender trust if not amity between states.

Of course, it is just such situations which pose the greatest problems for statesmen. In a world of sovereign states, each competing for the scarce resources demanded by societal needs and aspirations, is trust good enough? As in much of the classic writing, the answer must be no; but in the nuclear age, the no has a twist. Nuclear politics demands risk-taking in order to avoid a catastrophic garrison mentality, but the cost of being wrong – that is, in trusting a potential adversary's declared benign intent when in fact the opposite occurs – undermines any sense of generosity. This dilemma of the hypothetical, to use Wolfe Haefele's term of a decade ago, is insurmountable with any degree of certainty. Treaties (the NPT) and regulatory or supervisory instruments (review conferences, the IAEA) are open to unilateral abrogation, subversion and duplicity. Although there is, as yet, no technological fix which can overcome human ingenuity in pursuit of specific goals, treaties and instruments do offer a practical middle ground to anarchical order on the one hand and world government on the other. In spite of all the obvious problems attendant to treaty enforcement between unequal partners, the benefits probably outweigh the costs since uncertainty and ambiguity exist with or without treaties.

The following chapters address these and other issues concerning the problems of horizontal nuclear proliferation and global security. They provide the reader with breadth sufficient to introduce, if not cover, the central challenges facing a nuclearised world, with a depth of understanding possible only when you bring together leading policy-makers, scholars and representatives of the nuclear industries. These chapters cannot be comprehensive, but they definitely are insightful, challenging and authoritative. They also are troubling because they underline the continued realities of power and state self-interest in the face of the vexing set of problems posed by the confrontation between interdependence, inequality and the asymmetries of needs, demands and capabilities. Originally drafted between the conclusion of the preparatory committee meetings and the Third Review Conference and then selectively revised after the conclusion of the September meeting, these chapters reflect a sober and, at times, optimistic assessment of the role of the NPT (and IAEA) in harnessing nuclear technology for the betterment of mankind without undermining global security. But they also make clear the need to confront situations as they are, not as we might wish them to be. Hence, the anarchic qualities of the inter-state system, fostered by the continued need for governments to guarantee state security, will continue to challenge the most hopeful among us. The results of the Third Review Conference give one confidence in the process, however slow and tortuous, while reinforcing the need for continued multilateral efforts at addressing the twin dilemmas of the distribution of security and the security of distribution. It is unlikely that one can be resolved in isolation from the other.

ACKNOWLEDGEMENTS

The original drafts of these chapters, save for the retrospective of the Third Review Conference, were presented at the Conference on Global Security and the Future of the Non-Proliferation Treaty: A Time for Reassessment, at York University, Toronto, in May 1985. On behalf of the York University Research Programme in Strategic Studies, sponsor of the meeting, I would like to acknowledge the financial assistance provided for the conference and this publication by: the Department of External Affairs, Arms Control and Disarmament Division; the Department of National Defence, Military and Strategic Studies Programme; the Social Sciences and Humanities Research Council of Canada; The Donner Canadian Foundation; and the Offices of the President and the Dean of Arts, York University. My personal thanks to Kirsten Semple for her secretarial assistance during the conference preparation, to Elaine Holoboff for preparing the first drafts of the glossary and index, and to Michael Slack for his superb organisational and administrative skills. A special note of appreciation to Marianne Weide for both secretarial and editorial assistance and in the preparation of the final manuscript.

I would be remiss if I did not add the traditional comment concerning author responsibilities. In this case it is a pleasure to record the degree of co-operation I received from each contributor. This is particularly noteworthy since a number of them are senior representatives of their countries on nuclear non-proliferation and/or arms control and disarmament, and as such subject to both time and content constraints. Contributions reflect the opinions and analyses of the authors and not the governments, institutions or firms to which they are or have been associated. While each is ultimately responsible for the content of his specific contribution, I bear the overall responsibility for the organisation and content of the volume. My decision not to be an overly interventionist editor reflects my belief that when analysis is so often intertwined with policy prescription, each author should be allowed full room for expression. I have tried to ensure consistency of style and structure throughout the book.

On behalf of authors and readers alike, I must add a final note of appreciation to the 50 or so participants in the York University conference. The penetrating and oftentimes heated debate contributed in varying measure to the revision process and ultimately to the content of each of the chapters to which you now turn.

David B. Dewitt
York University
Toronto, Canada
March 1986

I.
GLOBAL SECURITY AND THE TREATY ON THE
NON-PROLIFERATION OF NUCLEAR WEAPONS:
THE AGENDA

THE THIRD NPT REVIEW CONFERENCE: ISSUES AND PROSPECTS

M.I. Shaker

In September 1985 the Third Review Conference on the Treaty on the Non-Proliferation of Nuclear Weapons (NPT) convened in Geneva. It was another opportunity for the parties to the treaty to review its operation with a view to ensuring that the purposes of the preamble and the provisions of the treaty are being realised. In our view, any assessment of the implementation of the treaty should be based on the five principles upon which the treaty itself had to be negotiated and concluded. These principles were the result of the efforts of a number of non-aligned states in 1965 and were adopted by the General Assembly of the United Nations that year. Three of these principles whose relevance is topical in the present context ought to be reiterated here:

1. the treaty should embody an acceptable balance of mutual responsibilities and obligations of the nuclear and non-nuclear powers;
2. the treaty should be a step towards the achievement of general and complete disarmament and more particularly nuclear disarmament; and
3. there should be acceptable and workable provisions to ensure the effectiveness of the treaty.

Any assessment of the implementation of the treaty has, therefore, to take into consideration how far a balance is being achieved between the responsibilities and obligations of the nuclear-weapon states and the non-nuclear-weapon states, how far the treaty has contributed to disarmament and how effective the treaty has become as an instrument to prevent nuclear proliferation.

By August 1985 the NPT had been ratified and acceded to by 130 states. This number is quite impressive. It should be recalled that at the First NPT Review Conference in 1975 the parties to the treaty were only 96 states and at the Second Review Conference in 1980 they increased to 114. But how long can we be confident that this trend will continue, and that the treaty will continue to be respected by those who have committed themselves to its provisions if no progress is achieved in the field of disarmament, and if co-operation in the peaceful uses of nuclear energy does not thrive to the benefit of all states party to the treaty and more particularly the developing countries without restrictions or hindrances. Just as disarmament and co-operation in the peaceful uses of nuclear energy dominated the discussions at previous review conferences, so they dominated discussions at the review conference in September 1985.

Against the background of the failure of the Second NPT Review Conference in 1980 to reach a consensus on disarmament issues, and in view of the lack of progress so far on these issues, the implementation of Article VI of the NPT received much greater attention at the September 1985 Review Conference when compared with the implementation of Article IV on peaceful nuclear co-operation. The conference, as expected, focused on nuclear disarmament.

It is quite clear from the five principles referred to earlier and, more particularly, the three principles quoted above that more is expected from the NPT than merely prohibiting the horizontal proliferation of nuclear weapons. That is why we have come to speak of a regime of the NPT and not just a treaty. Nuclear disarmament figures prominently in this regime. As one analyst puts it so well, the treaty is 'an omnibus compact that comprehends virtually every aspect of the new nuclear crisis: proliferation, nuclear energy, development and trade, international safeguards, peaceful nuclear explosions, *testings*, the *strategic arms race*'.[1]

The nuclear arms race continues unabated. Article VI of the NPT remains to be fully implemented. Without this the treaty will be endangered. As put by Ambassador Goldberg, the United States representative to the United Nations in 1968:

> My country believes that the permanent viability of this Treaty will depend in a large measure on our success in the further negotiations contemplated in Article VI.[2]

When the First NPT Review Conference met in 1975, SALT I agreements had been signed in 1972 and SALT II agreements were being negotiated. Moreover, the Seabed Treaty prohibiting nuclear weapons on the seabed was signed in 1971, followed by the Threshold Test Ban Agreement in 1974. The international atmosphere, therefore, was encouraging and conducive to making further progress on disarmament issues.

In the interval between the First and Second Review Conferences, apart from the Peaceful Nuclear Explosions (PNEs) agreement of 1976 and the SALT II agreements of 1979, there was no other major achievement in the field of disarmament. Even these agreements, along with the Threshold Test Ban Agreement, were not ratified before the 1980 NPT Review Conference and remain unratified to this date. This explains the tense atmosphere which prevailed during the 1980 conference and which led to a deadlock on reaching agreement on a Final Declaration.

As the 1985 NPT Review Conference approached, a very short time was left for the nuclear-weapon states to demonstrate their good faith in carrying out their obligations under Article VI. The critical question was: What are the disarmament measures which ought to be agreed upon in order to save the conference from failure to adopt a constructive and forward-looking Final Declaration enhancing the NPT regime?

Our view at the time was that any measure agreed upon, if it were to have a positive impact, should be in the field of nuclear disarmament. Future arms control and disarmament agreements must in the first place be related to the subject matter of the NPT, namely non-proliferation of nuclear weapons and, in this case, vertical non-proliferation.

Some argued that the ongoing Geneva negotiations between the United States and the Soviet Union indicated the seriousness and sincerity of the two superpowers in halting and reversing the nuclear arms race. These negotiations constituted an important step in this direction and created a favourable climate before the 1985 NPT Review Conference. However, in view of the intricacies of the issues which were under examination, the Geneva negotiations were not expected to yield concrete and drastic steps in the near future. It took almost seven years for SALT II agreements to be negotiated. They even remain unratified. Moreover, SALT I agreements and more particularly the Anti-Ballistic Missile Treaty (ABM), are being put to the test as a result of the United States Strategic Defense Initiative.

Against this background and apart from the necessity to honour the aforementioned unratified agreements, a comprehensive test ban would have been the ideal gift to the review conference. The political will to go ahead with such a measure is still lacking. When the Partial Test Ban Treaty of August 1963 was signed, it was apparent that certain tests in the three environments covered by the treaty (that is, the atmosphere, outer space and under water) could be carried out without being detected, but were considered to be too insignificant if they ever took place to have any effect on the military balance between the two superpowers. The political wills of the superpowers in 1963 overcame the technical hurdles. Why could it not be displayed once more?

The only alternative that was hoped for prior to the convening of the 1985 Review Conference was to agree on a moratorium on nuclear testing for a fixed but renewable duration. This certainly would have had a positive impact on the conference and would have facilitated its proceedings. Non-nuclear-weapon states party to the NPT are living up to their obligations under the treaty. They are committed to the NPT because it is to their national interest to do so. But they would also wish to see some substantive progress on nuclear disarmament to justify their continued affiliation with the treaty. With a moratorium this continued affiliation with the treaty would have been greatly enhanced.

A test ban is both a vertical and a horizontal non-proliferation measure. It would have a positive influence on a number of non-nuclear-weapon states not party to the NPT and/but interested in or contemplating the creation of nuclear-weapon free zones. For example, Brazil and Argentina, who are signatories to the 1967 Treaty of Tlatelolco but not yet full parties to the treaty, are urging the conclusion of a comprehensive test ban. Pakistan is sponsoring the idea of creating a nuclear-weapon-free zone in South East Asia. The advantages of the establishment of such zones need not be stressed in this context. Suffice it to say that they will enhance and bolster the NPT regime.

With regard to the implementation of Article IV of the NPT, it should be noted that after long and arduous negotiations at the Second NPT Review Conference, a fragile consensus was reached on issues of nuclear supply. That consensus was re-examined and enhanced at the 1985 Review Conference in light of developments in the field of peaceful uses of nuclear energy which have taken place since 1980.

The consensus reached in 1980 contained elements still valid today. Other elements have been worked upon and developed. For example, that conference considered that effective measures could and should be taken to meet the specific needs of developing countries in the field of peaceful uses of nuclear energy. Moreover, the 1980 conference considered the importance of energy back-up mechanisms. These have been elaborated upon in 1985, but much work remains.

In its meetings in Vienna the International Atomic Energy Agency (IAEA) Committee on Assurances and Supply (CAS) made some progress on emergency and back-up mechanisms in the case of supply disruption, as well as on the mechanism for revisions of co-operation agreements. CAS is still working on, with some diffi-culties, a set of principles on international co-operation in the peace-ful uses of nuclear energy.

An important point that ought to be made is that a relaxed atmos-phere of co-operation in the field of peaceful uses of nuclear energy is essential for the survival of the non-proliferation regime. It is impor-tant to reduce and eliminate constraints on access to nuclear tech-nology and to guarantee a reliable supply of nuclear material and equipment. For a great number of states party to the NPT it is unacceptable that they should be denied access to certain tech-nologies. IAEA safeguards should dispel any fears. The decision by any state to embark on a nuclear power programme is not an easy decision to make in the absence of firm guarantees with regard to supply of nuclear material and equipment.

The NPT Review Conference would have been an ideal forum to examine the results achieved at CAS. The conference also could have been an ideal occasion to examine the idea of a fund or a programme to finance the construction of nuclear power plants to the benefit of developing countries. A number of these countries are experiencing great difficulties in raising enough funds to embark on their very first nuclear power project. In this respect, it is to be noted that the largest share of the funds administered by the IAEA is spent on activities other than energy, such as the use of radio-isotopes and radiation to increase food production or develop water resources.

It is not enough to guarantee future supply or to provide assistance in financing nuclear power projects. Of equal importance is the protection of existing nuclear facilities built with great effort and sacrifice against attack or sabotage.

In 1975 the NPT Review Conference came up with the idea of an agreement for the physical protection of nuclear material. This idea materialised in 1980. In the field of peaceful uses of nuclear energy, the 1985 conference explored new ideas which would foster inter-national co-operation to the benefit of states party to the treaty. The idea of a fund or a programme to finance the establishment of nuclear power plants is but one such idea which might bear fruit in a few years to come. At the First Review Conference in 1975 one delegate noted that if 1 per cent of the amount spent on armaments each year by the developed countries were devoted to providing nuclear grants and loans to the developing countries for power reactors and training, it would amount to more than two billion dollars a year.

Now that certain security and promotional aspects both of the NPT and its implementation, which is closely related to the 1965 principles of the balance of obligations and responsibilities and of disarmament have been examined, some attention should be focused on the principle of effectiveness, which would touch upon NPT safeguards, universality of adherence to the treaty and its adaptability to changing circumstances.

With regard to the aspect of prohibitions contained in the NPT, it is quite significant that although the IAEA is not a party to the treaty, it is very much involved in the implementation of the safeguards provisions of Article III. The acceptance of IAEA safeguards by all parties to the treaty is a unique feature of ongoing efforts in the field of arms control and disarmament. So far, the agency has been satisfied with its performance in safeguarding peaceful nuclear activities of parties to the treaty. No diversion of nuclear material from peaceful purposes to weapon purposes has been detected and reported. Another encouraging development in the field of safeguards is the acceptance by the three nuclear-weapon states party to the treaty, the United Kingdom, the Soviet Union and the United States, to submit some of their peaceful nuclear activities to international safeguards. The basic objective of this gesture by the three nuclear-weapon states is to lessen the feeling of discrimination between them and the other parties to the treaty. This is a gesture of solidarity with non-nuclear-weapon states that hoped the treaty would intrinsically contribute directly to the cessation of the nuclear arms race. This gesture may encourage in the future the acceptance and introduction of on-site verification in other arms control and disarmament agreements involving the nuclear-weapon states.

It is hoped that the IAEA will continue to improve its safeguards techniques. More sophisticated measures such as Remote Continual Verification (Recover) are under development. The latter is a secure communication system using small computers and public telephone lines to remotely verify the status of safeguards devices.

IAEA safeguards could play an important role in future arms control and disarmament agreements. The IAEA is already involved in the implementation of the Treaty of Tlatelolco establishing a nuclear-weapon-free zone in Latin America. It can play a similar role with respect to a nuclear-weapon-free zone in Africa or in the Middle East. IAEA safeguards would be quite pertinent for the implementation of a cut-off for fissionable material for weapons purposes.

The review conference was another opportunity to assess and evaluate the role of the IAEA in the implementation of Article III of the NPT. The IAEA was not only commended for its delicate and dedicated performance, but also encouraged to pursue its task with greater effectiveness.

Another facet of the effectiveness of the NPT is its provisions allowing all states without any distinction or hindrance the right to become party to it, which is not the case in a great number of other international instruments. This principle of universality has allowed 130 states to adhere to the treaty, the largest number of signatories to any arms control and disarmament agreement, reflecting a steady increase since the First NPT Review Conference from 96 in 1975 to 114 in 1980 and 130 in 1985.

On the other hand, a number of threshold countries are gaining in strength and diversity in the nuclear field. They are steadfast in rejecting the NPT for a complex set of reasons ranging from conceptual to economic and security considerations. They are not expected to adhere to the treaty unless it undergoes a basic transformation in its conceptual outlook and/or if major results were to be achieved in nuclear disarmament.

As the Third NPT Review Conference approached, there was a concerted effort exerted to encourage more states to adhere to the treaty, especially those who have signed it. Efforts also concentrated on inducing all parties to the treaty to participate in the September 1985 review process. But before discussing the participation issue, the review process and its role in enhancing the effectiveness of the NPT ought to be examined.

It is quite clear from the provisions of Article VIII (3) of the NPT that the objective of a review conference is to review the operation of the treaty with a view to assuring that the purposes of the preamble and the provisions of the treaty are being realised. However, it should be underlined that the negotiating history of Article VIII (3) clearly indicates the relevance of the review conference to the achievement of measures to halt the nuclear arms race and nuclear disarmament. This has been emphasised by the nuclear-weapon states party to the treaty. Even the word 'Preamble' in Article VIII (3) was suggested by one of the nuclear-weapon states, the United Kingdom, which then explained that

> the Preamble is . . . wider than . . . Article VI in the disarmament field and indicates in some detail what needs to be done, as well as containing an important declaration of intent to achieve at the earliest possible date the cessation of the nuclear arms race.[3]

It is, therefore, not surprising that disarmament issues had been and would continue to be the centre of attention at the review conferences.

The review conference is not an amendment conference. Article VIII (1) prescribes certain provisions for this purpose. Many delegations in the past found it important to emphasise this fact as a warning to avoid misunderstanding on the part of any of the parties to the treaty or to refute certain proposals found to imply or implicate an amendment to the treaty.

With regard to the convening of the Third NPT Review Conference, the decision to open the membership of the Preparatory Committee to all parties of the treaty, and not merely to the parties serving on the Board of Governors of the IAEA or represented at the Conference on Disarmament, was a wise step. It allowed the opportunity for more smaller states to play a role in the important preparatory phase. The opportunity was seized, and the level of participation, more particularly at the third session of the preparatory committee in April 1985, was quite impressive. At the September 1985 Review Conference, almost 90 parties participated, the largest number to date.

It should be recalled that the non-nuclear-weapon states, and more particularly small states, played an important role in the different phases which led to the NPT. Ireland played a central role in the emergence of the non-proliferation concept as adopted by the so-called 'Irish Resolution' in 1961 which the treaty adopted in 1968. Eight non-aligned members of the Eighteen-Nation Committee on Disarmament (ENCD), namely Brazil, Burma, Egypt, Ethiopia, India, Mexico, Nigeria and Sweden, were responsible for the formulation of the five principles of 1965 on the basis of which the NPT had to be negotiated. The eight members played an active role in negotiating the treaty at the ENCD. They were joined at the United Nations General Assembly by a score of other non-nuclear-weapon states. Their role continued in implementing treaty provisions, particularly in working out NPT safeguards procedures.

In the two previous review conferences, parties to the treaty – members of the Group of 77 – played a very active role. At the First Review Conference they contributed to the making of the Final Declaration adopted by the conference. At the Second Review Conference, on the one hand they contributed to the fragile consensus reached on Articles III, IV and V, and on the other hand they resisted any attempt to dilute or weaken a statement on Article VI. The group was critical of the failure of the nuclear-weapon states to live up to their obligations under this article. The confrontation on this issue led to the failure of the conference to adopt a Final Declaration.

It was important that at the Third NPT Review Conference a greater number than before of non-nuclear-weapon states participated. If the NPT regime is to become a viable one, every party should play a role in reviewing the operation of the treaty. It is an opportunity which offers itself only once every five years. Apart from the Western and Eastern groups, a group of neutral and non-aligned states (NNA) had been meeting since the first session of the Preparatory Committee of the Third Review Conference. The membership of the group has increased since 1980 and there was no doubt that it did exert great influence at the conference.

A review conference has to be a forward-looking exercise. It is difficult to disagree with the conclusions of a recent study which indicated, *inter alia*, that the review conference should be an opportunity for major progress rather than a damage-limitation exercise.[4] Fortunately, the Third Review Conference did result in rendering the treaty more attractive to the parties to it, as well as to countries pondering upon their adherence to it. In order to continue to work towards this objective, steps such as those suggested in this chapter, whether in the field of nuclear disarmament or in the field of peaceful nuclear co-operation, should be set in motion.

The results of the September 1985 Review Conference are contained in a final document which includes a substantive declaration, as was the case at the First NPT Review Conference in 1975. The abortive experience of adopting a final declaration at the Second NPT Review Conference in 1980 did not dissuade parties to the treaty from trying hard to reach an agreement on a declaration. The failure in 1980 had led some to point out that there should be no need to have a final declaration. They went on to say that if there must be a declaration, then it should not necessarily be a substantive one. This view no longer prevails and a final substantive declaration was, with some effort, largely accepted. It was inconceivable that, after three sessions of the preparatory committee over a period of one year and a review conference convening for four weeks, the conference would end up in vacuum.

The length of any declaration is irrelevant as long as it contains what the parties believe it ought to contain. This declaration may generate new ideas which may bear fruit in years to come, as was the case with the idea of a convention on physical protection of nuclear material at the review conference of 1975. In other words, it is hoped that this declaration will contribute to the bolstering of the non-proliferation regime. Progress on nuclear disarmament and on the transfer of nuclear technology, as well as on the reliability of supply of nuclear material and equipment, should strengthen the regime.

The Third Review Conference was able to reach its decisions by consensus. Nuclear-weapon states and non-nuclear-weapon states worked together in order to agree on a Final Declaration acceptable to all. In this way, the declaration has gained in strength and thus should generate a process which will bolster the NPT regime. This is mostly needed in present circumstances marked by lack of progress on nuclear disarmament and a downward trend in investing in nuclear power. In conclusion, it is hoped that this latest conference will demonstrate that the review process is a vital element in enhancing the effectiveness of the NPT and its viability.

End Notes

1. Alan Geyer, 'The Nuclear Question Explodes', *Worldview* (September 1975), p. 27.
2. United Nations, Army Control Document A/C.1/1556, para. 71.
3. Eighteen-Nation Disarmament Committee, Document ENDC/PV.358 (23 January 1968), para. 26.
4. United States (Association of the) United Nations, *Nuclear Proliferation: Toward Global Restraint*, New York (1984), p. vi.

THE NPT AND FUTURE GLOBAL SECURITY

Lewis A. Dunn

More than 40 years ago, the first test of a nuclear explosive at Alamogordo, New Mexico, on 16 July 1945 demonstrated a new weapon of unprecedented destructiveness. Throughout the ensuing decades, the community of nations has wrestled with the problem of controlling the military threat of nuclear energy while harnessing the atom for peaceful purposes.

Both bilateral and multilateral arms control and disarmament negotiations have been undertaken in an effort to eliminate eventually the threat of nuclear weapons and, in the interim, at least to achieve more stable deterrence at drastically reduced nuclear-force levels. Beginning with President Dwight D. Eisenhower's Atoms for Peace Programme of 1953, the United States, followed by other industrialised countries, has fostered peaceful nuclear co-operation around the world in areas ranging from nuclear power generation to nuclear medicine. In addition, the United States, its allies and other nations have adopted increasingly stringent measures to prevent the spread of nuclear weapons to additional countries.

Since its entry into force in March 1970, the Treaty on the Non-Proliferation of Nuclear Weapons (NPT) has been an essential part of this decades-long endeavour. Recognition of the NPT's central role in fostering a safer world, moreover, was at the heart of the successfully concluded 1985 NPT Review Conference.

Despite predictions by some observers that this third conference to review the treaty's implementation would end in deadlock and confrontation or, even worse, threatened withdrawals from the treaty, the parties engaged in a full and constructive assessment of the NPT. They adopted a consensus Final Declaration, which unequivocally reaffirmed their support for the treaty, and concluded that the NPT is essential to international peace and security.

The Treaty: Goals and Undertakings

The treaty's specific undertakings have been carefully crafted to serve its three major objectives: preventing the further spread of nuclear weapons, fostering peaceful nuclear co-operation under safeguards, and good faith negotiations on the cessation of the nuclear arms race with a view to general and complete disarmament.

The first two articles of the treaty seek to help prevent the further spread of nuclear weapons, thereby strengthening the security and well-being of all countries. Under Article I, the nuclear-weapon states party to the treaty undertake not to transfer nuclear explosives to any other state, and not to assist, in any way, non-nuclear-weapon states to manufacture or acquire such devices. In turn, under Article II, more than 125 non-nuclear-weapon states have renounced the right to seek to acquire or manufacture nuclear explosives.

Article III obligates the non-nuclear-weapon state parties to accept international safeguards administered by the International Atomic Energy Agency (IAEA). These safeguards verify the fulfilment of these states' obligations under the treaty and help to deter diversion of nuclear materials from peaceful purposes to the manufacture of nuclear explosives. Acceptance of safeguards is also an important confidence-building measure; such a demonstration by neighbouring countries of their peaceful intentions can help lessen suspicions that could trigger reciprocal steps by regional rivals to the acquisition of a nuclear explosive capability. This article also contributes to the objective of preventing proliferation by requiring safeguards on nuclear exports to non-nuclear-weapon states.

An effective safeguards system is at the same time a critical precondition for the peaceful uses of the atom promoted by Article IV. That article's objective is to facilitate the fullest possible dissemination of nuclear technology for peaceful purposes. Thus nations which forswear nuclear weapons and accept safeguards can tap the benefits of the peaceful atom. And should there be any potential benefits of nuclear explosions for peaceful purposes, these benefits are to be made available under Article V on a non-discriminatory basis to non-nuclear-weapon state parties.[1]

Article VI commits all parties to pursue negotiations in good faith on effective measures leading to the cessation of the nuclear arms race at an early date and to nuclear disarmament, and on general and complete disarmament.

The Treaty on the Non-Proliferation of Nuclear Weapons, however, is more than the sum of its particular articles. With 130 parties, the treaty also embodies a developing international norm of non-proliferation.

In the 1950s and early 1960s, it was common to find references to the 'prestige' associated with developing nuclear weapons. There also was a tendency then to regard these weapons simply as more advanced conventional arms. Indeed, in some quarters, it was feared that by the mid-1970s all countries with major military capabilities would have acquired nuclear weapons. Instead, world opinion increasingly has come to regard the acquisition of nuclear weapons as no longer legitimate, with the accompanying conviction that pursuit of a nuclear weapon capability does not enhance either a nation's prestige or security. As was evident after India's 1974 detonation of a nuclear explosive device, such a step brings opprobrium, not applause. Not least, there is a growing recognition, evidenced in the NPT, that a world of many nuclear powers is not the inevitable wave of the future.

More is Not Better

The origins of the NPT are to be found largely in the wide-spread belief that the further spread of nuclear weapons would undermine the security of all countries and threaten world order. More recently, however, it has become fashionable in some academic circles to question this belief. Critics of the 'conventional wisdom' contend that the introduction of nuclear weapons to conflict-prone regions such as South Asia and the Middle East, rather than raising the risk of local nuclear conflict, would lead to restraint on the part of regional rivals. In their view, fear of escalation to nuclear destruction would contain minor clashes and foster more basic stability – if not peace settlements – in previously conflict-prone regions. In the words of one analyst, 'more may be better'.

These views are based on a simple, and overly simplistic, extrapolation from the non-use of nuclear weapons by the United States and the Soviet Union to their future non-use in quite different circumstances. Mere extrapolation from the United States-Soviet Union context overlooks the very particular mix of geopolitical and technical factors that have ensured nuclear peace over the past decades: the presence of cautious leaders; the fact that neither national survival nor ideological purity was immediately at stake;

the lack of common borders, thereby lessening flash-points for conflict and impeding escalation; and adequate technical means to prevent accidental or unauthorised use of nuclear weapons. Without these circumstances, the fear of atomic destruction, though itself important, might not have sufficed.

The spread of nuclear weapons to conflict-prone regions is far more likely to exacerbate long-standing suspicions and tensions among rivals than to encourage the peaceful settlement of traditional disputes. Moreover, if progress towards the acquisition of nuclear weapons is asymmetrical in a region, the country in the lead may contemplate using pre-emptive military force – most likely conventional, though not necessarily so – to prevent a rival from matching its budding capabilities. Furthermore, throughout these regions, past experience has repeatedly shown the great risk that conflict or border clashes would escalate to wider conflict now with possible use of nuclear weapons. And, given the stakes of many Third World conflicts, often calling into question an opponent's legitimate claim to national survival or involving pursuit of over-arching religious-ideological goals, there is far more chance that a leader might conclude that use of nuclear weapons is warranted.

Thus in evaluating the risks of nuclear proliferation, the lingering Persian Gulf war between Iran and Iraq is a better and more appropriate model than the post-war political competition between East and West. In this war, both sides have violated international norms: Iraq has used chemical weapons, and Iran has refused to allow the Red Cross into its prisoner-of-war camps. Each side has conducted deliberate shelling and air and rocket attacks against civilians. Only the relative military weaknesses of these two countries have dampened this conflict. Few can doubt that nuclear weapons would have been used in the war if either party had such weapons. More is not better.

The First and Second NPT Review Conferences – and the Third

As provided for under the Treaty on the Non-Proliferation of Nuclear Weapons (Article VIII (3)), the parties have conducted three major multilateral reviews of the treaty's operation. In 1975 the First NPT Review Conference was marked by a full, and sometimes heated, debate over how well the treaty's goals were being met. In the end, however, the conference president, Madame Inga Thorssen of

Sweden, produced and pushed through a lengthy final report which reviewed each of the treaty articles, recommended further steps to strengthen and improve their implementation and, importantly, reaffirmed the parties' strong support for the treaty.

Debate at the Second Review Conference in 1980 was difficult and contentious. This debate centred principally on Article VI dealing with nuclear arms limitation and disarmament and, to a lesser extent, on Article IV which concerned peaceful nuclear co-operation. Despite the best efforts of a number of participants, including the United States, the 1980 conference became deadlocked and eventually concluded without producing a consensus final document. Although participants expressed wide-spread support for the treaty, this outcome was generally regarded as a 'failure' and a threat to the treaty.

The Third NPT Review Conference met for four weeks in Geneva from 27 August through to the early morning of 21 September 1985. Eighty-six of the 130 parties to the treaty participated in its work. In addition, a number of non-parties, including Algeria, Argentina, Brazil, Cuba, Israel, Pakistan and Spain, were granted observer status by the conference. There was heavy attendance by various non-governmental organisations as well.

The conference conducted its work both in plenary sessions over which presided the president of the conference, Egyptian Ambassador Mohamed Shaker, and in three main committees established by the Review Conference Preparatory Committee. The three committees dealt respectively with arms limitation and disarmament, non-proliferation and safeguards, and peaceful nuclear co-operation.

The main task of these three committees and the Third Review Conference itself was a full and honest article-by-article review of the operation of the treaty. Woven throughout that review and ensuing debate were three major questions. First, had the treaty strengthened the security of the parties by helping prevent the further spread of nuclear explosives? Second, how well had the treaty facilitated co-operation in the peaceful uses of nuclear energy, and what can realistically be done to buttress further that co-operation? Third, what had been done to bring the nuclear arms race to an end?

Strengthened Security from the NPT

Speaker after speaker during the general debate, in which parties delivered national statements, acknowledged the treaty's important contribution to international security and warned that the further spread of nuclear weapons would add to regional and global tensions and increase the risk of nuclear war. Many states called it the most important arms control agreement in history.

Moreover, in its consensus Final Declaration, the conference reiterated this strong support for the security benefits of the NPT. It noted that the non-proliferation commitments of Article I and II had been met during the period under review, greatly helping to prevent the spread of nuclear weapons.

In turn, the conference concluded that the application of IAEA safeguards on the peaceful nuclear activities of non-nuclear-weapon state parties plays a key role in preventing the proliferation of nuclear weapons and other nuclear explosive devices; promotes confidence among states by providing assurance that states are complying with their non-proliferation obligations; and, thereby, helps to strengthen international security.

Looking to those countries which had not joined the NPT, the 1985 Review Conference called for heightened co-ordination to convince them to become NPT parties. From a different tack, it declared that unsafeguarded nuclear activities in non-nuclear-weapon states pose serious proliferation dangers and urged such countries to accept IAEA safeguards on their present and future peaceful nuclear facilities (so-called comprehensive or full-scope safeguards). To that end, President Reagan previously had urged all nuclear suppliers to agree to require comprehensive safeguards in non-nuclear-weapon states as a condition for any new nuclear supply commitment. Tilting in that direction, the Final Declaration calls on the parties, 'specifically as a basis for the transfer of relevant nuclear supplies to non-nuclear-weapon States . . . to take effective steps towards achieving . . . acceptance of such safeguards by those States'.

The bottom line of the conference was clear: as many speakers noted, since 1970 only one additional country is known to have detonated a nuclear explosive device. The treaty clearly is a success in helping check the further spread of nuclear weapons, serving the security of all its parties, indeed of all countries.

Realising the Atom's Peaceful Promise

A vision of the atom as a potential promise to help countries meet their various needs in the fields of health care, medicine, science, industry and agriculture also influenced the creation of the NPT. Here, too, the Review Conference gave the treaty good marks.

Despite calls from some developing nations for greater efforts to grant access to nuclear materials and technology, there was general acknowledgement that an appreciable level of technical assistance in the area of peaceful uses had been provided both bilaterally and multilaterally. Peaceful nuclear co-operation had steadily expanded in the 15 years since 1970 when the treaty entered into force, and many developing countries party to the treaty had taken steps towards using nuclear energy for peaceful purposes.

In addition, the acrimonious Article IV debate of the 1980 Review Conference was not repeated in 1985; nor did the final consensus statement on Article IV contain the criticism of nuclear export controls, the Nuclear Suppliers Group Guidelines and nuclear suppliers generally, which had been sought by some parties in 1980. On the contrary, the parties affirmed that the non-proliferation and safeguards commitments of the NPT provide an essential framework for peaceful nuclear co-operation and that the NPT fosters the world-wide peaceful use of nuclear energy.

But more can be done, and the conference reaffirmed the parties' commitment to help foster peaceful nuclear co-operation. In that regard, special attention was paid to the IAEA's technical assistance and co-operation programmes. Possible measures to strengthen peaceful assistance were identified as well for IAEA consideration: for example, assistance in securing outside financing for nuclear power projects; assistance in planning; and possible multi-year, multi-donor projects. It was agreed as well to ask the IAEA to set up an expert working group to study mechanisms to help developing countries' power programmes, including financing.

Ending the Nuclear Arms Race

As expected, review of the implementation of Article VI was the most disappointing area at the 1985 Review Conference, and there was a broad criticism of the nuclear-weapon states for lack of progress in meeting the NPT's nuclear arms limitation and disarmament goals. At the heart of the debate was an honest difference over whether negotiation and conclusion of a comprehensive ban on nuclear weapons testing (CTB) should be the next step towards the shared goal of the eventual elimination of nuclear weapons.

The great majority of participating countries, while welcoming the resumption in February 1985 of bilateral United States-Soviet Union nuclear and space negotiations in Geneva, sought the start of bilateral and multilateral negotiations on a CTB. They argued that such a test ban was the most urgent measure in the nuclear arms limitation and disarmament field, and called on the conference to endorse this view.

The United States stressed that it shared the concern of all states – non-nuclear-weapon and nuclear-weapon states alike – that greater progress be made in efforts to control and reduce substantially nuclear arsenals. Indeed, to that end, in the early 1980s at the Strategic Arms Reductions Talks (START), the United States had sought major reductions of ballistic missiles and warheads. Similarly, in the parallel Intermediate-range Nuclear Forces (INF) talks, the United States had tabled proposals aimed at the elimination of an entire category of nuclear weapons. And these proposals had been followed by a readiness to negotiate seriously and flexibly in the resumed Geneva nuclear and space talks.

But the United States also made clear during the conference that it could not agree with the majority's appraisal of a nuclear test ban. While a comprehensive nuclear test ban is a long-term goal, in the context of improved verification and of broad, deep and verifiable reductions of nuclear weapons, top priority now should be on achieving radical reductions in existing nuclear arsenals and strengthened stability. Only such reductions would represent true progress towards a world without nuclear weapons.

After intensive negotiations and in the spirit of co-operation that characterised the review, an accommodation was worked out in the closing days of the conference. In the conference's Final Declaration, the parties agreed to reflect these divergent views on the relative priority of a CTB in a straightforward, factual manner, which stopped short of a conference endorsement of a CTB. In particular, all of the conference participants, including the United States, first accepted language that regretted that the objectives of Article VI remained unfulfilled, and that welcomed the United States-Soviet bilateral arms control negotiations in Geneva. Then, the compromise language that followed made clear the strong belief of the great majority of the parties present that CTB negotiations should resume in 1985; in turn, it set out the United States conviction of putting first deep and verifiable reductions of existing nuclear arsenals.

Given the real and serious differences of a CTB, the reflection of both views was accepted by all the participants as the only basis for consensus. Some countries were frustrated, none the less, that the Third Review Conference as a whole had not endorsed a nuclear test ban. But the basic concern was clear despite differences on particulars: greater progress was needed in implementing Article VI.

A Successful Review

The results of the 1985 Review Conference are only partly to be measured, however, in these specific evaluations of implementation of the NPT's three goals and in the various recommendations of the Final Declaration for strengthening further the non-proliferation regime. Indeed, on a broader plane, the overall positive results are even more striking.

Weighing all considerations, the parties concluded that the treaty is vital to international peace and security, and reaffirmed their support for it. The NPT emerged from the Third Review Conference with an aura of success, strengthened, not weakened. In turn, the widely shared recognition that the NPT is an arms control success underscored the vitality of the treaty, a vitality already enhanced by the adherence of a dozen additional countries in the past couple of years. Consequently, the international norm of non-proliferation has been buttressed; it has become still harder politically for countries to set out on the path to acquire nuclear explosives.

Many factors contributed to this successful outcome of the 1985 Review Conference. For over two years, the United States and other parties had been preparing for the conference, consulting closely to gain a better understanding of each other's concerns and to build up a pattern of co-operation. The strong common interest of the United States and Soviet Union in the NPT helped to avoid polemical exchanges, which would have served only to distract attention from the many security benefits of the NPT. A general desire on the part of virtually all countries to avoid a repetition of the 1980 outcome also seemed important.

None the less, the most important factor which led to success in 1985, and clearly the most significant from the perspective of the long-term health of the treaty, was the recognition by all of the parties of their vital stake in this important arms control agreement. This was evident throughout the conference as the parties worked intensely to find the common ground to reach consensus. Put simply, even with less progress than desired on Article VI, there was more that united the parties than divided them. The NPT was too important to risk damaging in order to make a particular point – whether about regional politics, nuclear supply or disarmament. Above all, the participants in the third review believed that without this treaty every country would be less secure and the world a more dangerous place – and they are right.

A More Dangerous World

A weakening of the NPT, let alone its collapse, would undermine international confidence and generate increased uncertainty and suspicion in many quarters about the long-term nuclear intentions of other countries. The belief would begin to grow that a world of dozens of nuclear-armed states would be unavoidable. As a result, more countries would seek to hedge their bets and re-open a nuclear weapons option. In turn, regional tensions would increase, and rivals could resort to military action to maintain their lead in the nuclear arena and to prevent an opponent from taking steps seen as leading to nuclear weapons. Over time, nuclear weapons would spread, adversely affecting regional and global peace and security.

Moreover, without the NPT, one of the legal, institutional and normative foundations of nuclear export restraint would vanish. Countries no longer would be violating their legal obligations or standards of international responsible behaviour by making questionable nuclear deals. Nor is it clear that long term self-interest alone on the part of each nuclear supplier would be an adequate alternative restraint, especially in light of concerns about how other suppliers would act. As a result, countries seeking nuclear explosives might face fewer technical obstacles to acquiring a nuclear explosive capability. And in this new supplier environment there again would be heightened pressures not to be left behind regional rivals.

Weakening of the NPT would also greatly set back global peaceful nuclear co-operation, affecting adversely many countries' economic security. Domestic political pressures in some supplier countries probably would force a cut-off of nuclear co-operation, save with closest friends, on the grounds that any peaceful nuclear ties in this more uncertain environment simply were too dangerous. The likely undermining of the international safeguards system, were the NPT to collapse, would deal a blow as well to future international nuclear commerce. Those nuclear suppliers now relying on the safeguards system to provide credible assurance that their nuclear exports are not misused for non-peaceful purposes would confront the necessity of trying to put into place a system of bilateral safeguards or discontinuing nuclear exports. And, in many cases, there are no back-up safeguards commitments to replace those contained in the treaty.

Further, despite the slender progress in pursuit of the treaty's Article VI goals, those goals remain a legal, political and moral imperative in today's world. The nuclear-weapon states do recognise the need, as President Reagan stated, 'to meet the legitimate expectations of all nations that the Soviet Union and United States will substantially reduce their own nuclear arsenals'. Without the NPT, however, other countries would lack a critical legal and institutional basis to call on the nuclear-weapon states to act. And if the norm of non-proliferation were gradually to erode and nuclear weapons were to spread, the existing nuclear-weapon states would no longer be confronted with a world in which their own acquisition of nuclear weapons was perceived as illegitimate.

The Future of the NPT

Looking ahead, the United States, co-operating with other countries, should work on several fronts to enhance the effectiveness of the NPT and ensure its continued contribution to global security.

Various suggestions within the Final Declaration to strengthen the non-proliferation regime need to be followed up. Now also is the time to build on the successful 1985 review to convince wavering countries to join the treaty. Continued strong support equally is required for peaceful nuclear co-operation with NPT parties. And despite the fact that the parties' vital security interests carried the day in 1985, we cannot dismiss the great disappointment that more far-reaching results have not yet been achieved on nuclear arms limitation and disarmament. Implementation of Article VI will remain a major issue and, for its part, the United States must and will continue to negotiate flexibly and seriously in Geneva towards the goal of the eventual elimination of nuclear weapons.

Most important, as we look to the NPT's future, we should recall the words of the Third NPT Review Conference President Mohamed Shaker: 'We must build on the NPT's successes, not belittle them.'

The Third NPT Review Conference has reaffirmed broad international support for the NPT. There was an honest taking stock, and the NPT stood on its merits. This outcome will keep momentum behind the treaty and will support global non-proliferation efforts and international security in the coming years.

End Note

1. The United States and most other countries have maintained that there is no essential technical difference between nuclear explosives, whether used for weapons purposes or for peaceful purposes.

LEGITIMACY, CAPABILITY, EFFECTIVENESS AND THE FUTURE OF THE NPT

James F. Keeley

Introduction

> ... and what the king held to be right, all held to be right. Thus the world was properly ordered because the ruler was able to unify the standards of judgement throughout his realm.
>
> — Mo Tzu

Much of the public attention to non-proliferation seems to centre on two issues: (1) who will get the bomb?; and (2) the relationship between 'horizontal' and 'vertical' proliferation – the spread of nuclear weapons and the increase in nuclear arsenals in nuclear-weapon states. On the one hand, there are revelations about this or that country's nuclear capacity or intentions, and on the other, somber warnings that, unless the superpowers fulfil their responsibilities under Article VI of the Treaty on the Non-Proliferation of Nuclear Weapons (NPT), the attempt to check the spread of nuclear weapons may come to naught. These are legitimate concerns. This chapter, however, argues that there is a more general problem which could effectively destroy the non-proliferation regime and its centrepiece, the NPT, even if no other states acquire nuclear weapons or if the superpowers achieve significant nuclear arms reductions.

India's nuclear test of May 1974 and the Osiraq raid of 1981 suggested the vulnerability of the non-proliferation regime, but such specific events do not explain the general disarray that developed in the 1970s. The addition of another nuclear-weapon state (if we wish, by courtesy, to grant India this status) and even Israel's policy of 'active denial' of nuclear technological capabilities to its Middle East enemies were strains, to be sure, but the more general problem was the threat to the coherence and legitimacy of the non-proliferation regime. This threat arose from the more general dispute over the implications of, and the response to, the spread of nuclear technological capabilities.[1] India's nuclear test and the Osiraq raid were symptoms of these problems and occasions for these more basic factors to surface.

The forces leading to this strain continue to exist and to press on the regime, eroding its legitimacy and effectiveness. They are not, however, problems arising merely in non-proliferation; in fact, they arise from the very nature of politics. As such, they are unavoidable and subject only to temporary resolution. At the most general level, they arise from the relationship between legitimacy and capability in conceptually and politically contestable regimes. This chapter begins with a brief and general examination of this relationship. It then turns to two developments in the non-proliferation regime that have helped produce the more specific problems of that regime. These are the spread of nuclear technological capabilities and the development of complex co-operation networks. Finally, it looks quickly at prospects for the modification of the NPT in response to these challenges.

The Inherent Contestability of Regimes

An 'international regime' has been defined by one author as the 'principles, norms, rules and decision-making procedures around which actor expectations converge in a given issue-area'.[2] The creation of a regime, as of any social order, requires that certain questions be asked and answers be provided regarding purposes, specific objectives and mechanisms. These questions and answers must be connected to a construct of reality in order to establish their feasibility and desirability as solutions to defined problems. In providing one set of responses to these issues, the regime restricts, if not forecloses, further consideration of alternatives. If the maintenance of the regime thereafter depends in part on the ability of its mechanisms to perform in a technically adequate manner and to achieve the desired objectives, it will also depend on the political ability of the regime to resist challenges by parties advocating alternative questions or answers. Certain fundamental issues cannot readily be reopened if the regime is to function smoothly. Attempts to reopen them must be seen as illegitimate; those who attempt to reopen them may be defined as irresponsible or as deviants from an accepted order. Thus the strength of a regime will be measured in part by its resistance to and its ability to cope with diversity of judgements.

That the regime's questions and answers and the perception of the world on which they are based should be widely accepted as authoritative is therefore important. They provide a framework of shared judgements on which a coherent and rational order might be based. In the absence of such agreement, the regime will rest on mere coincidences of interest and on the abilities of particular parties to enforce their perceptions and interests. Yet there is no necessity for any one framework to recommend itself on its intrinsic merits to all concerned parties, much less do so on a permanent basis. The basic definition of the issue-area to be regulated and approaches to what might require regulation, to what ends, and how, may be capable of multiple interpretations,[3] and thus the answers to these questions may have to be 'negotiated'.[4]

If multiple sets of questions and answers are possible, any regime may be inherently contestable. The sources and nature of this contestability may vary. Key concepts may be 'essentially contested' in Gallie's terms; that is, they may be appraisive in character, internally complex, ambiguous in application and persistently vague.[5] Attempts to 'clarify' such concepts may only sharpen rather than resolve differences as the parties to the conceptual dispute become more aware of the implications of each other's meanings. Or the contestability may stem from a lack of 'consensual knowledge' in Haas's terms ('the sum of technical information and of theories about that information which commands sufficient consensus at a given time among interested actors to serve as a guide to public policy designed to achieve some goal'). Haas explicitly connects the strength of 'consensual knowledge' to the likelihood of formation and the stability of a regime. Where the regime lacks intellectual coherence but reflects merely politically opportune connections among issues, it is not only unlikely to form but also is unlikely to be stable. Where the regime has at least some basis in 'consensual knowledge', it might be both more likely to form and more stable in its existence.[6]

There is a third source of contestability. Regimes are means of organising parties and activities for certain ends. They are structures of power.[7] Since the questions and answers embodied in regimes are unlikely to be neutral in their consequences, they may also be contested on political grounds. These contests will reflect differences in preferences for objectives, purposes, mechanisms, outcomes and other components, as well as over the nature of the issue-area and the need for action. Disputes over regime-defining questions and answers may thus arise from a recognition and a differing political evaluation of their implications, however technically adequate they may be in their own terms. Even if a regime deals adequately with a generally acknowledged problem, it may do so in ways that have unacceptable side-effects. A regime's consequences are likely to be assessed, at least by the dissatisfied, in terms not merely of the attainment of its specified purposes, but also of the broader implications of the whole set of mechanisms and relationships it embodies: a regime never provides just one good to its members. The defenders of a regime, however, may tend to a view of disputes over it that implicitly or explicitly attempts to ignore or rule out discussions of basic and non-technical issues. Thus disputes over the merits of a given real or proposed regime may conceal, knowingly or not, a 'hidden agenda'. One state may defend 'the stability of the international monetary regime' while another attacks 'the domination of the American dollar'.

If regimes are inherently contestable, their creation and maintenance become exercises in power and interest, as well as in shared judgements. A main function of power is to make and enforce choices, including choices for others. This is particularly the case when choices are disputed. Whether the mechanism is persuasion, compromise, threats or promises, side-payments, mere imposition or some combination of these, an international regime may reflect above all the choices of a dominant state or dominant states. The results may take into some account the interests and perceptions of others, but the tendency for powerful actors to blur the distinction between their own interests and the interests of all should be noted.[8] The role of power in creating and maintaining specific regimes means, of course, that shifts in the identities of the strong, and shifts in the interests of the strong, will have implications for a regime.

Because a regime requires a choice among disputable questions and answers, and because this choice will be affected by power, the legitimacy of the regime will be a constant potential or actual problem. These choices, and the role of the strong in making them, may be defended by the satisfied with a variety of arguments which may be offered in good faith. The desirability of the service performed by the regime and its ability in technical terms to perform adequately may be widely proclaimed. Efforts may be made to show how the 'legitimate' interests of lesser parties have been taken into account, and how these parties might reasonably profit by the rules and consequences of the regime. Side-payments may be offered to sweeten the regime for at least some states. It will be noted that capable states must be involved in the regime if it is to function. One major theme of the international regime literature is the use of 'hegemony' or 'leadership' to overcome the problems inherent in the creation and maintenance of a regime.[9] The choice may be, then, between the regime proposed by the strong and no regime at all. This argument, of course, may imply more: that the specific regime is, or by right ought to be, desired and supported by all enlightened parties. 'Any regime is better than none (therefore my regime is better than yours).' There will also be tendencies for the satisfied to regard an existing regime as 'natural', if not ordained by God, and in need at worst of only minor or technical correction and of good will on the part of all members. There may be real problems in merely acknowledging that the regime is contestable.

Those who refuse to accept the regime or to contribute to its maintenance may be placed in the morally inferior position of 'free riders', in the terminology of collective goods theory (also widely used in academic discussions of international regimes). These are actors who enjoy a collective good, yet do not contribute to its supply. These 'free riders' may be responsible for the suboptimality of supply of the good or even the failure of the regime. The possibility of 'forced riding' or 'forced consumption' seems generally unremarked, but raises a fundamental question: how are we to regard parties which are forced to consume a collective good which they do not want (even if some others do want it), and which are subject, perhaps, to efforts to 'tax' them for its supply? Answering this question would require moving beyond the economic metaphor and reopening basic issues in the regime by challenging its legitimacy.[10]

If the regime is generally regarded as legitimate, and if it is seen as being effective in regulating behaviour, the probability of obtaining the voluntary compliance of parties will be increased and the problem and cost of enforcement will be reduced. Deviants, those which persist in questioning, are likely to be small in number, isolated and manageable. So long as the regime is widely accepted at least among those parties with the power to disrupt it, the regime will be able to survive discontent among the rest, although its legitimacy will now be challenged. As capabilities significant to the operation of the regime spread, however, the legitimacy problem may become more pressing. Judgements as to the desirability of any given rule or norm will be freer to vary in practice because the power to constrain will be weakened. The ability of specific actors to resist the regime and present challenges to its legitimacy will increase. The organisation of parties in defence of the regime will become more difficult since more parties, potentially of increasingly divergent views, will have to be organised. Thus the observance of rules will come to depend more significantly on voluntary compliance, yet that compliance may be less forthcoming.

The effectiveness of the regime, its ability to regulate its area of activity coherently and consistently and to achieve its ends, may diminish as a result of such strains. A failure to control deviants will lead to a wider range of tolerated behaviour and to the persistent stretching of at least some of the rules. This may strain voluntary compliance still further since deviance seems to go unpunished and may actually seem to be rewarded. Specific deviant behaviour may seem to be becoming a norm. The regime may be reduced to the status of merely one of a number of alternative arrangements, among which actors are reasonably free to choose as they please. If an attempt is made to co-opt challengers, barring some change in their perspectives once they are admitted to the inner circle (thus if the challenger is not simply reducible to an 'out' wanting to be 'in'), the cost is likely to be an alteration, if not a weakening, of the regime in order to achieve this accommodation. If the challengers are sufficiently estranged from the regime, however, no accommodation may be possible. Under any of these circumstances there may have to be a reworking of fundamental issues to obtain a reunion of power and interest and a renewing of legitimacy. Revolutions may occur in international as well as domestic politics.

All of this applies to regimes considered generally. In the case of the non-proliferation regime, more specifically, it suggests that the problems facing that regime do not arise simply from the question of whether proliferation is a technical or a political problem. Proliferation is a political problem, though it has technical components as well. More important, the problems of the non-proliferation regime draw on and reflect fundamental dynamics of any political order: they are based on deep-rooted problems of politics. Solutions may be found for specific technical problems and resolutions of particular political differences may be obtained, but there is no escape from the problems of politics as such. Thus the regime is bound by circumstances, always potentially vulnerable, always subject to dispute.

The non-proliferation regime readily displays the properties of contestability. What precisely is meant by 'proliferation' may be a matter of debate: the answers might range from the acquisition of a nuclear weapons force to the acquisition of a 'latent' nuclear technological capacity. The breadth of the definition will have implications for the nature of the regime. Is non-proliferation to be approached within the more general context of nuclear or complete disarmament, or is it a distinct problem of nuclear spread, best dealt with separately? The consequences of proliferation, however defined, may be debated: is it always undesirable, or does this vary with circumstances and with definitions of terms? Strategies for handling proliferation may vary: we may focus on technological capabilities as, if not driving forces of proliferation, at least the most accessible and manipulable factors in checking it, or we may stress decision and other political factors. Within either choice, differences may arise over specific approaches for the regime in general or for specific cases. Are certain technologies really more 'proliferation-prone' than others, or are arguments to this effect attempts to establish or destroy a commercial advantage in the guise of non-proliferation? The definition of the situation and the specific responses to these issues will generate a specific sort of non-proliferation regime which will, in turn, have consequences for broader political relations among states, whether or not it tends to confirm, alter marginally or transform those relations.[11]

A key factor in challenges to legitimacy seems to be the distribution of capabilities. The remainder of this chapter examines some of the implications for and effects on the non-proliferation regime of the spread of nuclear capabilities and the development of the nuclear co-operation network. It is not intended to argue that the problems of the regime are reducible to vulgar power politics, rather that these developments pose substantial problems for the regime. These problems include:

1. increased variance, or better, increased freedom to implement variance, allowed in judgements on nuclear and non-proliferation policies;
2. difficulties posed for the operation of the formal rules and institutions of the regime which are based on the regulation of nuclear technological capabilities;
3. the attempt by some states in the 1970s to rethink non-proliferation, since these developments posed questions for the regime, while the responses to that attempt testified to the rise of a legitimacy problem; and
4. the apparent shift of interest and emphasis to decision factors, thus to political factors as distinct from capabilities, raises significant difficulties for the creation of an acceptable and consistent

non-proliferation policy by individual states and by the international community as a whole.

It is not clear that recent interest in 'managing proliferation' offers a way out of this situation. We can look forward to persisting, possibly increasing, disagreement and fragmentation in the non-proliferation regime.

Nuclear Capabilities, Nuclear Co-operation and Non-Proliferation

The spread of nuclear capabilities has been widely and continuously documented. We are all familiar with lists of states that have a technical capacity to 'go nuclear' within certain periods after the decision is made. Meyer lists 29 states (other than the current five nuclear-weapon states, or states such as wartime Germany and Japan) that had such a 'latent capacity' as of 1980.[12] Other appraisals might provide different numbers or different names, but the general message of such studies is always the same: nuclear technological capabilities are more wide-spread and more accessible than formerly. An example of the concern aroused in the 1970s by the spread of such capabilities was that centred on the possible development of a 'plutonium economy'. This concern was based on the possibility of large-scale production of plutonium (including by breeder reactors) for fuel purposes, the relative accessibility of reprocessing technology, and the possibility that reactor-grade plutonium could be used to make at least crude nuclear weapons.[13] Somewhat less noted were advances in the more demanding technology of uranium enrichment which could lower the technical barriers to the production of weapons-grade material by that means.[14]

There have also been developments in the character of international nuclear co-operation networks.[15] Even if the population is narrowly defined, the number of civilian, bilateral, interstate nuclear co-operation agreements signed since 1955 could be, conservatively, as high as 250-300 and involve as many as 50 to 70 states. Over 100 of these agreements were probably in force by the early 1970s.[16] The involvement of many states, to be sure, is marginal in the number or the content of their agreements, but perhaps half of the countries have been substantial actors in the nuclear co-operation network, and many of these have acquired significant technological capabilities through international assistance.

Beyond these simple numerical estimates, we might also point to changes in the pattern of co-operation. Looking at new agreements only, in the period from 1955 to the end of 1965, the United States and the Soviet Union were clearly the dominant foci of co-operation networks, with some additional activity centred on Europe (the United Kingdom and France especially). After 1965 new centres of activity emerged, above all in Western Europe. France and the Federal Republic of Germany became major suppliers of nuclear assistance. In terms of both absolute and relative numbers of treaties in force, the United States' position as compared to all other states peaked before the early 1960s, well before the erosion of the overwhelming dominance of the United States as a supplier of reactors.

Of particular interest for the future is the pattern of co-operation and development among Third World states. India, Brazil and Argentina have been quite active and also are important states in the Third World (and outside the NPT) in terms of their nuclear infrastructures.[17] The South American states may lag somewhat behind India in terms of their infrastructures, but they may be more active in nuclear co-operation with other Third World states than is India. The example of these three states allows us to pose a question: will the next 10 to 15 years see the development of one or more significant civilian nuclear co-operation networks centred on accumulations of technological capabilities outside of the industrialised North and perhaps even outside of the ranks of NPT signatories?

Nuclear capabilities have been central to the formal rules and institutions of the non-proliferation regime. It follows that the changing distribution of nuclear technological capabilities and developments in international networks for the supply of nuclear goods and services must have an impact on the functioning of these formal rules and institutions. This impact follows from at least four aspects of the role of capabilities in the regime.

First, nuclear technological capabilities are a currency of power in the regime. The states with nuclear capabilities (civilian or military) have dominated the design and operation of the institutions and rules. It is a dilemma that those who are most influential in the attempt to regulate nuclear technology are also those who have this technology. Thus the very nature of politics in the regime encourages states to acquire the relevant capabilities, if only to increase their influence over the operation of the regime.

Bechhoefer and Wadsworth note how the drafting of the Statute of the International Atomic Energy Agency (IAEA) was dominated by a group of eight Western, relatively capable states, with later additions representing the East bloc and the Third World.[18] The composition of the Board of Governors of the IAEA consciously reflects in part the possession of nuclear capabilities.[19] Pendley and Scheinman note how control of the Board of Governors was important in the development of the IAEA's pre-NPT safeguards system. They also note the steps taken in the NPT safeguards to meet the objections of primarily the non-nuclear-weapon states with advanced nuclear technology.[20] Kapur notes the composition of both the Zangger Committee, which devised the safeguards system for the IAEA under the NPT, and the Nuclear Suppliers Group.[21] Both are dominated by major supplier states.

This first aspect points to a second. Control over the supply of capabilities has provided an incentive and control mechanism for, and a point of leverage on, the nuclear policies of recipient states. Suppliers of nuclear goods and services have placed conditions, including safeguards, on their provision of materials, equipment and even information. The pre-NPT practice was to impose safeguards, whether bilateral between supplier and recipient or applied by the IAEA, on specific items supplied or associated with supplied items. A recipient state was free to do without international assistance or to seek the most acceptable safeguards conditions. In the former case, it would be thrown back on its own, possibly quite expensive and perhaps inadequate capabilities, and in the latter it would confront attempts by suppliers to co-ordinate and standardise safeguards or to shift safeguarding duties to a single, centralised system in the IAEA or elsewhere. The NPT altered the relationship between supply and control for signatory states (non-nuclear weapons signatories place all their peaceful nuclear facilities under safeguards), but retained the older approach for flows from signatories to non-signatories. Some signatories may even go so far as to require full-scope safeguards of non-signatories as a condition of nuclear co-operation. This has become Canadian policy with respect to new agreements.

As the number of states with a nuclear technological capability has increased, the problem of organising and harmonising supplier policies has increased. There is an organisational problem created by the increasing numbers, in addition to the possible differences among suppliers on the definition of the situation and of the appropriate and desirable responses to it. While it would be premature to speak of the 'democratisation of the atom', the spread of the currency of power in the regime, and the possibility that alternative sources of supply may arise outside of the regime as well as within it, must be faced. Might new suppliers be brought within and kept within the regime? If so, by what means and at what cost to the regime itself?

The multi-centred nature of the nuclear co-operation network was reflected in the 1970s in the debates surrounding the control of exports of 'sensitive' technologies, with the Europeans tending to resist American attempts to strengthen technology controls. The disputes within the Nuclear Suppliers Group demonstrated the difficulties of reaching agreement among this expanding group, while nuclear recipients resented what they saw as a possible cartelisation of nuclear supply and a potential reneging on Article IV of the NPT.[22] If cores for supplier networks develop in the Third World, possibly outside of the NPT, what will be the consequences for the NPT-centred regime? It would not directly affect the safeguards assumed by non-nuclear NPT parties, but it could increase the leverage of these states or of non-signatory suppliers against more-established suppliers who may favour different interpretations of their non-proliferation duties. For those outside the treaty, it will reduce whatever incentives exist to adhere to the NPT.

Third, the regime is ultimately aimed at slowing, if not halting, the spread of a specific capability, nuclear weapons. To this end, it has developed a programme and a set of mechanisms, such as safeguards, aimed at controlling more immediate capabilities. The safeguards system at the heart of the non-proliferation regime is not so much intended to prevent physical diversion of nuclear goods and services as to monitor their use, to detect diversions from acceptable uses and to deter diversion through the threat of high-confidence and timely detection. There are other, more intrusive, forms of monitoring and control, such as attempts to regulate levels of uranium enrichment or the accumulation of stockpiles of fissionable materials or attempts to control the distribution of and access to 'sensitive' technologies and facilities. These are geared not to detecting misuses of goods and services, but rather to the physical control of these goods and services. Their focus is not on defining and detecting inappropriate use, but instead on defining, detecting and controlling capabilities which, by their nature or in certain circumstances, might be considered inappropriate or at least suspect.

Fourth, in focusing on capabilities, the regime focuses on relatively tangible and regulable items. Nuclear facilities and materials have a concrete existence. Facilities are designed, built and operated in concrete terms, not as intellectual constructs. Nuclear material exists as stockpiles and throughputs. Thus designs can be reviewed, construction detected, and the operation of facilities monitored. Changes in the physical character of a plant or in its mode of operation may be detectable: fuel burn-up rates, rearrangements of equipment, changes in power-generation levels, and losses of materials may be checked through appropriate devices and inspection schemes. These system checks have understood technical characteristics. Materials accounting procedures, for example, are able to detect a certain level of variation in materials flows with a certain level of confidence. Interpreting the technical information produced by a safeguards system will not necessarily be an automatic exercise, but the exercise is still relatively technical-rational in nature.

The spread of capabilities in particular has led to a problem of defining and then responding to proliferation. The NPT used a simple criterion: the test of a nuclear device. The ambiguity of proliferation, however, and the ability of states to profit from ambiguous proliferation, have been much commented upon. The 1970s saw a further definitional development in response to the actual and the anticipated spread of nuclear technological capabilities. Some states begin to define proliferation as being the acquisition of 'latent capacities'. Proliferation became a matter of degree or, as Schelling put it, became proliferation in a time-schedule sense.[23]

The difficulties created in this attempted redefinition did not arise merely from attempts by some states to renegotiate and to stiffen existing agreements and contracts, to bring these into line with their new perception of the proliferation problem. The expansive character of the new definition and the sorts of approaches to non-proliferation offered under it also created problems. The broader definition pointed to the spread of capabilities as such, not merely to their misuse, as the proliferation problem. The policy of controlling access to 'sensitive' technology which followed from this new definition implied attempting to block or at least to control the development of full national fuel cycles and to institutionalise the adaptation of national policies to, and their dependence on, the international supply of nuclear goods and services. These policies have been resented as interference in domestic energy policies, as well as possible attempts to renege on Article IV of the NPT. By focusing on spreading capabilities, the new definition also greatly expanded the number of states theoretically at issue in attempting to check proliferation. Thus this attempt redefined certain previously legitimate policies and capabilities as suspect; in so doing, it expanded the number of states likely to challenge this reconceptualisation of proliferation. To the extent that this effort attempted to be 'non-discriminatory', it also confused and complicated the problem of dealing with specific states.

The attempted definitional shift and the spread of capabilities also put strains on safeguarding as the regulatory approach of the regime. The 'latent capacity' problem is not particularly manageable by safeguarding. As well, the ability of safeguards to deal in a timely fashion, or at all, with high-volume flows of materials such as plutonium, may be suspect. One might argue, further, that the spread of nuclear capabilities changes the basic nature of the safeguarding function: where once it was above all a means for suppliers to guard against the misuse of nuclear assistance by others, now perhaps it is better regarded as a means by which nuclear recipients might offer public assurances, partially symbolic given the limits of safeguarding, of their peaceful intentions. That this may be insufficient is amply demonstrated by the Osiraq raid.[24]

By complicating and challenging a capabilities-based approach to non-proliferation, the spread of nuclear technological capabilities and the development of the nuclear co-operation network have contributed to an increased awareness of factors other than simple technological capabilities in the proliferation process. Where capabilities were concentrated and closely controlled, a concentration on the physical means of producing nuclear weapons was reasonable even if one did not espouse a 'technological' view of the proliferation process. Once capabilities are wide-spread, and thus available from a variety of sources, either hope or the 'technological' theory must be abandoned. Thus we now have increased attention to the incentives and disincentives that might affect the decision to 'go nuclear'.

The importance of these factors is not new, but this new emphasis on them marks a shift away from the tangible, technical, relatively regulable capabilities approach to non-proliferation towards a less tangible and regulable, and a more highly political, conceptualisation of proliferation. The nature of these factors makes it unlikely that a formalised regime to deal with them could either be created or work with great effectiveness. Instead, their character points to inconsistency both within and across state policies, to divisiveness, and to the existence of severe constraints on the regime. The first and most obvious characteristic of these decision factors is their sheer quantity. Meyer suggests 15 motivational variables (including both incentives and disincentives) and notes that these offer 32,768 possible combinations.[25] Kegley, Raymond and Skinner[26] and Potter[27] note 13 and 23 motivational factors respectively, organised into incentives, disincentives and precipitating factors or situational variables. This multiplicity of factors suggests that developing coherent and consistent policies to cope with specific target states would be difficult for one country, let alone a large number of countries acting in or through an international regime. To this we must add an additional consideration: attempts to redefine and expand the concept of proliferation to include 'latent capacity' add economic and energy policy motivations to the list of decision factors, motivations particularly likely to cause difficulties through their inclusion.

A variety of more specific difficulties arises from the number of incentives and disincentives to be dealt with. Since they may face different combinations in concrete circumstances, policies suitable for one target, one potential proliferator, may not be suitable for another. Worse, they may be counter-productive. If, because of a hypothesised link between 'vertical' and 'horizontal' proliferation, the superpowers reduce one state's propensity to go nuclear by reducing their own strategic arsenals, they might simultaneously increase the 'nuclear propensity' of another that fears a loss of its 'nuclear umbrella'. Thus policy instruments aimed at motivational factors will have to be tailored for specific occasions rather than used in a broad-brush way.

Consider also that different states will have differing relationships with a given target state, and their policies towards that target will therefore reflect different goals, priorities and instruments of influence. These states will probably differ in how they would be affected by the target's nuclear decision and may differ in their perceptions of the appropriate actions even if they agree on everything else. Indeed, some actions which might tend to reduce the target's 'nuclear propensity' might be regarded by a third state as undesirable or even hostile: for example, providing the target with conventional arms or extending a nuclear guarantee to cover it. There is no inherent reason, therefore, to anticipate that two or more states might agree on a policy towards a given potential proliferator though all might agree in general terms on the desirability of constraining proliferation. In the absence of a very strong consensus that proliferation is an overriding threat and thus that non-proliferation is an overriding policy priority, the identity of the target and the identities of states concerned in actions to affect the target will be crucial to the content of policy and therefore to state responses.

There are two arguments in response to the effects of this numerical abundance of decision factors. The first is that some factors may well be much more important than others, or at least much more amenable to leverage. Thus the operational set of factors may be smaller, perhaps very significantly smaller, than the theoretical set. Second, while we may construct long lists of various states with certain levels of nuclear technological capabilities, the list of states arousing real concern is substantially shorter, though the naming of names may be impolite. Thus both initial lists of factors and countries according to capabilities may be deceptively large. Weighted by some measure of risk or propensity, the population of real targets and thus the combinations of decision factors may be much more manageable.

Let us ignore the question of whether the manipulable factors may be the most important ones and look only at the target states. Unfortunately, the population of real targets will be composed precisely of those states that will be most difficult to handle: how else would they have survived the selection procedure? By definition, we will be dealing with the hard cases. Others of less concern might be manageable by more broadly applied policies, but for these hard cases in particular specifically designed policies may be required. Here the problems noted above do not vanish but rather arise in their sharpest form, although in a smaller set of states.

This argument tends to restrict the usefulness, possibility and even desirability of a formalised and routinised non-proliferation regime to deal with decision factors. The difficulties of such a regime are compounded if we adopt non-discrimination as a primary norm for the regime. The regime could then be led to develop broadly applied rules that are directed at a mere handful of states which might, however, impinge harmfully on a much wider set, or to develop rules which are more readily acceptable to the larger set, but which may be of diminished effectiveness with respect to the real target set.[28]

A final set of problems arises from the connection between nuclear weapons and nuclear technology on the one hand, and fundamental issues of regional and global order on the other. No regime provides just one good or just one service. The very mechanism of supply has additional implications and may itself be regarded as another good or service of the regime. Consider an example. Meyer suggests that

having a nuclear ally may be the most effective disincentive to proliferation. This challenges the thesis that 'vertical' proliferation
stimulates 'horizontal' proliferation.[29] In many cases this might well
work, but in some it could mean the creation of a superpower
relationship with the target state that might be resented by the other
superpower or by other states in the area, or that might be resisted by
the target state itself. If the superpowers disagree on the response to
a given case, the target state will have greater freedom of action. If
they agree, others could become alarmed by the possibility of a
superpower condominium in non-proliferation that could have effects
in other areas.

It is unlikely in the extreme, given the nature of these issues, that
the non-proliferation regime would be allowed to address them in
any but a subordinate manner, working out its rules subject to
parameters set by these 'higher' issues. The increased variation in
judgements allowed by the spread of nuclear technological capabilities and the development of complex co-operation networks will
merely increase the subordination of non-proliferation to other policy
considerations. Supply control will be more difficult to organise and
apply because of differences among supplier states. Attempts to
induce or coerce target states to conform to the rules of the regime
will be more sensitive to political considerations within the target
state and between the target and those attempting to maintain the
regime, and among other 'interested parties'.

The sense of increased difficulties with non-proliferation seems to
underlie interest in the idea of 'managing proliferation'. In a recent
volume this approach was differentiated from other attitudes to
nuclear proliferation on the following bases:

1. it notes the importance of preventing proliferation, but goes on to
   ask how proliferation might best be handled if and when it has
   occurred, as well as before the fact;
2. it takes as one theme the newer nuclear states and their progress
   from a demonstrated weapons capacity to a nuclear weapon
   force;
3. it reduces the emphasis on the control of nuclear technological
   capabilities and increases that on decisional factors; and
4. it attempts, through a more sophisticated methodology, to predict
   potential proliferators, and to guide the response to them.[30]

Does 'managing proliferation' point to a way out of the situation

facing the non-proliferation regime? Not really. One of these differences between 'management' and 'older' approaches to non-
proliferation is purely methodological, although it may have implications for substantive policy. One recognises the increased overt
importance of decisional factors. One records the concern with a
particular group of states, perhaps downplaying the implications of
the long-standing possession of nuclear weapons by another group.
One argues that dealing with proliferation does not, cannot, stop
with non-proliferation. Where the differences are substantive rather
than methodological, they echo the problems noted above, to some
extent responding to them, but to some extent illustrating them by
ignoring aspects of the legitimacy problem that is the central theme
of this chapter.

'Managing proliferation' may make two contributions to non-
proliferation. First, it says the unspeakable: contrary to the rhetoric
of non-proliferation, nuclear weapons will spread, though we hope
and will attempt to ensure that they do not. Second, it suggests an
extended repertoire of policies to match an extended field for their
application. It opens up to some extent the range of discussion of
nuclear proliferation, but does this necessarily mark an expansion of
that range in terms of real policy? Could it be that, like M. Jourdain,
we are in the process of discovering that we have been speaking prose
all our lives? The benefits offered by the 'management' perspective
are those of potentially recognising the full scope of a problem. They
are not, in themselves, the solutions to the problem.

The Future of the NPT: Life in a Disputed Regime

The spread of nuclear technological capabilities and the development of the nuclear co-operation network has had the effect of
increasing the scope for and the effects of sustained substantive disagreement over the nature of the non-proliferation regime. Attempts
to rework the concepts and rules of the regime have demonstrated
this rather than overcome it. These developments have also increased
the importance of factors inherently less susceptible to handling
through formalised rules, whether by individual states or by the
international community. The control of nuclear capabilities, whether
through safeguarding or other devices, is amenable to routinisation,
and has advantages of working to some degree within an existing, if
strained, consensus. This strategy will retain a basic and crucial

place in non-proliferation, but will be increasingly insufficient. Once we move beyond a capabilities-centred formal regime the chances for the maintenance of a consensus on non-proliferation, much less the chances for the creation of a new consensus, seem to decline. The substantive issues separating states are many and often complex, the differences are deep and the progress in dealing with them seems generally to be slow at best.

In substantive terms, it appears that the future non-proliferation regime will be centred on an agreed capabilities-oriented core based on the NPT. Despite disagreements about its adequacy and about attempts to strengthen it, the NPT represents a strong, if strained, consensus on the nature of the formal non-proliferation regime. Around this formal core will be a fragmented set of policies, unilateral or agreed among some states, directed at specific capabilities, specific motivations and specific targets. The future, in other words, may be very much like the past, but raised to a higher degree of disorder.

This conclusion is supported not only by the possibilities for substantive disagreement over the regime, but also by the procedural difficulties of revising the current regime, above all of revising the NPT itself. The treaty provides an amendment procedure and provides for review conferences. The amendment procedure specifically requires the approval of all nuclear-weapon states that are parties and of all states that are on the IAEA Board of Governors when the amendment is circulated, as well as the approval of a majority of parties to the treaty.[31] This underlines the power of the nuclear-weapon states and the members of the IAEA board. Whether the differences among states on any amendment of substance could be sufficiently resolved so as to meet this triple requirement is questionable. A further difficulty arises from the toleration of reservations and of the non-acceptance of amendments in the law of treaties. An attempt to amend the treaty, if successful, could create not a consistent and agreed set of modifications, but rather a patchwork of agreements holding among some parties but not among others. In the absence of an overwhelming consensus, modifying the written terms of the treaty thus may be impossible or, if possible, undesirable.

The formal problem could be avoided to some degree if the practice of states with respect to various issues could be informally co-ordinated, so long as that practice was consistent with or represented an evolving informal understanding of the terms of the NPT. Here, the review conferences theoretically could play a role. A positive feature of the review conferences in this regard is that non-signatories of the NPT have been allowed to attend as observers. Unfortunately, the history of the conferences does not suggest that this sort of informal understanding is likely to be readily forthcoming. Instead of helping to create agreement, it would seem that the reviews have very largely been fora for the expression of dissatisfaction; they reflect the problem of legitimacy rather than provide a means by which to resolve it.[32]

Argues David Fischer: 'The early 1970s marked the peak point of international consensus on what to do about horizontal proliferation. The situation will never recur.'[33] If, as this suggests, the NPT may express the strongest degree of consensus obtainable, and if the treaty remains at the heart of the non-proliferation regime, the problem of its revision, whether formally or informally, will bedevil any attempt to revise the non-proliferation regime as a whole. Changes made elsewhere in the regime in an attempt to restore order will have to be linked back to its terms for reasons of both substance and legitimacy. Thus the treaty may act as a basic constraint on the future formal development of a coherent regime.

For reasons of both substance and procedure, then, the NPT is unlikely to be revised successfully, and it is similarly unlikely that a substantially altered, coherent regime, strongly centred on the treaty will evolve. The treaty will not be the core of a new consensus, rather the remnant of an old consensus. In this capacity it will become further encrusted with understandings on specific issues among specific states and with unilateral interpretations and actions by particular states. It will retain its position at the centre of the regime as the single most widely applicable agreement on non-proliferation, but its terms will be increasingly obscured and overtaken by newer, less extensive agreements and policies.

This may, as some suggest, open up the possibility of a new, more flexible non-proliferation regime, one better equipped to deal with the complexities of non-proliferation and the requirements for carefully tailored policies.[34] The non-proliferation regime, after all, consists of more than the NPT. Difficulties in the NPT core may be compensated for by developments in other components – the IAEA, the Treaty of Tlatelolco, the Nuclear Suppliers Group, national policies, etc., as well as by the apparent strength of the norm of non-proliferation. This is possible; it could also be terribly deceptive. Developments in regional, national or other partial elements of the regime could further strain its overall coherence unless they are linked to an agreed core. The IAEA non-NPT safeguards constitute a fall-back position at best. Constant invocation of the norm of non-proliferation cannot disguise the existence of disputes over the content of that norm and how it is to be served. Nor does it meet the contention of this paper that the regime and the NPT are under threat, even if no additional states acquire nuclear weapons.

The erosion of consensus in the 1970s affected not only the question of where non-proliferation should go in the future, but also the question of the sufficiency of the existing regime. It reflected retroactive doubt as well as concerns for the future. 'Flexibility' anchored in a solid, widely accepted core of understanding about proliferation might be a significant source of effectiveness for the regime. 'Flexibility' that merely reflects or exacerbates wide disagreement is at best another word for 'incoherence'.

End Notes

The author would like to thank Barry Cooper, Tom Heilke and Nancy Pearson for their comments on portions of earlier drafts.

1. The International Nuclear Fuel Cycle Evaluation was an attempt to restore some degree of consensus on matters nuclear. As such, it may have had some success, although it also seems that many issues were left unresolved. P. Gummett, 'From NPT to INFCE: Developments in Thinking About Nuclear Non-Proliferation', *International Affairs*, vol. 57, no. 4 (1981), pp. 549-67.
2. S.D. Krasner, 'Structural Causes and Regime Consequences: Regimes as Intervening Variables', *International Organization*, vol. 36, no. 2 (1982), p. 185.
3. E.B. Haas demonstrates this with respect to the Law of the Sea in 'Is There a Hole in the Whole? Knowledge, Technology, Interdependence, and the Construction of International Regimes', *International Organization*, vol. 29, no. 3 (1975), pp. 834-8.
4. J.G. Ruggie, 'International Responses to Technology: Concepts and Trends', *International Organization*, vol. 29, no. 3 (1975), pp. 567-8, 574. Winham suggests that such negotiations are an increasingly important aspect of modern diplomacy. G.R. Winham, 'Negotiation as a Management Process', *World Politics*, vol. 30, no. 1 (1977), pp. 87-114.
5. W.B. Gallie, 'Essentially Contested Concepts', in M. Black (ed.), *The Importance of Language* (Prentice-Hall, Englewood Cliffs, New Jersey, 1962), pp. 121-46. See also W.E. Connolly, *The Terms of Political Discourse* (Princeton University Press, Princeton, 1983).
6. E.B. Haas, 'Why Collaborate? Issue-Linkage and International Regimes', *World Politics*, vol. 22, no. 3 (1980), pp. 357-405.
7. For example, see P. Bachrach and M.S. Baratz, 'Two Faces of Power', *American Political Science Review*, vol. 56, no. 4 (1962), pp. 947-52.
8. K.N. Waltz, *Theory of International Politics* (Addison-Wesley, Reading, Massachusetts, 1979), p. 198:
   The greater the relative size of a unit the more it identifies its own interest with the interest of the system.

At least two readings can be understood from this statement.

9. For example, see C.P. Kindleberger, 'Domination and Leadership in the International Economy', *International Studies Quarterly*, vol. 25, no. 2 (1981), pp. 242-54.

10. Sandler, Loehr and Cauley, who briefly note this problem, suggest a 'negative tax' to compensate such parties, but this solution is both quite abstract and quite limited. It does not and cannot, within the limits of the theory, approach the basic legitimacy problem in such a situation. T.M. Sandler, W. Loehr and J.T. Cauley, *The Political Economy of Public Goods and International Co-operation*, University of Denver Graduate School of International Studies, Monograph Series in World Affairs, vol. 15, bk. 3 (University of Denver, Denver, 1978), pp. 40-1.

11. For example, see B.N. Schiff, *International Nuclear Technology Transfer: Dilemmas of Dissemination and Control* (Rowman and Allanheld, Totowa, New Jersey, 1983), pp. 9-32.

12. S.M. Meyer, *The Dynamics of Nuclear Proliferation* (University of Chicago Press, Chicago, 1984), pp. 40-2.

13. For example, A. Wohlstetter et al., *Swords from Plowshares: The Military Potential of Civilian Nuclear Energy* (University of Chicago Press, Chicago, 1979).

14. For example, see T. Greenwood, G.W. Rathjens and J. Ruina, 'Nuclear Power and Weapons Proliferation', *Adelphi Papers*, no. 130 (IISS, London, 1976).

15. These estimates and all other claims in this paragraph and the next two (save where otherwise noted) are based on research on the pattern and content of civilian nuclear co-operation being carried out by the author. They reflect 161 original agreements and 145 amendments, the texts of which are in his possession, and a list of 203 known or suspected agreements compiled from various sources. The numbers and patterns, of course, are extremely rough and should be considered only as at best 'ballpark' estimates. For further information on the research, see J.F. Keeley, 'Coding Treaties: An Example From Nuclear Co-operation', *International Studies Quarterly*, vol. 29, no. 1, 1985, pp. 103-8.

16. A 1980 estimate states that by mid-1976 14 supplier states had over 100 agreements in force. Stockholm International Peace Research Institute, *The NPT: The Main Political Barrier to Nuclear Weapon Proliferation* (Taylor and Francis, London, 1980), p. 25.

17. For brief overviews of these three states, see D.L. Tweedale, 'Argentina', V. Johnson, 'Brazil', and R.R. Subramanian and C.R. Mohan, 'India', in J.E. Katz and O.S. Marwah (eds.), *Nuclear Power in Developing Countries: An Analysis of Decision Making* (Lexington Books, Lexington, Massachusetts, 1982), pp. 79-95, 96-117 and 161-79 respectively.

18. B.G. Bechhoefer, 'Negotiating the Statute of the International Atomic Energy Agency', *International Organization*, vol. 13, no. 1 (1959), pp. 45-6; J.J. Wadsworth, 'Atoms for Peace', in J.G. Stoessinger and A.F. Whiting (eds.), *Power and Order: Six Cases in World Politics* (Harcourt, Brace and World, New York, 1964), p. 37.

19. Article VI.A.1 of the Statute of the IAEA reads, in part, as follows:
    > The outgoing Board of Governors shall designate for membership on the Board the five members most advanced in the technology of atomic energy including the production of source materials and the member most advanced in the technology of atomic energy including the production of source materials in each of . . . eight geographic areas listed . . . in which none of the aforesaid five is located . . .

    There are, in addition, members elected from the General Conference.

20. A basic problem was the obtrusiveness of safeguards and other controls in the

IAEA safeguards system. R. Pendley and L. Scheinman, with the collaboration of R.W. Butler, 'International Safeguarding as Institutionalized Collective Behavior', *International Organization*, vol. 29, no. 3 (1975), pp. 585-616.
21. Members of the Zangger Committee are: Australia, Austria, Belgium, Canada, Czechoslovakia, Denmark, Finland, the Federal Republic of Germany, the Democratic Republic of Germany, Ireland, Italy, Japan, Luxembourg, the Netherlands, Norway, Poland, Sweden, Switzerland, the United Kingdom, the United States, the Soviet Union and South Africa. The NSG apparently contains somewhat fewer members, but virtually all are on the Zangger Committee. A. Kapur, *International Nuclear Proliferation: Multilateral Diplomacy and Regional Aspects* (Praeger, New York, 1979), p. 70.
22. A. Wohlstetter, 'Spreading the Bomb Without Quite Breaking the Rules', *Foreign Policy*, no. 25 (1976-77), pp. 88-96, 145-79; P. Lellouche, 'Breaking the Rules Without Quite Stopping the Bomb: European Views', *International Organization*, vol. 35, no. 1 (1981), pp. 39-58; M.A. Khan, 'Nuclear Energy and International Cooperation: A Third World Perception of the Erosion of Confidence', in I. Smart (ed.), *World Nuclear Energy: Toward a Bargain of Confidence* (Johns Hopkins University Press, Baltimore, 1982), pp. 49-68.
23. T.C. Schelling, 'Who Will Have the Bomb?', *International Security*, vol. 1, no. 1 (1976), p. 79.
24. The Israeli attack on the Osiraq reactor underlines both this function of safeguards and the problems of their limits in fulfilling this function. For example, see S. Feldman, 'The Bombing of Osiraq – Revisited', *International Security*, vol. 7, no. 2 (1982), pp. 114-42; C. Herzig, 'Correspondence: IAEA Safeguards', *International Security*, vol. 7, no. 4 (1983), pp. 195-99; A. D'Amato, 'Israel's Air Strike Upon the Iraqi Nuclear Reactor', *American Journal of International Law*, vol. 77, no. 3 (1983), pp. 584-8.
25. Meyer, *Dynamics*, pp. 91-8.
26. C.W. Kegley, Jr, G.A. Raymond and R.A. Skinner, 'A Comparative Analysis of Nuclear Armament', in P. McGowan and C.W. Kegley, Jr (eds.), *Threats, Weapons, and Foreign Policy* (Sage Publications, Beverly Hills, 1980), pp. 235-6.
27. W.C. Potter, *Nuclear Power and Nonproliferation: An Interdisciplinary Perspective* (Oelgeschlager, Gunn and Hain, Cambridge, Massachusetts, 1982), pp. 132-5.
28. This problem arises with capabilities as well as with decision factors, most particularly if a 'latent capacity' definition of proliferation is used.
29. Meyer, *Dynamics*, pp. 101-4.
30. D.L. Brito, M.D. Intriligator and A.E. Wick, 'Preface and Acknowledgements', and T. Greenwood, 'Comments', in D.L. Brito, M.D. Intriligator and A.E. Wick (eds.), *Strategies for Managing Nuclear Proliferation: Economic and Political Issues* (Lexington Books, Lexington, Massachusetts, 1983), pp. xi-xii and 291-5 respectively.
31. Article VIII (2) of the NPT reads:
    Any amendment to this Treaty must be approved by a majority of the votes of all the Parties to the Treaty including the votes of all nuclear-weapon states Party to the treaty and all other Parties which, on the date the amendment is circulated, are members of the Board of Governors of the International Atomic Energy Agency. The amendment shall enter into force for each Party that deposits its instrument of ratification of the amendment upon the deposit of such instruments of ratification by a majority of all the Parties, including the instruments of ratification of all nuclear-weapon States Party to the Treaty and all other Parties which, on the date the amendment is circulated, are members of the Board of Governors of the International Atomic Energy Agency.

Thereafter, it shall enter into force for any other Party upon the deposit of its instrument of ratification of the amendment.

32. For example, see Stockholm International Peace Research Institute, *Postures for Non-Proliferation: Arms Limitation and Security Policies to Minimize Nuclear Proliferation* (Taylor and Francis, London, 1979), pp. 130-45, for the 1975 Review Conference. The 1980 Review Conference failed to produce an agreed Final Declaration.

33. D.A.V. Fischer, 'Preventing Nuclear Proliferation: Scope and Limitations of International Action', in E. Meller (ed.), *Internationalization: An Alternative to Nuclear Proliferation?* (Oelgeschlager, Gunn and Hain, Cambridge, Massachusetts, 1980), p. 156.

34. For example, see R.K. Lester, 'Revising the NPT Regime', in W.H. Kincade and C. Bertram (eds.), *Nuclear Proliferation in the 1980s: Perspectives and Proposals* (Macmillan, London, 1982), pp. 217-29.

THE SECURITY FACTOR
IN NUCLEAR PROLIFERATION

Michael Brenner

For more than a generation, the prevailing view of the military utility of nuclear weapons has held that they serve no other purpose than to deter an opponent from using them against oneself.[1] The great power experience with large, sophisticated arsenals has confirmed the conviction that nuclear weapons are ill-suited to the traditional ends of defeating an enemy on the battlefield and compelling behaviour. Despite the successful employment of nuclear weapons by the United States to force Japanese capitulation at the close of World War II (or, perhaps, because of it), the world has seen the emergence of a strong non-nuclear norm that both deprecates the value of nuclear weapons and stigmatises their possible use. The ethical judgement that weapons of mass destruction lie beyond the pale of acceptable morality tends to be reinforced by the widespread belief that the reasoned deliberation of military ways and means can find little or no place for them.

These commonly made assessments of the practical value of nuclear weapons are doubtless coloured by the superpowers' labours in fashioning stable configurations to ensure that weapons without apparent utility will not be used. In the absence of a manifest security threat, they seem more an unwieldy burden than a valued military asset.

It is an understandable, if not necessary, extrapolation to conclude that sober and prudent governments elsewhere will be similarly sceptical about the benefits that accrue from taking up a nuclear option. In truth, though, we have a very imperfect understanding of what minor powers might do with a rudimentary nuclear force. Even more important, we do not know how the leaders of prospective nuclear-weapon states view their utility. The historical record is not sufficient basis for making an assessment. The circumstances of the superpowers have been exceptional. As a number of commentators have pointed out, they are geographically distant, none of their vital interests have been threatened, they have had the liberty of an extended learning period for coming to terms with weapons of mass destruction, and – thanks to those factors already cited – they have not engaged each other in direct hostilities.[2]

By contrast, the countries that figure prominently on the list of candidate members to the nuclear club – Pakistan, Iraq, Taiwan, South Korea (as well as Israel and South Africa which are presumed to have a nuclear capability already) – face genuine security problems. Moreover, most form part of a hostile pairing with another nuclear state. It does not require exceptional imagination to visualise confrontations over basic national interests that lead to a lowering of inhibitions on the use of atomic arms while offering opportunity for their employment.

The perceptions of security risk and the strategic assessments that may result in the acquisition, development and use of nuclear weapons will surely vary from instance to instance. There are no hard and fast rules, and any generalisation will call for qualification. With those disclaimers in mind, an examination of the security conditions faced by possible entrants to the nuclear ranks nevertheless remains a necessary undertaking. A more confident assessment of the possible ends to which small nuclear arsenals may be put is crucial to a proper evaluation of what they portend for regional stability, for great power interests and for international peace. Without it, the policy-maker cannot appraise accurately a candidate nuclear-weapon state's interest in building a nuclear force, the size and characteristics of such a force that would be militarily significant, and what approaches aimed at blocking a weapons programme might have the best chance of working.

Catalogue of Prospective Proliferations

Three criteria suggest themselves as being of greatest importance for classifying prospective nuclear-weapon states: (1) their relationship to the great powers; (2) their regional security positions; and (3) their stability of government and political leadership.[3] By referring to these factors, it should be possible to better assess how security concerns would bear on a decision to acquire nuclear weapons; whether and how they might be used; and the manner of threat they pose to the interests of other parties.

Great Power Ties

It is by no means coincidental that among the countries high on the proliferation worry list are states that have depended heavily on the United States for their security. The power of the United States has been waning for more than a decade. The long recessional from Vietnam and the inhibitions about the engagement of United States forces abroad that followed have raised understandable doubts about the credibility of Washington's defence commitments to nations not obviously of central interest to the United States. Taiwan, Pakistan, South Korea and, to a lesser extent, Israel have felt cause for concern on this account. Anxiety has been only partially assuaged by the military build-up of the Reagan Administration undertaken to the accompaniment of brave rhetoric. The reliability of the United States as a protective ally remains impaired.

Allies' flirtation with the idea of acquiring nuclear weapons is entirely natural. The essential stability of the global security system that emerged after World War II under the aegis of the two Cold War rivals tended to obscure a basic truth of international politics; that is, states prefer to ground their security on self-reliant means wherever possible. It is not an either-or question. The security value of great power ties is still acknowledged even as an uneasy ally explores unilateral measures. The interest in nuclear weapons evinced by Seoul, Taipei and Jerusalem does not auger an abandonment of alliance with the United States. Rather, they are signs of a perceived need to reinforce the effectiveness of the United States deterrent and the defence potential it provides. We should bear in mind a cardinal truth about extended deterrence: 'it takes more credibility to keep an ally than to deter an adversary'.[4]

Pakistan's security ties with the United States are of a somewhat different character than those of South Korea, Israel or Taiwan. In the aftermath of the 1971 war with India that resulted in the loss of its East Bengal province, Islamabad downgraded the value of its United States ally and relations cooled. India's explosion of a nuclear device in 1974 prompted a clear decision to acquire nuclear weapons of its own. Suspicion of Pakistani nuclear intentions, and later appearance of confirming evidence, added to the chill as Washington sought to pressure the Pakistanis into altering their course.

The latter's ability to resist United States pressure owes something to the more tolerant attitude in Washington brought on by the Soviet invasion of Afghanistan. However, it also is indicative of two other factors that distinguish Pakistan from other nuclear-minded allies of the United States: (1) its stronger desire to maintain an independent political course that diverges in significant respects from that of the United States; and (2) the greater number and variety of its friends. Pakistan is not a state anxious about its legitimacy (except perhaps in the eyes of India) and diplomatically isolated, although it does share with the more isolated states (Israel, South Africa, Taiwan) fear of a threatening and powerful neighbour.[5]

The fact of alliance, whatever its exact form, presumes mutual interest. The implications are several. First, as far as the ability of the United States to restrain an ally's move towards developing a nuclear capability is concerned, two things stand out. Washington, being the dominant partner, has potential leverage to exert on its dependant. At the same time, the United States must take care not to alienate a valued friend and/or lose influence on the shape and direction of its defence programme. As Michael Nacht has pointed out in discussing the United States reaction to Israel's putative nuclear force, not only did its acknowledged existence fail to evoke either United States sanctions or a weakening of defence guarantees, it actually resulted in a strengthening of United States commitment.[6] In part, Washington's reaction reflects Israel's unique place in United States domestic politics and foreign policy. But the reaction was also based on a judgement in Washington that the gravest danger to United States interests in the Middle East would arise were a diplomatically isolated Israel challenged successfully by its military enemies and forced to use its nuclear option. (In addition, Israel's tacit observance of the nuclear taboo by refraining from testing its bomb made it easier for the United States to continue diplomatic business as usual while not faced with the need to deal with an immediate Arab response in kind.)

Although there are unique features to the Israeli case, the general point remains. Any alliance is based on mutual dependence and mutual interest, however asymmetrical the strengths and vulnerabilities may be. Constraining influence flows in both directions.

The second implication is that the acquisition of nuclear weapons by an ally increases the possibility of becoming involved in hostilities with the other superpower through the catalyst of a local conflict. The intentional employment of nuclear weapons as a device for forcing the intervention of a protective ally may be improbable. However, it is not an eventuality to be dismissed out of hand. In some parts of the world – for example the Middle East and South Asia – the accumulation of clients and obligations by the Soviet Union and the United States, associated with substantial geostrategic stakes, creates combustible conditions. The exact paths by which conflict between local parties can escalate to include nuclear weapons and to engage the superpowers are unknowable, no matter how many scenarios we sketch and how often they point to a resolution short of catastrophe. In most cases, on balance, nuclear weapons may indeed be expected to induce prudence and conservative behaviour, especially on the part of the superpowers. The chances of a less satisfactory outcome are too uncertain, though, and the implications too dreadful not to warrant the concern and close attention of officials in Washington and Moscow.

On the Soviet Union's side, there is no exact counterpart to the United States alliance ties with would-be proliferators. Moscow's formal defence commitments are restricted to those countries where it has an incontrovertible veto over military programmes (that is, the Warsaw Pact states, Cuba). Those commitments have been specific and unwavering, without the ambivalence that has marked United States undertakings to countries on the margins of its central security interests. India, and less clearly Iraq, are the two important exceptions. The entente between Moscow and Delhi is a prominent fact of political life for both countries. India has looked to the Soviet Union for diplomatic backing in its ongoing rivalry with Pakistan. It has received military aid, technical assistance and advantageous trade opportunities as well. For the Soviet Union's part, the relationship provides Moscow with a sympathetic friend and political ally who holds the dominant position in South Asia and enjoys high standing among non-aligned Less Developed Countries (LDCs) in the world at large. India's value as an ally has grown since the Afghan invasion and rebellion. With Pakistan playing the key role as refuge and supply base for the rebels, the presence of a potentially hostile, pro-Soviet Union neighbour on its eastern flank acts as a constraint on Pakistani support for the Afghans and, at some future point, could make Islamabad more susceptible to Soviet pressure.

The Soviet Union's attitude towards the Indian nuclear programme conforms to a more general pattern of nuclear relations between a dominant and a weaker ally. First, whatever protection close ties with Moscow offered, they obviously were insufficient to dissolve the Indian interest in developing a nuclear weapon capability. Second, while all indications are that Moscow was unhappy about the 1974 test, it was very restrained in voicing its displeasure. It did not even go so far as to match the very mild sanctions imposed by the Western powers on India's nuclear programme; and, indeed, has attempted to mitigate their effect at times.

Indian dependence on the Soviet Union has not been so total as to give Moscow the leverage that the United States has been able to exert on Taiwan and South Korea. Yet Soviet interests in maintaining close ties with Delhi make it tolerant of the latter's transgression of the non-proliferation norm. Those same interests give reason to be concerned about great power entanglement in an Indo-Pakistan nuclear arms race on the subcontinent. A significant stake and unsure influence is a condition that may permit miscalculation, leading to conflict by inadvertence.

The Soviet Union's connection with Iraq has been neither as close nor as unwavering. Before the outbreak of the war with Iran, Moscow was a major arms supplier and diplomatic ally of the Baghdad government. Friendly relations grew in importance for the Soviet Union after Sadat broke with the Soviet Union to seek his own peace with Israel and rapprochement with the United States. But they have been unsettled by the revolution next door in Iran and the opportunities for political gain Moscow saw there. Relations cooled noticeably as the Soviet Union equivocated in selecting its favourite in the Iran-Iraq conflict. Soviet-Iraq friendship did re-emerge in the latter half of 1983 as the Soviet Union, frustrated in Teheran, resumed its position as a major arms supplier to Baghdad, now desperate to bolster its capabilities to deal with the relentless Iranian counteroffensive.

Sadam Hussein's avowed interest in acquiring nuclear weapons does not seem to have had a bearing on these twists and turns in the Soviet-Iraq quasi-alliance. Whatever Moscow's feelings about the Iraqi intentions that surfaced in the wake of the Osiraq affair, they have not been well publicised. While there is little reason to doubt that the Soviet Union would be unhappy about the spread of nuclear arms in the Middle East, what it would do to oppose them remains obscure. Political alliances do serve the dual ends of expanding Soviet Union influence and creating potential leverage on a nuclear-inclined partner. They also imply stakes that could limit the amount of political capital Moscow might be prepared to invest in support of its non-proliferation interest.

As in the case of India, great power ties can both assuage security anxieties and act as a constraining influence on a nuclear weapons programme without precluding it altogether. The net effect of greater power interests in regional conflicts is uncertain, however.

Their presence restrains combatants which may now be or could later come into possession of nuclear weapons; but at the same time it creates the latent danger that local nuclear forces could trigger a general larger war.

Ties with great powers are an ambiguous factor from a proliferation perspective. There is no doubt that the reciprocal interests embodied in an alliance give comfort and instill confidence in the more vulnerable partner and create pressures counteracting any disposition to acquire nuclear arms. Conversely, the absence of close political relations with the United States or Soviet Union gives a threatened and/or ambitious regional power more freedom to meet its security needs as it sees fit. Political distance from the great powers is clearly of central importance in pessimistic projections of whether and how the Iraq-Iran war will whet future appetites of both protagonists for nuclear weapons.[7]

There is a middle ground of limited or qualified alliance that in some ways is potentially most troubling. The embrace by a protective ally may not be strong enough to discourage a dependant state from seeking a nuclear option; yet the former may retain enough of a stake in a regional security situation so as to create a risk of its inadvertent involvement in a local clash made more hazardous by the presence of nuclear arms. This logic applied to the Arab-Israeli conflict suggests that the greatest danger of an escalating war would arise when the diverted attention or flagging interest of the great powers give local parties room to nurture exaggerated fears and unrealistic aspirations. In a similar way, it could be argued that the importance of the Persian Gulf does not allow either Washington or Moscow to ignore politico-strategic developments in the region even as their ability to influence the security decisions in Baghdad and Teheran remains diminished.

Regional Security Position

The premiss of this analysis is that security concerns are the essence of the proliferation problem. Whatever the importance we attach to spreading capabilities, efforts to regulate them and incremental paths to weapons development, in the end the primary determinant of whether a state goes nuclear will be a governmental judgement that there is need for atomic weapons. It is in the nature of states in an unruly political environment to seek the means required for their own protection and preservation. A self-denying injunction on arms, as embodied in the Treaty on the Non-Proliferation of Nuclear

Weapons (NPT), is an exceptional act. Its value is magnified, and its accomplishment all the more remarkable, in that it contradicts the traditional wisdom that arms make the state. The treaty's acceptance by the vast majority of nations is testimony to the uniqueness of nuclear weapons. Yet, the failure to win the adhesion of many prospective nuclear-weapon states is a constant reminder of how jealously governments guard their sovereign prerogatives. Security needs give cause for them to do so.

The level of danger and degree of risk vary. For Israel there exists a threat to the survival of a nation and its people. For the apartheid regime of South Africa the stake is the continued dominance by the country's white population and its control over the state's future. Political support from the Western powers, especially the United States, can mitigate the varied threats but cannot remove them. Taiwan, too, sees its continued political existence at risk, although its people are not endangered to the same extent. Their worry is that of absorption by China. Their fate most likely will be decided through great power agreements that leave the regime no recourse except surrendering power or seeking protection behind a barrier of nuclear weapons.[8] Not only might nuclear weapons help the Taipei government resist military pressure, but their very presence would add an uncomfortable new element to the calculations of Beijing and Washington.

Other states that figure prominently on proliferation worry-lists are faced with something less than physical dismemberment or political destruction. South Korea frets about the hostile regime in the north which invaded it once before and whose staunch backing by the Soviet Union is contrasted unfavourably with the perceived inconstancy of Seoul's United States protector. Pakistan remains preoccupied with its unreconciled and more powerful neighbour, India. The atavistic rivalry between them has evoked the spectre of an aggressive Hindu imperialism threatening Pakistan's existence, although there appear to be slim grounds for judging India either capable or desirous of reabsorbing a bitterly hostile nation of Muslims. A war to establish Indian hegemony and force resolution of the Kashmir issue on its own terms, however, is not wholly unimaginable. Nor is its centrifugal effect on Pakistan's uneasy union of nationalities.

As for the Middle East, the intensity of the Arab-Israeli conflict and the fierce character of internecine Arab rivalries present a picture in which significant security threats are the rule rather than the exception. Iraq's interest in nuclear weapons, aroused initially by a desire to enhance its prestige as a leader of the confrontational bloc opposing Israel and its dominant status in the Gulf, now gains greater cogency as a means to protect itself against the intransigence of its truculent enemy, Iran. Any move in that direction, real or imagined, can be expected to prompt parallel action in Teheran.[9]

The Iranians must be attentive as well to nuclear developments in Pakistan, where an acknowledged nuclear capability could be viewed in quite different ways. Positively, it may be seen as offering a measure of indirect protection against possible intimidation by Iraq. Negatively, it underscores the prospective danger of Iran becoming an isolated non-nuclear island surrounded by powers with established or emerging nuclear forces. This is a situation where indeed one can be paranoid and still have real enemies to be worried about.

In reviewing the security problems by possible nuclear-weapon states, we should take care to avoid the common fault of interpreting conditions and assessing threats as we perceive them. Security, as much as beauty, is in the eye of the beholder. Our idea as to the kind of stake that may warrant resort to nuclear weapons can be distorted by our preoccupation with the security concerns of the great powers threatened mainly by each other's nuclear arsenals. For the states cited above, the risks of nuclear weapons are not self-evidently greater than the risks of dealing with military challenges without them.

If we were to acknowledge that in a hostile environment it is plausible for political leaders to weigh seriously the nuclear option, the question remains whether atomic arms, in fact, can be employed to meet perceived security needs. Were disinterested observers to conclude that they could not, the task then would be to persuade decision-makers of this logic. However, were sober assessment to conclude otherwise, we must confront the disturbing prospect that not only is there reason for a nuclear-capable state to pay close attention to its options, but that it may find ways to take practical advantage of such weapons.

There are several ways in which small nuclear forces could be put to military use. First, there are circumstances in which nuclear weapons logically could serve a strategy of compelling by intimidation. The Iraq-Iran war is a case in point. Arms of mass destruction instil caution; they also can bolster self-esteem. Swaggering behaviour tends to induce self-intoxication. In a regime such as Khomeini's, the effect could lead to even greater self-righteousness and a more aggressive attitude towards external foes. In an environment of impassioned conflict, they might well encourage the more assertive use of other coercive means, including conventional military force.

Iraq and Iran have been protagonists in a contest where the stake is regime survival. High stakes, high emotions (plus vulnerability) raise a serious possibility that all available instruments of intimidation, and perhaps physical coercion, would be brought into play to achieve overriding national objectives. Had either country possessed a rudimentary nuclear force at the time of their initial confrontation, prudence might have prevailed. It might equally have resulted in an exaggeration of strength across-the-board and heightened ambition. Which set of attitudes would have prevailed is not self-evident. Nor is it certain whether primary objectives, as the governments saw them, could have been attained without a reversion to nuclear weapons used as coercive sanction or in retaliation.

Second, intimidation as part of a deterrent strategy is another possible mode of use. With reference once again to the Iraq-Iran case, the greatest incentive to the use of hypothetical nuclear weapons would have come when Iraq's conventional defences seemed on the verge of collapse (in mid-1962) and the regime's survival – as well as its territorial integrity – at risk. In that setting inhibitions about violating an unspoken nuclear taboo could be expected to be sharply lowered. Nuclear weapons might have been employed to force the Iranian enemy to cease and desist from pursuing an intolerable (to Iraq) course of action. The shock effect of being on the receiving end of a nuclear attack is perhaps the only thing sufficient to break the emotional thrust of an ideologically-driven holy war.

The struggle between these two bitter rivals provides a particularly graphic illustration of circumstances discernible as well in other parts of the world where nuclear weapons threaten to make an appearance. Israel's envisaged security predicament is even more severe. Pakistan's *vis-à-vis* India may not match that of the Gulf antagonists (the Delhi government is certainly not as single-minded or ambitious; Pakistan is far less isolated diplomatically). But it is by no means far-fetched for its leaders to contemplate alternative futures darkly to seek a nuclear antidote to their fears. That option is not, of course, risk-free. There is a real danger of setting off a nuclear arms race and ending up with less security. However, we cannot simply assume that it is a course of action to be rejected by all reasonable persons.

Third, nuclear weapons in support of a deterrent and/or defence strategy can play yet another role; that is, as a catalyst to external intervention. Where the involvement of outside powers is seen as a means to ward off total defeat (or break a deadlock viewed as a prelude to collapse), then the detonation of a nuclear explosive could do the trick. It is the best attention-getter around; surely more effective albeit dangerous than Iraq's attacks on shipping around Kharg Island or an attempted blockade of the Straits of Hormuz. Arguably, it is more likely to bring outsiders – the Western powers – into the picture. They might be prompted to act in concert to bring things under control. Of course, they might just as well be encouraged to back as far away as possible and accept the costs. To a government in dire straits seeking outside intervention, it could be seen as worth the try, especially when the same act serves both a strategy for coercing outside parties to intervene and a strategy for deterring a conventionally superior foe from giving the *coup de grace*. For a government that seeks to keep third parties out of the conflict, the threatened use of nuclear weapons might also appear as an effective way to discourage military intervention. In either case, possession of nuclear weapons would carry potential diplomatic value.

Fourth, nuclear weapons can be seen as the most effective means for stalemating another nuclear-armed, hostile state. To the extent that we credit the potential uses of nuclear arms catalogued above (with the probable exception of the third), there is some incentive to counter them by reciprocation. The protection of a superior ally may be more desirable, but there is no assurance of its always being readily available or sufficiently reliable. India's acquisition of a nuclear capability has spurred Pakistan's single-minded, relentless pursuit of the same. A similar logic is likely to prevail in other situations of hostile states where the nuclear factor exists now or could be present.

Any binary nuclear relationship between nuclear-armed regional rivals most probably will be unstable. It is unlikely that mutual deterrence will set in, expressing what some view as the inherent logic of weapons of mass destruction imposing itself on paired states.[10] Rather, we can expect to view the greater incentives to use, the lowered inhibitions, and the systemic instabilities when two passionate foes have atomic bombs in their arsenals. Their possession could serve to arouse bellicose feelings as well to sober decision-makers. Swaggering tendencies could make it more difficult to terminate a conventional war once begun, while reinforcing an unwillingness to accept adverse outcomes. Moreover, the vulnerability of small nuclear arsenals and unsophisticated delivery systems encourages hair-trigger contingency plans, thereby raising an already high risk of pre-emption. Fear, anxiety, pride and ambition would be contending emotions on both sides. In the atmosphere of a high stakes confrontation where ideology may be the driving force and where the nuclear balance is so easily tipped, there is a fair chance that the psychological balance will tilt towards use of nuclear weapons.

A definitive answer to the question of whether nuclear weapons have utility is impossible to give, even in particular situations. More important, it is not necessary for a government to make a precise, confident judgement before deciding to build the bomb. So long as the costs of abstinence are seen as outweighing the costs of possession, there is a good chance that the choice regarding acquisition will be the preferred choice.

Looking back at the history of the nuclear age, it is apparent that the pace of nuclear weapons spread has been slower than many predicted and feared. Nevertheless, it can be argued that nearly all countries capable of building the bomb and having outstanding security problems did in fact take up the nuclear options. (The possible exceptions are South Korea and Taiwan whose plans were scrapped under intense United States pressure in the mid-1970s.) The implications for future proliferation are sobering. Clearly, several states have believed their security to be enhanced by the possession of nuclear weapons. Thoughts of possible use surely figured in those decisions.

Stability of Government and Political Leadership

The structure and character of political leadership has a major bearing on the question of whether a country takes up the nuclear option and the likelihood of using nuclear arms if acquired. There is a dense literature that addresses both these issues.[11] Much of the writing devoted to the first question examines multiple policy paths, including several that see the outcome as emerging from a policy process where no critical points of deliberate choice are identified. That is to say, the ultimate act of building or not building a bomb may register, or conclude, a series of incremental steps whose impetus is provided by organisational inertia, the steady progression of technological advances and, perhaps, the machinations of strong-willed bureaucrats.

There is cause for concern about such a process predisposing a government to make a final affirmative decision. Keeping a check on technical capabilities is an important and worthwhile goal of a non-proliferation strategy. But in the end it is the motivations of a nation's leadership that will determine what it does.[12] A number of propositions can be offered about leadership:

1. Its decision will be based primarily on a judgement that nuclear weapons can meet the military and political needs of the country as it perceives them.
2. These needs will be mainly of a classic security/defence nature.
3. Ideology could have a significant influence on the way national interests are defined, the priorities accorded them and the threats identified.
4. Recent military experience, especially those resulting in defeat and national humiliation, will be especially salient in militating towards a positive decision on nuclear weapons acquisition.
5. Continuity of political leadership is not a pre-condition for maintaining a sustained nuclear development programme, but can be expected to accelerate programmes where a positive decision already has been made.
6. A government that enjoys strong domestic support and exercises broad discretionary powers is better able to resist external pressures to forgo or abandon commitment to the acquisition of nuclear weapons. A government so constituted also is in a stronger position to resist domestic pressure to initiate or to continue a weapons programme which it judges a net liability to the country's interest.
7. Fear that nuclear weapons might become pawns in internecine power struggles and/or used without authorisation does not appear to be a major concern of governments deliberating whether to take up the nuclear option.

These propositions are not offered as universal truths. Most require amendment or qualification when applied to individual cases. They are, however, valid generalisations whose value can be judged in the evaluation of each prospective nuclear-weapon state.

The connection between the nature of governmental leadership and possible use of nuclear weapons is even more difficult to make. The diversity of conjectured conditions in which they might figure and the multiplicity of factors that could affect decisions do not allow for blanket assertions. A number of points, however, are worth making.

First, domestic political weakness may lower the odds on a resort to nuclear arms in a setting of military crisis. As Lewis Dunn has suggested, a leader uncertain of his position could be tempted to escalate hostilities rather than accept an embarrassingly unsatisfactory outcome.[13] Pressure from hawkish advisors or military commitments making urgent entreaties not to concede without at least threatening use of available nuclear arms may add to this disposition. Weakness also can encourage an opponent to take an uncompromising stance in the expectation that its foe lacks the will to escalate or would be deterred from doing so by the fear of retaliation (if both sides are nuclear-armed).

Second, a nuclear-weapon state must have a high level of governmental discipline and organisational sophistication in order to exercise effective powers of command, control and communication. While there is no reason to think that anyone would take a casual approach towards the deployment and disposition of nuclear arms, the technical means and institutional capacity for their management may be inadequate. This is an especially salient problem for small, probably rudimentary nuclear forces whose dispersal to minimise risk of a first strike runs counter to the needs for central political control.

Finally, our earlier propositions regarding susceptibility to outside influence on the decision to go nuclear apply as well to the question of how open a government may be to diplomatic pressure aimed at keeping it from using its atomic arms. On balance, it is probable that strong political leadership would be easier to deal with in so far as the locus of authority could be more readily identified; one's messages communicated in the confidence that they will register; and the range of proposals that might be considered would be wider as well as the time frames they cover. Weak governments, seemingly more responsive to pressure, often have proven exceedingly difficult to control, much less the outcomes of conditions for which they are nominally responsible. The United States experience in Vietnam and the Middle East (and that of the Soviet Union in the latter region) give cause for concern as to the ability of great powers to affect the behaviour of small nuclear states which may be over-armed and under-controlled.

Implications for Great Power Policies

Much of the analysis presented to this point may be interpreted as leading to the conclusion that the pace of proliferation is likely to quicken; and, further, that there is a fair chance of those nuclear arms being used in regional conflicts. The chances of such an eventuality coming to pass are good enough that it behoves us to ponder the implications for the great powers and for the larger security system of which they are custodian in some sense.

The first thing to say is that the developments we have conjectured will not threaten directly either the United States or the Soviet Union. As John Weltman has noted: '[f]or at least until the end of this century, the stability of the central strategic balance will remain substantially unaffected by any force that could be deployed by Nth countries'.[14] Most of the proliferation that can be foreseen would be in locations more proximate to the Soviet Union than the United States (for example, Pakistan and Iraq). The Soviet Union, though, has managed to accommodate itself with the advent of the far more threatening Chinese force and to tolerate India's crossing the nuclear threshold. Other developments of that kind would be unwelcome but in fact little more than strategic pin pricks.

The risk of minor nuclear forces acting as a catalyst to general nuclear war between the great powers is only somewhat more troubling. With the deployment of sophisticated technical means for surveillance, the dangers of misapprehension leading to unintended hostilities have been markedly reduced, if not entirely eliminated.[15]

More worrisome is the impetus to ballistic missile defence which might be given by the spread of nuclear weapons. However negligible the danger they pose, the presence of third nuclear parties does provide a supporting argument for proponents in Washington and Moscow of strategic defences, which are seen by many as destabilising of the central balance and an obstacle to efforts at avoiding nuclear war.

The chance that the great powers might be drawn into a regional nuclear conflict is more troubling. Unless we conclude that the availability of nuclear arms in these circumstances will act as a constraint on the use of military force, then any crisis becomes inherently more dangerous; the Arab-Israeli confrontation and the Indo-Pakistan stand-off being the most prominent examples and causes for concern. How the United States and Soviet Union might respond in such a circumstance is problematic.

Conceivably, the United States and Soviet Union would be sufficiently sobered by the hazardousness of the situation to adjust their
objectives downward and to redouble their efforts to reach a compromise while restraining their local allies. The stakes, though, will
remain high. The presence of nuclear weapons in the hands of the
regional foes could make them more recalcitrant. Moreover, as
Dunn has argued, nuclear weapons can be expected to increase the
tempo of events and, thereby, the risk of miscalculation.[16] The
challenge to the diplomatic skills of Moscow and Washington would
be daunting, to say the least.

The last point deserving mention is that the spread of nuclear
weapons into an area such as the Middle East could make it more difficult for the United States to defend interests other than those of a
security nature. It is, for example, committed to maintaining access
to Persian Gulf oil and, by implication, has a paramount stake in preserving the independence of friendly regimes in the region. A threat
to Saudi Arabia or the Gulf principalities, whether through aggression or externally sponsored insurrection, is a threat to the economic
well-being of the West and Japan. So, too, any attempt to interfere
with the shipment of oil from Gulf suppliers would be viewed gravely.
An Iranian victory in its protracted war with Iraq would magnify
the danger.

The United States has proclaimed its readiness to use force if
necessary to defend its interests against a range of challenges. Were
the actual contingency to take the form of hostile action by a belli-
gerent Iran, the credibility of United States pledges to protect friends
and secure oil resources would be drastically affected by the former's possession of nuclear arms. Even the most rudimentary force
would dictate a sober reappraisal of what and how it might intervene, for atomic arms in the hands of a local power cannot fail to
act as deterrents against unwelcome great power intervention.

This is admittedly a remote contingency, but there seems no
denying the general proposition that the spread of nuclear capabilities not only raises the risk of nuclear conflict, it also could constrain the use of force by the great powers in support of highly
valued interests. The presence of nuclear arms introduces a factor
of capital importance, wherever they appear, whatever their
calibre.

Prescription

The title of this concluding section is somewhat misleading. It does not propose an outline of a comprehensive set of definitive proposals for warding off the danger of security nuclear arms. The focus of this chapter has been to discuss the security factor in proliferation. Therefore, there is little by way of examination of how growing capabilities influence weapons-related choices or what might be done to curb that growth. On that score there clearly is important work to be done in tightening supplier guidelines, in closing the gaps that remain, and in bringing the second- and third-tier suppliers into the fold.

Looking specifically at security considerations, one can identify two issues that require the attention of the nuclear-weapon states, above all, the United States and the Soviet Union. The first concerns the bearing that their own nuclear arms policies have on the perceptions and dispositions of possible proliferators. The other is the question of what might be done collectively or individually to alleviate the causes of security anxieties.

One of the distinguishing features of non-proliferation as an arms control problem is the presumption of a fundamental line of discrimination between those states that are allowed to retain nuclear weapons and those that are asked to abjure them. As a consequence, the behaviour of nuclear-weapon states is under constant scrutiny by non-nuclear-weapon states. Vertical proliferation – that is, the expansion and qualitative improvement of the nuclear arsenals of the great powers – is frequently pointed to as undermining the force and credibility of the campaign against horizontal proliferation. (Other contributors to this volume make that connection with a passion that testifies to the political significance, if not cogency, of the argument.) While it has never been quite clear how dangerous armsracing at one level could be used to justify the acquisition of these horrific weapons by others, there is no denying the emotional tie that is made in the thinking of governments that are candidate proliferators.

Strategic arms control may not be a logical pre-condition to strengthening prohibitions against nuclear weapons spread, but it understandably helps. It performs its most valuable service by reinforcing the conviction that nuclear weapons are indeed something new under the sun, deserving to be treated with exceptional caution and requiring extraordinary action by the nations of the world. The collapse of SALT II, followed by a return to confrontational postures by the United States and the Soviet Union, creates inauspicious conditions for the launching of other major arms control proposals. Revival of talks to control strategic arms is itself a favourable development. Further non-proliferation dividends would accrue were the superpowers to act positively on the one item that actually bridges the two levels of arms control, that is, a Comprehensive Test Ban (CTB).

From a non-proliferation standpoint, the value of a CTB is considerable. A general prohibition on nuclear explosions means that the onus of breaking an international norm would fall on any state that tests a weapon, however it may be represented. The CTB would permit drawing an unmistakable line between acceptable and unacceptable behaviour. Being able to draw such a line, it becomes possible at least to think in terms of collective sanctions against transgression of a non-proliferation norm. Without a clear guidepost no such action is feasible, even were there a superpower disposition to oppose actively nuclear weapons spread.

Organising collective sanctions would be facilitated by another great power accord: acceptance of a 'no-first-use of nuclear weapons' doctrine. It would have a twofold effect. By implicitly rejecting a war-fighting role for nuclear weapons, it would diminish their theoretical attractiveness as a useful mode of arms. By pledging the United States and the Soviet Union (and, desirably, other nuclear-weapon states as well) to refrain from initiating atomic warfare, it would strengthen collective norms as to what is and is not acceptable nuclear conduct.[17] To the extent that the utility of nuclear arms is thereby devalued, the interest in acquiring them may be somewhat muted. Similarly, the implied cost of violating a general prohibition on first use could help to discourage a minor nuclear power from employing nuclear weapons in battle, and reduce the risk that their successful use would spur near-nuclear states, with comparable security needs, to develop their own nuclear weapons.

Dealing with the security problems that may motivate a state to take up the nuclear option is, if anything, more vital to avoiding further proliferation, and more difficult. We must acknowledge that the weakening of great power influence in the world, especially of the United States, although welcomed by many, carries with it a diminution of their ability to aid in the resolution of regional conflicts. (Admittedly, their ability to aggravate them is also reduced, if not proportionally.) The security worries of Pakistan, Israel and its

Arab neighbours, Iran or South Africa cannot be removed by action of the United States, the Soviet Union or the other nuclear-armed states, China, France and the United Kingdom. Even with the best of intentions, based on a sense of mutual interest, a significant level of threat and the reasons for them would remain. As a practical matter, we cannot count on either an enlightened view of interests or the constructive behaviour they may prompt.

Of course, we each could draw up a list of initiatives and proposals that we earnestly believe would serve the cause of peace and stability in conflict-ridden regions of the world. We may rightly hope that they figure on the diplomatic agenda both of local powers and external parties, and bend our shoulders to that end. But it is unreasonable to place our faith in panaceas that promise either instant or complete success. We can reasonably aspire, though, to the mitigation of conflict that lowers security concerns below the threshold that is likely to encourage the acquisition and use of nuclear weapons. That is the task of international diplomacy on which, for better or worse, we must rely.

While much can be done by each of the great powers along these lines, there are very definite limits imposed by the absence of the other as a collaborative partner. Pakistan is a case in point. Its interest in nuclear weapons is prompted unmistakably by the demonstrated capacity of India. Its sense of insecurity has been accentuated by what Islamabad sees as the uncertain reliability and inadequacy of the protection offered by the United States. It has been suggested that Washington could have deflected Pakistan from the current course through a more adroit use of aid as carrot and/or stick. The question of conventional arms transfers to would-be nuclear-weapon states has been dubbed the dove's dilemma. The Pakistan situation suggests an even deeper dilemma. Experience since the Afghan invasion holds the lesson that arms sales cannot easily be designed to slow the move to acquire nuclear weapons, nor are they effective.

The United States government operates under too many constraints to provide Pakistan with iron-clad security guarantees. It cannot eliminate the latent threat of India. Short of doing either, transfers are relatively weak tools of anti-proliferation diplomacy. Moreover, the desired quid-pro-quo arrangement is obviated in this instance by Pakistan's having already given the quo of succouring the Afghan rebels in exchange for the quid of United States assistance.

Only the Soviet Union could complete the bargain by accommodating the Afghani opposition. Only the Soviet Union could make the United States offer of security guarantees acceptable by working towards a settlement with India which both powers would join in underwriting. Unfortunately, neither in this case nor other proliferation-relevant regional conflicts do other great power interests converge enough to favour this kind of collaboration. One last question remains to be asked. Do we have reason to believe that the two great powers might co-operate to prevent first use of nuclear weapons by third parties and to impose penalties on whomever did? Is their stake in preserving the norm of no-nuclear-use so strong as to call forth a concerted effort?

A great power condominium to police the world's nuclear affairs often has been raised. The idea has been dormant for three obvious reasons. First, it requires a degree of trust that they have yet to achieve. Second, it presumes a mutual interest in avoiding third-party use of nuclear arms that outweighs differences of interest they may have in the situation in question. Third, it demands agreement on appropriate measures and the means to implement them. Only the second condition could be met in selective cases, for example the Iraq-Iran war. The other two conditions depend on a kind of collaboration that the present level of tension precludes. The great powers' fundamentally adverse relationship would make it difficult to reach it even under relatively more relaxed circumstances.

Co-operation in the future most probably will be partial and imperfect, adding further to the formidable diplomatic burden borne by those who are responsible for non-proliferation policy.

End Notes

1. See Robert S. McNamara's illuminating reflections in 'The Military Role of Nuclear Weapons', *Foreign Affairs*, vol. 62, no. 1 (1983).
2. For example, Lewis A. Dunn, *Controlling the Bomb* (Yale University Press, New Haven, 1982).
3. This formulation benefits in some respects from that offered by Michael Nacht, 'The Future Unlike the Past: Nuclear Proliferation and American Security Policy' in George H. Quester (ed.), *Nuclear Proliferation* (University of Wisconsin Press, Madison, 1981).
4. Earl C. Ravenal, 'Europe Without America', *Foreign Affairs*, vol. 63, no. 5 (1985).
5. The notion of pariah state is discussed by Robert Harkavy, 'Pariah States and Nuclear Proliferation' in Quester, *Nuclear Proliferation*.
6. Nacht, 'The Future Unlike the Past'.
7. A salient feature of this regional power rivalry is the relatively weak ties between either protagonist and the great powers. Iraq, whose off-again, on-again relationship with the Soviet Union we have noted, never has been susceptible to dictation

from Moscow. Its ties with the United States are minimal. The Khomeini regime in Teheran fulminates against the United States and the Soviet Union in turn. Both enjoy an exceptional level of diplomatic independence and freedom from external constraint. It is reinforced by a high degree of financial self-sufficiency (although Iraq has had to be subsidised by the Gulf states with its port at Basra blocked and the war of attrition dragging on). Hence the decision whether to pursue the nuclear option, on either side or both, is likely to be taken in a security environment where the principle of self-reliant defence prevails. It is also an environment in which threats to security are manifest and serious.

8. One consideration of this issue is offered by John J. Weltman, 'Managing Nuclear Multipolarity', *International Security*, vol. 6, no. 3 (Winter 1981-82).

9. I discuss the nuclear implications of the Iraq-Iran war in 'Iraq-Iran War: Speculations About a Nuclear Rerun', *Journal of Strategic Studies* (March 1985).

10. A number of analysts have taken the sanguine view that the spread of nuclear weapons is likely to quiet regional conflicts and further international stability. Neither the logic nor the evidence offered in support of this view strikes me as persuasive. See especially Kenneth Waltz, 'The Spread of Nuclear Weapons: More May Be Better', *Adelphi Paper*, no. 171 (IISS, London, 1981). Also, Ali Mazrui, 'Changing The Guards from Hindus to Moslems: Collective Third World Security in Cultural Perspective', *International Affairs*, vol. 57, no. 1 (Winter 1980-81).

11. See Stephen M. Meyer, *The Dynamics of Nuclear Proliferation* (University of Chicago Press, Chicago, 1984); Dunn, *Controlling the Bomb*; and the introduction by David Gompert to Ted Greenwood, Harold A. Feiveson and Theodore B. Taylor, *Nuclear Proliferation: Motivations, Capabilities and Strategies for Control* (McGraw-Hill, New York, 1977).

12. Meyer, *The Dynamics of Nuclear Proliferation*, Ch. 5, analyses exhaustively all known cases of decisions by national governments whether to seek nuclear weapons and reaches a similar conclusion.

13. Dunn, *Controlling the Bomb*, p. 85.

14. Weltman, 'Managing Nuclear Multiplicity', p. 186.

15. Dunn, *Controlling the Bomb*, p. 79.

16. The agreement reached by the United States and the Soviet Union in the summer of 1985 to consult through the Washington-Moscow hotline in case of a nuclear explosion or a threat by a third party is evidence of the assiduous efforts they are making to avoid catalytic nuclear war. See the *New York Times*, 6 July 1985.

17. A no-first-use doctrine has benefits in its own right, as argued in the provocative article by McGeorge Bundy, George F. Kennan, Robert S. McNamara and Gerard Smith, 'Nuclear Weapons and the Atlantic Alliance', *Foreign Affairs*, vol. 60, no. 4 (1982).

II.
NUCLEAR NON-PROLIFERATION:
POLICIES AND PERSPECTIVES

THE IAEA, INTERNATIONAL SAFEGUARDS AND THE FUTURE OF THE NPT

Jon Jennekens

Introduction

For almost four decades international initiatives to limit the spread of nuclear weapons have included two or more of the following fundamental concepts:

1. concerted efforts to lessen international tensions by general disarmament, and reduction and eventual elimination of all weapons of mass destruction are required if a lasting, universal peace is to be achieved;
2. all nations should enjoy the manifold benefits of the peaceful uses of nuclear materials, equipment and facilities;
3. national and international control measures, including binding treaties, are needed to provide the world community with meaningful assurances regarding the peaceful objectives of national and multi-national nuclear programmes; and
4. a credible and therefore effective system of international safeguards is required to verify compliance with the aforementioned control measures and continued fulfilment of the obligations undertaken by sovereign governments pursuant to the provisions of formal treaties.

The first nuclear non-proliferation initiative of consequence was the 16 November 1945 declaration by the United States, the United Kingdom and Canada. It is known formally as The Agreed Declaration of 1945 and it led to the creation of the soon-forgotten United Nations Atomic Energy Commission (UNAEC) in January 1946. Although the commission was short-lived, due to substantive and not surprisingly recurrent disagreement between the United States and the Soviet Union on a number of critical issues, it did prepare a series of reports which both helped and hindered the subsequent development of the nuclear non-proliferation regime.

The first report of the UNAEC was submitted to the United

Nations Security Council on 31 December 1946. Not unexpectedly, it contained many of the elements of a United States' proposal presented to the commission on 14 June 1946 by Ambassador Bernard Baruch. The commission recommended the establishment of an international organisation for control and inspection of atomic energy activities by means of a system of safeguards which would detect and prevent diversion of materials from declared facilities to non-peaceful purposes. Moreover, it was proposed that the organisation would implement measures to detect the existence of clandestine facilities. Nuclear non-proliferation proponents and safeguards practitioners of today will quickly recognise the particular significance of the words 'prohibit', 'disposal', 'control', 'detect', 'prevent', 'declare' and 'clandestine'.

More than 38 years have passed since the first report of the UNAEC and, despite the considerable efforts of many nations, 1985 has arrived without:

1. the existence of a universally accepted treaty prohibiting the development or acquisition of nuclear weapons nor one providing for the disposal of existing stocks of nuclear weapons; or
2. the existence of an international organisation with the mandate and means to control all nuclear programmes and to prevent the diversion of nuclear materials to non-peaceful purposes and to detect the existence of clandestine nuclear facilities.

Notwithstanding the delays in achieving some of the long-standing objectives of non-proliferation and general disarmament, it is important to recognise that a number of directly related bilateral and multilateral treaties have been negotiated during this 38-year period. These include the Limited Test Ban Treaty of 1963, the Treaty for the Prohibition of Nuclear Weapons in Latin America which was opened for signature in 1967, the Outer Space Treaty of 1967, the Seabed Treaty of 1972 and, of course, the Treaty on the Non-Proliferation of Nuclear Weapons (NPT) itself. Although quite clearly the NPT has not attracted the universality of acceptance which its drafters had hoped for initially, the broad support that it has received is indicative of the importance which most nations of the world attach to the continuing development of the nuclear non-proliferation regime. An equally essential element of the regime is the International Atomic Energy Agency (IAEA), whose very existence facilitated the task of the Eighteen-Nation Disarmament

Committee which drafted the NPT.

The negotiations which led to the drafting of the IAEA statute and the NPT were both long and complex. They provided ample opportunity for misunderstandings to arise and for misconceptions to develop, particularly with respect to the mandate of the IAEA. These misunderstandings and misconceptions, in turn, have provided substantial fuel for critics of the non-proliferation regime.

The purpose of this chapter is to reiterate the clear and unequivocal objectives of the IAEA as stated in its statute, to outline some of the most problematic misconceptions about these objectives, and to underline the agency's successes, recognising the importance of its many functions in the context of Articles III and IV of the NPT.

The Statutory Mandate of the IAEA

In the ten years which followed the first report of the UNAEC, several important events occurred which kept alive international interest in pursuing the development of a nuclear non-proliferation regime. Undoubtedly, the most significant of these was the Atoms for Peace proposal of President Eisenhower, which he advanced in 1953. These events culminated in the drafting of the statute of the IAEA which was approved on 23 October 1956 by the Conference on the Statute of the International Atomic Energy Agency at the headquarters of the United Nations. It entered into force on 29 July 1957, a year that witnessed the first hydrogen bomb test by the United Kingdom and the launching of Sputnik I by the Soviet Union.

The twofold objectives of the IAEA are set forth in Article II of its statute which reads as follows:

> The Agency shall seek to accelerate and enlarge the contribution of atomic energy to peace, health and prosperity throughout the world. It shall ensure, so far as it is able, that assistance provided by it or at its request or under its supervision or control is not used in such a way as to further any military purpose.

It is essential to the understanding of the agency's achievements and the nature of its activities to note the qualifying words 'so far as it is able' and to examine carefully the seven-point statement of its functions which appears in Article III of its statute.

Article III(A)5 of the statute states that one of the agency's functions is:

> To establish and administer safeguards designed to ensure that special fissionable and other materials, services, equipment, facilities, and information made available by the Agency or at its request or under its supervision or control are not used in such a way as to further any military purpose; and to apply safeguards, at the request of the parties, to any bilateral or multilateral arrangement, or at the request of a state, to any of that State's activities, in the field of atomic energy.

In view of the emphasis to be placed in this chapter on international safeguards, the other six points of sub-section A of Article III of the statute will not be repeated. However, this should not be misconstrued as suggesting that they have little or no relevance to the future of the NPT. In fact, all seven of the clarifying statements of the agency's functions are relevant to the continued viability of the NPT.

Misconceptions, Difficulties and Achievements

As an initial step towards the establishment of the safeguards required under Article III of the statute, the agency's Board of Governors commissioned a committee-of-the-whole to draft a set of principles and procedures which would provide guidance to the secretariat in administering safeguards. The committee prepared a document[1] that proved to be of considerable value in terms of the safeguards principles it prescribed, but of limited value in terms of safeguards implementation because of the narrowness of its application, which was restricted to small research reactors. The document was extended to cover large reactor facilities in 1964; however, the magnitude of the agency's safeguards programme was still very small. Fortunately, the Board of Governors recognised that it had only begun what was to become an iterative, time-consuming and extremely controversial process in further defining and arranging for the implementation of the agency's safeguards system. The committee-of-the-whole was instructed to pursue its efforts and to widen the applicability of the safeguards principles, criteria and procedures which it developed. In 1965 the Board of Governors approved the issuance of a further document[2] which, as intended, specified general provisions applicable to all nuclear facilities and special procedures for reactors. This document was revised in 1966 and 1968.

In 1970 the Board of Governors commissioned a 'new' committee-of-the-whole with much the same membership as its predecessor, although substantially enlarged to prepare recommendations to be used by the director general as the basis for negotiating safeguards agreements between the agency and non-nuclear-weapon states party to the NPT. The recommendations are recorded in a document entitled, The Structure and Content of Agreements Between the Agency and States, required in connection with the Treaty on the Non-Proliferation of Nuclear Weapons, INFCIRC 153. In disregard of the historical and evolutionary development of safeguards principles, criteria and procedures, INFCIRC 153 has been portrayed frequently as the statement of 'NPT safeguards' as distinct from 'agency safeguards', the claim being made that the 1968 version of the agency's safeguards system (documented in INFCIRC 66 (Rev. 2)) constitutes the sole and definitive statement of 'agency safeguards' and that the safeguards principles and provisions stipulated in INFCIRC 153 are only applicable to NPT parties. Such attitudes hinder and, in certain instances, frustrate the effective implementation of safeguards. The agency's safeguards system is a dynamic combination of principles, practices, human resources and a number of technologies. Needless to say, the safeguards system must retain its dynamic character and, through an iterative process of development and implementation, it must continue to evolve in order to best serve the interests of the member states for which it exists.

In the enthusiasm of the first few years of the agency's existence, a few member states, including Canada, made available to the agency token quantities of source and special fissionable material as well as certain research equipment and facilities for delivery to predetermined recipient member states. This 'technical assistance' was subject to agency 'supervision and control' in that both health and safety considerations and safeguards provisions were applied. However, physical, operational and managerial control by the agency were not involved. This form of limited 'control' is a far cry from that initially envisaged by the UNAEC, but is in keeping with the limitations imposed by Article II of the statute, wherein the qualifier 'so far as it is able' appears. In subsequent years (that is, the 1970s and 1980s) the placement of 'source and special fissionable materials . . . etc.'

under agency 'supervision and control' dried to a trickle. Consequently, the opportunity for the IAEA to exercise 'supervision and control' over atomic energy activities in its member states reduced coincidentally. Several attempts have been made to develop agreement among member states on various institutional arrangements for strengthening the non-proliferation regime, which would involve an expansion of the agency's role in the 'supervision and control' of nuclear materials, equipment and facilities. Notable among these is the International Fuel Cycle Evaluation (INFCE). This study produced a number of significant conclusions, perhaps the most important of which are:

1. there is no easy technical means of preventing the acquisition of nuclear explosive material;
2. it is not possible to rank various fuel cycles according to the risk proliferation they entail; and
3. proliferation is chiefly a political problem requiring new institutional and other internationally acceptable measures, in particular the improvement and strengthening of the international safeguards system.

Other initiatives such as the Committee on Assurances of Supply (CAS), International Plutonium Storage (IPS), and International Fuel Cycle Centres (IFCC) would also involve the enhancement of the agency's 'supervision and control' role if brought to fruition. Pending the achievement of agreement on such measures, reinforcing the viability and credibility of current agency activities is the best means of enabling the agency to realise its full potential.

To return to the 1960s, it is evident that these years were characterised by a gradual evolution of ideas and experience as the fledgling agency endeavoured to fulfil its very heavy responsibilities. Safeguards agreements of the 'project' type were concluded with individual member states, as well as 'trilateral' agreements under which the agency's safeguards replaced bilaterally administered safeguards. In most instances small quantities of source and special fissionable materials were involved, and the nuclear facilities in which these materials were used or processed tended to be of the research, teaching or demonstration variety. Nevertheless, a number of very important lessons were learned by the agency's secretariat and officials in member states in which 'Agency safeguards' were being applied. From the standpoint of the pragmatist, perhaps one of the most significant of these lessons was that for the long-term it is not realistic to assert, assume or assure that a given atom of uranium or plutonium can easily be tagged with a national identity. Unrealistic and impractical as it may be, there continues to exist a school of thought which insists that a given atom of uranium or plutonium, or an identical and therefore equivalent proxy can be rationally, realistically and reasonably identified, measured, recorded and safeguarded along its peripatetic journey throughout the nuclear fuel cycle. For a brief period some 15 years ago, a flash of enlightenment illuminated the corridors of officialdom and an obvious and much needed concept was advanced. The 'unified inventory concept', as initially proposed, would have required the agency and each member state to establish a single record of all nuclear material in the state subject to safeguards irrespective of its origin and to maintain and update this inventory record on the basis of subsequent nuclear materials accounting reports and the results of the agency's verification activities. More importantly, the 'unified inventory concept' envisaged the development of a single, universally accepted set of conditions which would govern the supply of nuclear materials, equipment, facilities, technology and services.

For many years following World War II, the United States, Soviet Union and United Kingdom imposed strict controls over the provision of assistance in the nuclear field. As previously indicated, the 1953 Atoms for Peace proposal of President Eisenhower and the subsequent 1955 United Nations Conference on the Peaceful Uses of Atomic Energy reversed the acknowledged 'policy of denial', albeit insufficiently in the eyes of some nations.

Notwithstanding the relaxation of export controls by the principal suppliers of nuclear assistance, there remained quite rigorous national and international guidelines which were in effect during the drafting of INFCIRC 153. These guidelines and the national policies of many suppliers required keeping individual inventories of nuclear materials, etc., according to their country of origin. As a consequence, the 'multiple labelling' of such material and equipment, and subsequent generations of nuclear material produced therefrom, began to impose an unreasonable administrative burden on the recipients. However, this was only a minor irritant in comparison to the perceived intrusion into the sovereign rights of recipient states which found it necessary to seek the prior consent of from one to several suppliers of their plans for retransfer, storage, reprocessing or enrichment of nuclear materials. These 'prior consent' requirements also applied to supplied equipment, facilities and technology, and to nuclear materials produced therein or thereby.

The unified inventory concept was advanced in the hope that all member states of the agency and all of the adherents to the NPT would agree to develop the necessary conditions that would govern the international supply of all forms of nuclear assistance. Unfortunately, the gap between the requirements of some supplier states proved to be too large, at least in the early 1970s. Certain developments, including India's explosion of a nuclear device in 1974, prompted the majority of supplier states to negotiate an informal agreement on a set of nuclear export guidelines. These are known as the 'London Guidelines' and are published in IAEA document INFCIRC 254 (1977).

Further attempts have been made to develop a broader understanding of the linkage and essential concurrence between Articles III and IV of the NPT. The most important of these attempts is that of the previously mentioned Committee on Assurances of Supply of the IAEA's Board of Governors. Although stalemate and delay have been the order of the day, recent initiatives by the committee have encouraged many of the participants to renew their efforts to develop a broad consensus. Without question, universal adherence to the NPT would facilitate the early achievement of this consensus.

The congruence between the recommendations of the UNAEC's first report, the Atoms for Peace plan, the statute of the IAEA and the NPT is best illustrated by the title of the previously mentioned 1955 United Nations Conference on the Peaceful Uses of Atomic Energy. The conference marked the first substantive attempt by the United States, the Soviet Union and other member states of the United Nations to open their doors to the rapidly expanding medical, agricultural, industrial, research and teaching applications of the peaceful atom. Soon after its establishment, the IAEA assumed a position of acknowledged and continuing leadership. A current example of this leadership is the agency's joint programme with the Food and Agriculture Organisation (FAO) in agricultural biotechnology which spans a broad range of projects. These projects include measures for insect and pest control, animal production and health, plant breeding and genetics, soil fertility, irrigation and crop production, the improved use of agrochemicals, the control of chemical residues and, of course, food preservation. In connection with the latter, Canada is one of the many member states of the agency actively supporting the International Facility for Food Irradiation, which has been established under the leadership of the Netherlands and the Joint FAO/IAEA Division. Scientists from 40 developing countries have completed training courses at the facility and dozens more will participate in such courses annually. Certainly, the agency's achievements in accelerating and enlarging the contribution of atomic energy to the health and prosperity of people throughout the world have been remarkable and, equally, so have been its contributions to world peace.

It is somewhat difficult to speak about world peace in light of past and current events. Nevertheless, the fact remains that the IAEA's safeguards system undoubtedly has contributed substantially to the assurance and reassurances which are essential to the avoidance of conflict. Before mentioning some of the agency's many achievements in continuing to fulfil the second of its twofold objectives, it is important to note that the agency is not authorised to attempt to prevent the diversion of nuclear materials to non-peaceful purposes, nor do agency safeguards embrace investigations intended to uncover the existence of clandestine nuclear materials or facilities. Agency safeguards agreements are not entered into by member states as a means of self-deterrence or as a result of coercion by others. The sole purpose of agency safeguards is to verify retrospectively the fulfilment of obligations undertaken by member states pursuant to the provisions of safeguards agreements to which they are a party.

In the context of the agency's safeguards achievements, a somewhat startling statistic, at least at first glance, is that 40 of the 125 non-nuclear-weapon states which have ratified the NPT have not yet complied with the provisions of Article III of the treaty, which requires each such state to enter into a safeguards agreement with the agency, pursuant to which safeguards are to be applied to all source and fissionable material in all peaceful nuclear activities in the state.[3] Upon closer examination, it becomes evident that none of these 40 states have initiated activities which would call for the application of safeguards. The 85 member states which have concluded safeguards agreements pursuant to the provisions of the NPT and the Treaty for the Prohibition of Nuclear Weapons in Latin America (Treaty of Tlatelolco), together with eleven additional member states which have concluded safeguards agreements in accordance with INFCIRC 66 (Rev. 2), constitute powerful testimony to the contributions of the agency to world peace. The safeguards agreements which they have concluded stipulate formal undertakings and obligations that provide for the mutual assurance so important to the shared objective of non-proliferation. The safeguards applied in accordance with these agreements are a technical means of providing the desired mutual assurance by verifying the fulfilment of the political obligations assumed by sovereign states.

Approximately 1,900 IAEA safeguards inspections were carried out at well over 500 nuclear facilities in 1984. These facilities ranged from small experimental and research reactors to major installations employing several hundred persons engaged in a broad spectrum of research, production and operational activities. The inspections at these facilities included an audit of accounting records and reports as well as direct physical verification of materials in accordance with previously determined inspection goals. These goals are derived on the basis of a number of considerations including the significance of the quantity, form, condition and isotopic composition of the materials involved, the important notions of timeliness and totality of information available to the agency about the design and operating characteristics of nuclear facilities, the effectiveness of the state's own system of accounting and control, the extent of import, export and indigenous transfers of nuclear material, and the availability of containment and surveillance devices which enable the continuity of information about nuclear materials to be maintained in certain instances. Not all inspection goals were attained in 1984, nor is it likely that 100 per cent attainment will ever be achieved in an absolute sense.

As one would expect, this non-attainment of all inspection goals could be, and sometimes is, misconstrued as failure of the safeguards system to achieve its objectives. Aside from the realisation of the magnitude of the task, an appreciation of the mechanics of the system aids in understanding why 100 per cent attainment is not likely. Unlike the auditing of banking operations which only involve very discreet, easily identifiable and totally quantifiable items of interest, the conduct of a safeguards inspection invariably involves a host of destructive and non-destructive measurement techniques and the verification of a multitude of different materials in bulk quantities. Varying chemical and isotopic compositions and differing physical forms add significant dimensions of complexity, as does the interpretation of the outputs from containment and surveillance devices. Equipment failure, human error and all the usual complications are involved. However, the agency's safeguards system does, nevertheless, provide sufficient information on which to base the all-important conclusion as to whether the nuclear material under safeguards is being used for peaceful purposes.

A fact also not fully appreciated is that by accepting IAEA safeguards, sovereign states also have accepted inspection teams made up of persons of many nationalities, cultural backgrounds and political persuasions, despite the fact that most states are very sensitive about the potential impact of a foreign presence. To accept a foreign presence on a visitor basis is one thing, but to accept a foreign presence on an inspection basis is quite another. This latter basis is precisely what is involved in IAEA safeguards. Acceptance of IAEA safeguards demonstrates that states are willing to subordinate their sovereignty in the cause of global peace and security.

Conclusions

Although the fundamental concepts embodied in the early recommendations of the UNAEC have not all been accepted, much has been achieved. Further steps can and must be taken to bring about the ultimate objectives of nuclear non-proliferation, arms control and general disarmament. However, in striving for these noble objectives, it will be important to ensure that we do not allow anyone to weaken the fabric of the non-proliferation regime which has been painstakingly developed to date and which will continue to evolve and be strengthened. Nor can we allow anyone to emasculate the only credible, broadly international institution that has contributed so much to the betterment of mankind by assisting its 112 member states to initiate and to expand their peaceful nuclear activities within the framework of this non-proliferation regime.

Hopefully, this chapter will have clarified some of the misconceptions about the role of the IAEA, highlighted some of the difficulties experienced by the agency in carrying out its responsibilities, and recorded some of the achievements which it has accomplished in spite of the limitations imposed.

How firmly we are committed as individuals and nations to non-proliferation and to the peaceful uses of nuclear energy will become quite apparent when we are seen to be alleviating rather than contributing to the difficulties and misconceptions that the IAEA is encountering. By further assisting and encouraging the IAEA, the evolutionary development of its safeguards system will continue. The linkage between the future viability of the IAEA and of non-proliferation initiatives, such as the NPT, should be apparent to all.

End Notes

1. International Atomic Energy Agency, 'The Agency's Safeguards System (1961)', *Information Circular/26* (Vienna).
2. International Atomic Energy Agency, 'The Agency's Safeguards System (1965)', *Information Circular/66* (Vienna). The document was further extended in 1966 (Rev. 1) and 1968 (Rev. 2) to cover reprocessing, conversion and fuel fabrication facilities.
3. Editor's note: Between May 1985 when the author prepared this chapter and the end of the Third Review Conference, the statistics changed. As of October 1985, 130 countries had ratified the NPT, of which 127 were non-nuclear-weapon states and 42 had not yet entered into a safeguards agreement with the IAEA.

THE POLICIES OF SUPPLIER NATIONS

Mark J. Moher

The policies of supplier nations cover a wide range of interests and concerns: political, economic, commercial, resource management, financial, technological and nuclear non-proliferation among others. This chapter concentrates on the nuclear non-proliferation element of those policies. While it is recognised that nuclear proliferation is primarily a result of political factors often pertaining to regional security, and that those factors must be recognised in pursuing any coherent long-term non-proliferation policy, this is not the focus in this chapter. Rather, the focus here is on the specific policies that nuclear suppliers have implemented and should implement from a non-proliferation perspective as regards their nuclear exports.

In this context, the evolution of the nuclear export policies of supplier nations has been moulded by the tension between alarm over the dangers of nuclear proliferation on the one hand, and on the other by the desire of supplier nations to share the benefits of the peaceful uses of nuclear energy and to secure economic return by exporting nuclear products. Considerable progress has been made in this evolution, but challenges remain and further progress is essential. These three words – evolution, challenges and progress – identify the purpose and structure of this chapter.

In preparing this chapter, a number of assumptions have been made. First, the use of nuclear energy and international nuclear commerce are both realities which cannot be dismissed. Thus the question is not whether nuclear energy will be used, but within what framework it will be used. Second, it is taken as given that nuclear weapons and other nuclear explosive devices are unacceptable uses of nuclear energy and that nuclear proliferation, either 'vertical' by the existing recognised nuclear-weapon states (NWS) or 'horizontal' beyond those five states, must be strongly resisted. The argument that nuclear weapons are or can be stabilising in security terms, and thus that further 'horizontal' proliferation is not necessarily undesirable in itself, finds no welcome in this chapter. In addition, 'vertical' proliferation *per se* is not dealt with except in a tangential way, but this chapter does assume that nuclear co-operation with NWS should be for peaceful, non-explosive purposes only and therefore should, to the maximum extent possible, also take place within an effective non-proliferation framework. It also assumes that one major contribution to efforts to prevent 'horizontal' proliferation will be progress in negotiations on nuclear disarmament. Finally, the chapter is written from the perspective of the major nuclear suppliers which, it is assumed, have a special responsibility with regard to international nuclear co-operation. This is not to ignore the fact that no country is a supplier only, nor to discount the rights or responsibilities of recipients, but solely to recognise that special responsibility.

The tension, creative in some cases and destructive in others, between alarm over nuclear proliferation and the desire to secure political and economic benefits from nuclear co-operation has characterised not only the evolution of supplier policies, but also efforts to establish an international framework for nuclear co-operation. The November 1945 Agreed Declaration on Atomic Energy, the Atoms for Peace proposal in 1953, the Statute of the International Atomic Energy Agency in 1957 and the Treaty on the Non-Proliferation of Nuclear Weapons (NPT) in 1968 have all reflected that tension. The balance at various stages between these two forces, and hence the course of the framework's evolution, has in turn been influenced by the experience gained in nuclear co-operation over the past 30 years.

Evolution

The evolution of supplier policies can be broken down into the three general periods: from the early 1950s to 1968; from 1968 to 1978; and from 1978 to the present.

First Period

The first period was marked by a strong desire to share the benefits of the peaceful use of nuclear energy under generalised commitments by recipient governments to use the supplied material, nuclear material, equipment and technology for 'peaceful purposes' only. In some agreements provision for bilateral verification of that commitment was made, frequently with anticipatory language looking forward to the establishment and implementation of the safeguards system envisaged in the statute of the International Atomic Energy Agency (IAEA). The outstanding example of nuclear co-operation under this kind of framework, from Canada's perspective, was that with India under which the CIRUS research reactor and the RAPP I and RAPP II power reactors, as well as associated training and know-how, were provided. It is worth noting that the non-proliferation or 'peaceful uses only' commitment applied only to specific items provided by Canada or to nuclear material produced in or by those items. This approach was similar to that followed by other suppliers at the time and was reflected in the evolution of the IAEA safeguards system, culminating in the issuance of IAEA document INFCIRC 66 Rev. 2 in its final revised form in 1968. This document specified the safeguards regime to be applied to individual nuclear facilities pursuant to the statute of the agency. In 1971 Canada, India and the IAEA concluded an agreement for the application of such safeguards to the RAPP power reactors.

Second Period

The subsequent period, 1968 to 1978, saw two different processes take place. First was the negotiation and ratification of the NPT and the consequent effort to establish some multilaterally agreed supplier procedures or guidelines for the implementation of Article III (2) of the treaty. Several aspects of this development are worth emphasising, most important of which is that the international community, in response to an increasing concern over the nuclear proliferation which had occurred, had agreed on an instrument specifically designed to provide a comprehensive commitment to non-proliferation by non-nuclear-weapon states (NNWS) party to the treaty, as well as for verification of observance of this commitment. In other words, NNWS party to the NPT committed themselves through an international instrument not to develop or acquire, directly or indirectly, nuclear weapons or other nuclear explosive devices. To verify observance of that commitment, they agreed to accept IAEA safeguards on source or special fissionable material in all their peaceful activities (implicitly current and future): this is called NPT full-scope safeguards (FSS). The fundamental shift was therefore from a focus only on individual nuclear facilities and some nuclear material in a particular country to one on all nuclear material in all nuclear activities, thereby providing a much more comprehensive non-proliferation assurance.

In addition to this commitment, all state parties, whether NNWS or NWS, also undertook to ensure that their nuclear exports would be subject to IAEA safeguards. It was pursuant to this undertaking that a group of NPT parties decided to consult on, and subsequently in 1974 agreed to, common procedures covering the export of source or special fissionable material as well as certain categories of equipment and material especially designed or prepared for the processing, use or production of special fissionable material. This was the Zangger Committee 'trigger list', published in the IAEA document INFCIRC 209. It marked the first concerted effort by a group of nuclear suppliers to establish an agreed list of nuclear 'items' which would require the application of a multilaterally agreed export control mechanism.

In sum, the results of this first process were: (1) an international instrument providing a comprehensive commitment to non-proliferation by states acceding to it; (2) an undertaking within that instrument to submit all peaceful nuclear activities in an NNWS party to IAEA safeguards; and (3) a multilateral agreement to ensure that certain nuclear exports would only take place when subject to IAEA safeguards. Two significant non-proliferation steps accordingly had been taken: first was the significant upgrading of an NNWS commitment to non-proliferation covering all indigenous and imported activities; second was the agreement among a major group of nuclear suppliers on a common approach to an agreed list of nuclear exports.

As an aside, it is noteworthy that an additional major step in the evolution of the agency's safeguards system was also taken in this period. In September 1973 the IAEA Board of Governors approved document Gov/1621 which recommended:

1. that the *duration* of the IAEA's safeguards agreements concluded under INFCIRC 66 Rev. 2 should be related to the period of actual use of the items in the recipient state; and
2. that the provisions for terminating such agreements should be formulated in such a way that the rights and obligations of the parties would *continue* to apply in connection with the items subject to safeguards until such time as the agency terminated the application of safeguards, as provided for in INFCIRC 66 Rev. 2.

The adoption by the IAEA of these duration-and-coverage provisions provided yet another significant building block for the non-proliferation regime and provided further protection for nuclear suppliers against the possible misuse of supplied material, nuclear material and equipment.

The second process built upon, but went beyond, the progress made in the first. The trigger for the process was the Indian 'peaceful' nuclear explosion of 18 May 1974. The ensuing shock was international in scope, but was felt particularly strongly in Canada.

Canada had agreed in 1956 to supply, under the Colombo aid programme, a research reactor to India subject to a 'peaceful uses only' commitment. The United States supplied the heavy water for the reactor. The Federal Republic of Germany assisted India in the construction of a small heavy water plant, and an Indian reprocessing facility was built with assistance from United States and French companies. Concern over the possible use of these facilities to build a nuclear explosive device led both the United States and Canada to communicate officially to India in 1970 that neither government accepted nuclear explosive devices as constituting 'peaceful uses' of nuclear energy. This interpretation had, of course, been reinforced by the international community in the drafting of the NPT, which cited both nuclear weapons and other nuclear explosive devices as being unacceptable. In reply, Indira Gandhi, then-prime minister of India, wrote to Pierre Elliott Trudeau, prime minister of Canada at that time, agreeing that Canada-India nuclear co-operation had been dedicated to 'the development and application of nuclear energy for peaceful purposes', but that

> The obligations undertaken by our two governments are mutual and they cannot be unilaterally varied. In these circumstances it would not be necessary, in our view, to interpret these agreements in a particular way based on the development of a hypothetical contingency.

Despite these exchanges, India detonated the May 1974 nuclear explosive device, claiming that the action was solely for peaceful purposes and that, while plutonium produced in the CIRUS reactor had been used, the origins of this plutonium were in non-Canadian nuclear material, and thus there had been no breach of its undertakings to Canada.

This event, which demonstrated in dramatic fashion the connection between nuclear facilities supplied for 'peaceful purposes only' and the potential for misuse of these facilities, confirmed the trend towards a requirement for a clear non-proliferation commitment, not just the earlier 'peaceful uses' or 'non-military uses' formulation thereof, as well as the movement towards an explicit non-proliferation connection between material and equipment exported by a supplier and any special fissionable material produced by or with that material and equipment. The fact that the lesson was not ignored by the international community was revealed in 1975 when the IAEA Board of Governors decided that all safeguards agreements concluded by the agency, whether under the NPT or not, would preclude the use of safeguarded items for any kind of nuclear explosive devices. The May 1974 explosion also certainly accelerated the publication in September 1974 of the Zangger trigger list, referred to above. But was that enough?

The mid-1970s saw a congruence of factors which provided for many nuclear suppliers a negative answer to that question. There was a strong and growing domestic concern in many supplier countries over the potential misuse of nuclear exports. Could another 'India' happen? This concern had to be satisfied if the political and economic benefits of continuing international nuclear co-operation were to be enjoyed. At the same time, there was recognition of the enhanced interest, perhaps for economic and technological objectives (for example, energy security and efficiency) but also perhaps for other purposes in accelerating the development of the nuclear fuel cycle involving reprocessing and plutonium use. This recognition focused on efforts by Korea, Taiwan, Pakistan (in India's footsteps), Argentina and Brazil to develop or acquire reprocessing facilities and technology. The potential for national competition in the acquisition of such nuclear facilities with their potential contribution to a state's capability to develop or acquire a nuclear explosive capability, together with the real possibility of non-proliferation requirements for supply becoming a factor in commercial competitions, were additional considerations. The conclusion reached was that further refinement of the terms under which nuclear suppliers should operate was required.

Fifteen of the major nuclear suppliers (that is, the Nuclear Suppliers Group (NSG) or the London Club) began meeting for this purpose in late 1974, and in early 1978 the results of their common efforts – the NSG Guidelines – were published by the IAEA in its document, INFCIRC 254. The guidelines reflected the earlier Zangger trigger list, but went significantly further in a number of respects (emphasis added):

1. the guidelines contained 'fundamental principles for safeguards *and export controls*' which should 'apply to nuclear transfer to *any* non-nuclear-weapon state for peaceful purposes', and went on to define an export trigger list including material, nuclear material, and equipment and common criteria for *technology* transfers;
2. any uses which would result in any nuclear explosive device were to be *explicitly* excluded by *formal* governmental assurances;
3. effective *physical protection measures* on all nuclear materials and facilities on the trigger list were to be required, and the levels of those measures were to be the subject of agreement between supplier and recipient;
4. the duration and coverage provisions for IAEA safeguards were established in conformity with the Gov/1621 guidelines;
5. *certain technologies* (that is, heavy water production, enrichment and reprocessing), either directly transferred *or derived from* transferred facilities, were to be covered by the non-proliferation commitment, physical protection requirement and safeguards provisions of the guidelines;
6. *restraint* was to be exercised in the transfer of *sensitive* (that is, enrichment or reprocessing) *facilities, technology and weapons-usable materials.* A specific requirement was included, limiting the use of transferred enrichment equipment, facilities or technology to the production of no greater than 20 per cent enriched uranium unless the supplier gave its consent otherwise;
7. suppliers were encouraged to include in their agreements, 'whenever appropriate and practicable', provisions calling for *mutual agreement* between the supplier and the recipients on arrangements for reprocessing, storage, alteration, use, transfer or re-transfer of any weapons-usable material arising from the supply of nuclear materials or of facilities which produce weapons-usable material; and
8. additional definition of *controls over retransfers*, particularly a requirement for the supplier's consent for the retransfer of the certain technologies and facilities identified in sub-paragraph 5 above, was given.

Also important was the recognition of the need for ongoing consultation between the suppliers.

The NSG Guidelines reflect the current high-water mark of agreement by a significant group of the major suppliers on non-proliferation conditions for nuclear supply. Efforts to refine these guidelines continue with particular examples being the recent identification for export control purposes of 'equipment especially designed or prepared' for centrifuge enrichment and reprocessing facilities. It should be noted, however, that the guidelines have their weaknesses, political as well as technical. Their underlying concept is that a nuclear supplier's non-proliferation concern need only focus on its nuclear exports and not necessarily take into account current or potential indigenous activities in the recipient country. The need for consistent application of the guidelines also has not received the necessary attention, thereby leaving open the way for subjective judgements as regards the nature and extent of their implementation. Export controls on technology remain a difficult question while implementation of the 'derived from' provision (sub-paragraph 5 above) as regards the three technologies identified in paragraph 6 of the guidelines remains ill-defined. These are only some of the aspects requiring further consideration.

Third Period

The third, or current, period from 1978 to the present also has been characterised by two basic exercises. The first has been the implementation of the NSG Guidelines and national policies related thereto, an exercise during which the weaknesses identified in the preceding paragraph have emerged clearly. It has, however, been a period of relative success in that suppliers have been able to feel increased certainty that their nuclear exports will not contribute to nuclear proliferation. National efforts to strengthen nuclear export control procedures also have been successful. Moreover, the potential for competition between suppliers on the basis of differing non-proliferation requirements, while not eliminated, has been reduced.

The second exercise has been based on a different concept from that upon which the NSG Guidelines are based. This concept is that a nuclear supplier must take into account the overall non-proliferation status of a recipient, not just its undertakings with regard to specific imported material, nuclear material, equipment and technology. This concept thus requires nuclear suppliers to pose as a fundamental requirement for nuclear supply that the recipient NNWS must make a comprehensive, binding commitment to non-proliferation and accept IAEA safeguards on all nuclear activities in that country. As by far the most common way to satisfy this requirement is to ratify the NPT, this requirement is commonly labelled the NPT-FSS, or *de jure*-FSS approach. This approach was endorsed as an objective at the First NPT Review Conference in 1975, was discussed but not agreed to during the negotiation of the NSG Guidelines, and recently has been discussed further between suppliers on an informal basis pursuant to the 1983 'comprehensive safeguards' initiative of United States President Reagan. In the interim several nuclear suppliers, including Canada, have moved in their national policies to establish this requirement as a condition for their nuclear exports to go abroad. (Canada, in fact, took this step in 1976.)

The third period from 1978 to the present therefore has been one of implementation and consolidation as far as the NSG Guidelines (and national policies) are concerned, but also one of continuing reflection and consideration as to whether further steps are required. The non-proliferation regime as of 1985 consists of the basic elements of the IAEA's statute and safeguards system, the NPT-FSS system, the Zangger Committee 'trigger list', the NSG Guidelines and a range of national nuclear export policies. Even more important has been the emergence of a wide-spread consensus that nuclear proliferation is highly undesirable and that firm action should be taken to prevent it. Significant progress, therefore, has been made; however, there is a need to harmonise and integrate these elements to ensure the effectiveness of the regime, to increase international acceptance, and to enable it to respond to the challenges confronting it. What are the challenges to which that evolution will have to respond?

Challenges

The international non-proliferation regime is confronted in the 1980s with a complex and overlapping set of old and new challenges, challenges which will require hard decisions to be taken.

The single most important challenge is to governments, certainly those of the major nuclear suppliers, but also those of the international community more generally, to maintain the political will and commitment which allocate to the non-proliferation objective the political priority it requires. Many factors mitigate against this being done. Ten years have passed since the Indian nuclear explosion of May 1974, and public memory, hence pressure on governments, has faded. At the same time, the inability to date to persuade those key states remaining outside the regime – Israel, South Africa, India, Pakistan, Argentina, Brazil – to modify their positions can lead to frustration and, even worse, to resignation. A difficult nuclear market with consequent pressures on nuclear industries places further pressures on supplier governments, if not to relax their standards, then at least to resist any upgrading thereof. These and other similar factors weaken the resolve of governments to allocate to non-proliferation the priority it deserves. This in turn encourages the tendency, particularly strong in some states, to regard non-proliferation as just one more objective of foreign policy – an objective to be subordinated as circumstances warrant to other considerations. While it would be foolish for any government to direct its foreign policy towards promoting the non-proliferation objective to the exclusion of all else, that objective can easily become irrelevant if it is too readily subordinated or found inconvenient.

A second challenge – a political/psychological one – originates from the inability of the NWS to attain any significant progress in their efforts to secure nuclear disarmament. While this chapter is not the place to explore why this is so, it must be recognised that continuing 'vertical' proliferation creates a climate in which it is difficult to persuade some NNWS to forgo the nuclear weapons option. A circuitous argument then arises: Pakistan will move if India moves; India will move if China does; China will if the Soviet Union and United States do; and so on. The 'equality-of-sovereign-states' and the 'power-status' arguments advanced by some states are also reinforced. Even more invidious is the currency being given to the argument that as nuclear weapons have contributed to superpower stability, perhaps the spread of such weapons to various regions would enhance stability therein. A twofold response to this challenge is necessary: progress must be made in negotiations between the NWS while, in the meantime, sincere efforts to prevent the further spread of nuclear weapons (a development which will only complicate further nuclear disarmament negotiations) must be made.

A further challenge arises from the nature of nuclear co-operation itself. A nuclear programme requires a major political, economic, technological and industrial investment. Moreover, it involves nuclear facilities with lifetimes extending into decades and nuclear material with significantly longer lifetimes. The challenge is to define a framework within which that relationship can develop in a stable, predictable and mutually beneficial way over the time spans involved. Surely this framework must be international, not bilateral, and one which provides the international community as well as the supplier and the recipient with the degree of security – political, economic and technological – required. Furthermore, a nuclear relationship provides a flow not only of material, nuclear material, equipment and technology, but also of technological skills and know-how. The latter cannot be kept hermetically sealed in one (safeguarded) sector of a nuclear programme. Thus the nature of nuclear co-operation leads inevitably to the challenge of defining a non-proliferation regime which, as well as being international, is comprehensive in nature.

The nuclear fuel cycle is itself a challenge. A nuclear energy programme, whether indigenous or based on a supplier-recipient relationship, will develop over time to the point where the more sensitive nuclear fuel cycle activities, for example reprocessing and plutonium storage and use, will be involved. The complexity of these activities, as well as the volume and nature of the nuclear materials involved, provide a further challenge which enhances the need for an effective non-proliferation regime.

Despite efforts to the contrary, there are now, and will likely continue to be, countries which will remain outside any comprehensive and effective non-proliferation regime. Some of those countries will in turn undoubtedly wish to source material, nuclear material, equipment and/or technology indirectly or even clandestinely from nuclear suppliers. The challenge posed is again multifaceted. Nuclear suppliers must develop national and multilateral systems of nuclear export control which forestall such efforts. Here the problems of dual-use equipment and of how to control technology transfers have raised their heads. Moreover, a non-proliferation regime must respond to the challenge of possible retransfers, intentional or unintentional, to third parties.

A new challenge which has arisen in the 1980s is that of the so-called 'new suppliers'. This emergence is an expected and inevitable result of three decades of nuclear co-operation; the major or traditional nuclear suppliers cannot and should not expect that they would continue to fill the same role in the 1980s and 1990s that they filled in the 1950s and 1960s. While too much can be made of this development and the extent of the capabilities of these 'new suppliers' can be exaggerated for various reasons, their emergence poses the challenge to the non-proliferation regime of how to encourage them to adhere to the regime and not to supply outside that regime.

A word used frequently in this chapter to describe one attribute of a non-proliferation regime is 'international'. It is a word which characterises both a positive and negative challenge to that regime. On the positive side, it is self-evident that the more universal the international community which adheres to a particular regime, the more effective that regime can be over the time spans involved. No small group of nations, and definitely no one nation, no matter how powerful, can devise and enforce a regime that will be effective over the period of time envisaged. Thus for the regime to be as effective as possible, it must be as international as possible; in turn, this means it must be based on widely accepted international instruments and mechanisms.

On the negative side, it has to be recognised that there may well be some NNWS which, for a variety of reasons, refuse to adhere to an international non-proliferation regime. This conscious decision carries with it at least an implicit willingness to pay a price for maintaining a nuclear option. This is regrettable, and efforts to remove the motivation for that decision obviously should not stop. It is highly arguable, however, whether the NNWS in question should continue to enjoy the benefits of participation in the international nuclear economy developing within the framework of the non-proliferation regime. Too often, arguments are advanced that it is futile from a non-proliferation perspective to exclude such states from international nuclear co-operation (since they are bound to proliferate anyway if they so wish), or that the lines of co-operation must be kept open to provide an opportunity for dialogue and persuasion as justification to continue nuclear supply arrangements. These arguments carry with them the risk that such NNWS will secure the benefits of international nuclear co-operation without being required to contribute to the international non-proliferation regime. This in turn may well encourage other countries to ask why they should pay the alleged non-proliferation 'price', when they can receive the benefits of such nuclear co-operation without doing so. The challenge, therefore, is to ensure that the regime has a demonstrable value for those inside it as well as political and economic costs for those which remain outside. Those NNWS that wish to remain outside the regime are willing to pay the price; certainly those suppliers supportive of the regime must be equally willing to pay a price, for example to forgo commercial contracts if necessary.

One additional argument often used to justify a supplier's decision to initiate or to maintain nuclear co-operation with an NNWS remaining outside a comprehensive international non-proliferation regime is that not only does such a course of action enable the supplier to continue efforts to persuade the NNWS to adhere to the regime, but it also enables the supplier (through the contamination and deeming provisions of the NSG Guidelines) to make more and more of the NNWS's nuclear programme subject to IAEA safeguards and possibly other non-proliferation provisions. This approach, which can be labelled the 'incentive/contamination' approach, should not be dismissed too quickly. A number of suppliers, including Canada, have applied it; however, care has to be exercised that it does not become a convenient basis merely to secure the benefits of nuclear co-operation. If it is to be employed, it should be consciously and deliberately employed with the identification of a clear point beyond which the nuclear relationship in question will not be allowed to develop without a modification in the non-proliferation status of the recipient. This is far from an easy task; the challenge is not only to make the original decision, but to stand by it over time.

Finally, there is the challenge of continuing *to enhance and expand support* for an effective international non-proliferation regime. Both current adherents and additional states, especially the 'new suppliers' as pointed out above, must be convinced of the value of the various elements of that regime. Thus a much more deliberate and conscious effort has to go into making that regime function smoothly and positively for those countries which support it. Currently, many NNWS, particularly developing country NNWS, are led to believe that even though they support non-proliferation, they must continue to pay a price despite that support. The answer to this is not to scrap those elements of the current non-proliferation regime, for example the NSG Guidelines singled out for criticism, or to provide power reactors or research reactors at highly discounted prices, but to formulate and implement together with those states an international non-proliferation regime which responds as much as possible to their concerns while serving the non-proliferation objective.

This is only a partial survey of the challenges facing the non-proliferation regime today. Each one of those identified could be the subject of a lengthy study; each in turn impacts on the other, making the overall situation more complex. However, this admittedly limited survey does provide some clear signals as to what should constitute an effective international non-proliferation regime and, by doing so, outlines the objective for the major nuclear suppliers to pursue in considering the effectiveness of the current non-proliferation regime. In sum, that regime should:

1. receive the political commitment and priority required;
2. pursue the 'horizontal' non-proliferation objective vigorously in parallel with efforts to reduce and ultimately eliminate 'vertical' proliferation;
3. be as international as possible as regards its support, coverage, instruments and mechanisms;
4. be based on a comprehensive and verified non-proliferation commitment;
5. be effective from both the political and technological perspective;
6. incorporate effective nuclear export control measures; and
7. have a demonstrable value (political and economic) for its adherents.

To create such a regime will not be an easy task; both the major nuclear suppliers and other states committed to nuclear non-proliferation will have to make hard decisions and to accept political and economic penalties. Despite this difficulty, the alternative of the further spread of nuclear weapons or nuclear explosive capability – or even the degree of international insecurity caused by the possibility thereof – merits a concerted effort to tackle that task.

The NPT

The NPT is an essential component of any non-proliferation regime if that regime is to possess the characteristics identified in the preceding section. Why is this so?

First of all, the NPT is an international instrument; in fact, its 130 state parties, including three NWS, give it the largest adherence of any international security treaty. Incorporation of the NPT in a non-proliferation regime therefore gives that regime a major claim to being international in nature. Moreover, it provides a binding non-proliferation commitment by all NNWS parties (Article II) not to develop or acquire nuclear weapons or other nuclear explosive devices, reinforced by the commitment by NWS in Article I not to transfer, directly or indirectly, to any recipient nuclear weapons or other nuclear explosive devices. This commitment is to the international community at large (that is, not bilateral), as is the requirement for withdrawing from the treaty set out in Article X. It is therefore immune from the whims and vagaries of bilateral relations between states.

The non-proliferation commitment made by NNWS through the NPT is *comprehensive* and *verified*, applying as it does to *all* nuclear material in *all* peaceful nuclear activities in NNWS parties and, given that, it requires the acceptance of IAEA safeguards on all that nuclear material in both current and future activities. By relying on the IAEA safeguards system, moreover, the NPT incorporates even more firmly another international element into a non-proliferation regime.

Article III (2) of the NPT also provides a basis for an effective nuclear export control system by requiring all state parties not to provide source or special fissionable material or, especially, designed or prepared material or equipment to any NNWS without ensuring that the nuclear material provided, or nuclear material produced by or used with the material or equipment, will be subject to IAEA safeguards. While falling short in its coverage (for example, technology is not covered) and failing to provide weighting as regards the proliferation risks associated with particular fuel cycle activities, this fundamental international recognition of a nuclear supplier's responsibilities underlies the concept of any nuclear export control system.

Finally, the NPT attempts to deal with the dangers of both 'vertical' and 'horizontal' proliferation. While efforts to secure the objective of nuclear disarmament are pursued in fora outside the NPT itself, Article VI does contain a commitment by NWS parties to negotiate in good faith to this end. As already pointed out, efforts to prevent 'horizontal' proliferation live in and by the NPT.

In sum, the NPT is an essential element of any non-proliferation regime if that regime is to be effective, comprehensive and international. The principles upon which it is based clearly provide common grounds upon which all states committed to nuclear non-proliferation can meet to establish that regime, as well as the core around which the integration and harmonisation of additional non-proliferation measures into the regime can take place. But is there further action necessary for progress in this regard to be made?

The answer to that question is, yes. It is a major contention of this chapter that it is essential for the major nuclear suppliers and other countries sharing the non-proliferation objective to decide that they will only engage in nuclear co-operation with NNWS which have made a comprehensive binding non-proliferation commitment to the international community and have agreed to accept IAEA safeguards on all their peaceful nuclear activities, current and future. It is this question which, as noted in the section on the evolution of the current conditions of supply for nuclear suppliers, is now before those suppliers.

Some nuclear suppliers, including Canada, have already decided to incorporate this requirement in their national nuclear export policies. Reasons advanced for this approach, in addition to and in expansion upon those already given, are:

1. as the long-term evolutionary nature of a nuclear relationship will inevitably involve the transfer of technology and know-how, a nuclear supplier must recognise the equally inevitable transfer of know-how from the safeguarded portion of a national fuel cycle programme to the non-safeguarded portion;
2. the acceptance of IAEA safeguards on all nuclear activities is an international norm which, at this date, 127 NNWS have done voluntarily (for example, pursuant to the NPT), a step which is a major contribution to the security of all nations;
3. the effectiveness of IAEA safeguards is greater when safeguards are applied to all nuclear activities in NNWS on a continuous basis than when they are applied only to a limited number of facilities in a country or to individual facilities on a non-continuous basis;
4. in order to contribute to international security, NNWS which have taken the step referred to in sub-paragraph 2 must expect a similar commitment to non-proliferation by other NNWS with which they engage in nuclear co-operation;
5. such a requirement promotes adherence to the NPT by non-NPT NNWS, since being a party to that treaty is the clearest way of expressing agreement to adopt FSS and being eligible for participation to a greater degree in nuclear co-operation with all major supplier states;
6. such a requirement by all suppliers creates an incentive for NNWS to accept FSS, since the advantages of inclusion in a growing and multi-faceted international nuclear economy would be offered; and
7. such a requirement recognises the basic argument that international security and the minimisation of the risks of nuclear proliferation are of sufficient importance that even exclusion from international nuclear co-operation of those few NNWS which remain unwilling to accept FSS is justified; the price – political and economic – of such a move is considered worthwhile, even as

those NNWS which wish to remain outside the regime are willing to pay a price to do so.

Securing acceptance of this condition as a key element of their national policies and, by extension, of the international non-proliferation regime by all the major nuclear suppliers and other countries will not be easy. It is considered, however, that only within a framework based on such an NPT-type FSS commitment can the non-proliferation objective be truly served.

Conclusion

Since the 1950s the major nuclear suppliers have led the way in establishing elements of a non-proliferation regime designed to pre-vent nuclear proliferation while encouraging international nuclear co-operation. The evolution of that regime has resulted in a set of instruments and measures – the IAEA's statute and safeguards sys-tem, the NPT, the NSG Guidelines, national nuclear export policies – which to a significant extent have been successful. However, the 1980s, 1990s and beyond will see a series of complex and overlap-ping challenges from both inside and outside the regime which will require its further evolution.

The objective of the major suppliers, as well as of other participat-ing states, must be to encourage that evolution so as to:

1. ensure that international nuclear co-operation will not increase the risk of further nuclear proliferation; and
2. encourage the emergence of an effective, comprehensive and international non-proliferation regime of benefit to all states.

The challenges of today and the future will require at the minimum that this regime be based on a binding, comprehensive commitment to non-proliferation and acceptance of IAEA safeguards on all nuclear activities. All NNWS should be encouraged to take this step; all states should undertake to engage in nuclear co-operation only with other states which have done so. The value and role of the NPT in this context cannot be over-emphasised.

In sum, considerable progress in halting nuclear proliferation has been made, but further work is necessary. Time is not unlimited; there is a real danger that if progress is not made, the existing elements of an effective, comprehensive and international non-proliferation regime could begin to deteriorate: that must be prevented. The goal of the major nuclear suppliers and the international community at large must be the establishment of an effective, comprehensive and international non-proliferation regime, one capable of withstanding the challenges with which it will be faced, while providing that climate of confidence within which nuclear co-operation of benefit to all states can take place.

Postscript

Since the preceding chapter was written, the Third NPT Review Conference took place in Geneva during September 1985. The importance of the results of that successful conference merit attention here in the light of the subject matter addressed in this chapter.

The most important result of the conference is that it produced a Final Document by consensus of the 86 state parties participating. While the outcome of any NPT Review Conference should not have as its sole measurement the production of a Final Declaration (note: the 1975 Review Conference did; the 1980 Review Conference did not), it must be admitted that the public perception of the 1980 conference as a failure placed an additional burden on the 1985 conference. That the 86 participating states were willing, despite various pressures and strains, to reach a consensus provides evidence that the majority of the international community continue to attach great priority to efforts to prevent nuclear proliferation. Moreover, the NPT itself is seen as a fundamental element of those efforts; the Final Declaration states:

> The Conference affirms its determination *to strengthen further* the barriers against the proliferation of nuclear weapons and other nuclear explosive devices to additional States. The spread of nuclear explosive capabilities would add *immeasurably* to regional and international tensions and suspicions. . . . The Parties remain convinced that *universal adherence* to the [NPT] is the best way to strengthen the barriers against proliferation and they urge all States not party to the Treaty to accede to it . . . (emphasis added)

Thus the political will and priority evoked in the preceding chapter exists; the challenge will be to use it wisely and well.

The conference also clearly identified those key features of the NPT which it considered as essential to any non-proliferation regime:

> The Conference therefore specifically urges all [NNWS] not party to the Treaty to make an *international legally-binding commitment* not to acquire *nuclear weapons or other nuclear explosive devices* and to accept *IAEA safeguards on all their peaceful nuclear activities, both current and future*, to verify that commitment. (emphasis added)

The conference also unequivocally stated that 'unsafeguarded nuclear activities in (NNWS) pose serious proliferation dangers'. The conference therefore gave a clear signal as to the political will of the participating states.

The conference, moreover, did not avoid dealing with one of the most contentious issues before it – what essential non-proliferation commitment should be required for international nuclear co-operation to take place? While no clear decision in this regard was possible, the conference did indicate the direction in which it thought the answer should evolve. Thus:

> The Conference further urges *all* States in their international nuclear cooperation and in their nuclear export policies and, *specifically as a necessary basis for the transfer of relevant nuclear supplies to all [NNWS]*, to take effective steps towards achieving *such a commitment* to non-proliferation and acceptance of *such safeguards* by those States. The Conference expresses its view that accession to the [NPT] is the best way to achieve that objective. (emphasis added)

The commitment and safeguards verification thereof are, of course, those defined above.

Having dealt with the non-proliferation basis for nuclear co-operation with the NNWS, the conference then turned its attention to NWS. The conference expressed its satisfaction that four of the five NWS had voluntarily concluded safeguards agreements with the IAEA, covering all or part of their peaceful nuclear activities, and called on the fifth to do likewise (note: the People's Republic of China made a 'voluntary safeguards offer' to the IAEA at the Agency's General Conference immediately after the NPT Review Conference). The gradual extension of this safeguards coverage as well as the further separation of civil and military facilities in NWS were also endorsed. Finally, the conference

> affirmed the great value to the non-proliferation regime of commitments by the [NWS] that nuclear supplies provided for peaceful use will not be used for nuclear weapons or other nuclear explosive purposes.

The results of the Third NPT Review Conference cited above are only a few of those drawn together in the Final Declaration. They are, however, of great importance in terms of the continuing evolution of the non-proliferation regime as advocated in this chapter. Canada played a major role at the Third NPT Review Conference in securing these results; Canada should now devote equal effort and priority to building on those results. Canada's political commitment to nuclear non-proliferation, and the value of an effective non-proliferation regime for its approximately one-billion-dollars-a-year nuclear commerce, merit such devotion:

> The Treaty and the regime of non-proliferation it supports play a central role in promoting regional and international peace and security, *inter alia*, by helping to prevent the spread of nuclear explosives. The non-proliferation and safeguards commitments in the Treaty are essential also for peaceful nuclear commerce and co-operation.

THE NON-PROLIFERATION POLICIES OF NON-NUCLEAR-WEAPON STATES

Onkar Marwah

Introduction

Of the 127 non-nuclear-weapon states (NNWS) which have signed the Treaty on the Non-Proliferation of Nuclear Weapons (NPT), a limited number are capable of producing nuclear weapons but abjure the option for a variety of reasons – the main one being that their participation in alliance relations assures them against nuclear threats or attack; for example, the European states of NATO and the Warsaw Pact, Australia, Canada and Japan. Another 15 or so NNWS that have not signed the NPT probably possess the means in varying measure and time to produce nuclear weapons but have not done so. However, their intentions remain suspect. Among the latter, some states are more suspect than others, due primarily to an assessment of their incentives to 'go nuclear' in the short term, given capabilities and intent. The countries usually included in the 'real suspects' class are eight in number: Argentina, Brazil, India, Pakistan, Israel, South Africa, the Republic of Korea and Taiwan. At various times, the intent and activities of states such as Iran, Iraq and Libya have led to their inclusion in the suspect list, although these states have never possessed the ability to produce nuclear weapons.

It appears reasonable, in the circumstances, to study the policies of the eight suspect NNWS as indicative of their individual objectives; and, perhaps, as explanatory of the attitudes of other NNWS, should they also happen to be included in the suspect list. This study is undertaken in three parts. The first part assesses the non-proliferation (or proliferation) policies of the eight suspect NNWS. The second evaluates their differences in approach from the policies urged upon them by the nuclear-weapon states (NWS). In the third section, an attempt is made to understand the future evolution of NNWS's policies in the nuclear-military field.

Non-Proliferation Policies of the NNWS

No NNWS has ever stated that its nuclear activities are designed to provide it with a weapons option. Nor were such proclivities adduced against the NNWS in the early post-war period by the NWS. Indeed, the NWS were the providers of nuclear technology, materials and engineering facilities to the rest of the world through the decades of the fifties and the sixties. Further, no distinction was made – or possible, then – between civilian and military-related nuclear assistance, either by the suppliers or by the recipients. For the most part, the assistance was of a rudimentary nature, consisting of training facilities, small experimental research reactors and the provision of non-military technical information.

It is worth noting that at this early stage, the Soviets probably supplied more militarily significant nuclear assistance to their (then) fraternal Chinese allies – in the form of a gaseous diffusion plant, plutonium-producing reactors and the training of hundreds of scientists – than did the West to countries such as India, Brazil or Israel. While China has escaped the odium and the pressures against 'going nuclear' because of its artificially accredited great power status during and after the Second World War, it is probably the most significant example of an NNWS deliberately aided by an ally in a focused effort to acquire nuclear weapons (and a missile delivery system).

In hindsight, it seems that, among the sample of the eight suspect NNWS, only Israel and South Africa embarked from the outset upon a military-related nuclear-technology acquisitions process. While South Africa has built nuclear power generating plants, this civilian aspect of the programme was preceded by clandestine uranium enrichment facilities and the like, about which little is known and much is suspected.[1] In the case of Israel, all the available information suggests that the Dimona plutonium reactor from the very beginning has been of a dedicated nature, used to provide bomb-grade fissionable material, and has no other use.[2] Additionally, there is scattered evidence in relation to both the South African and the Israeli nuclear programmes that, despite (or because of) their military implications, a variety of official and non-official organisations in the Western countries have continued to provide nuclear informatory and materials aid to the two countries. While such charges in relation to South Africa and Israel cannot be proved conclusively, the perception is wide-spread among the decision-makers in other NNWS that, like the Soviet Union, the Western states early on chose their clients for a 'selective proliferation' of nuclear weapons even as they adopted public stances against a general proliferation of nuclear weapons by other states.

Unlike the Israeli and South African nuclear programmes, the nuclear programmes of the remaining suspect NNWS have been relatively open, and were still more so in the period up to the mid-sixties. In the case of India, a civilian nuclear power programme, first outlined in the fifties, still remains intact. Despite delays and shortfalls due to political or material exigencies, the Indian civilian nuclear programme has been implemented as planned, proceeding from the construction of natural uranium fuelled CANDU reactors of 220-megawatt capacity in the initial stages; to their upscaling to 500-megawatt capacity in the next stage; and the acquisition of breeder-reactor technology based on plutonium and thorium charges. An experimental breeder-reactor of 15-megawatt capacity, the first one in the Third World, is already in operation at Kalpakkam in South India, and a commercial one of 500-megawatt capacity is to commence construction. A 10,000-megawatt nuclear power capacity is to be acquired by the turn of the century[3].

The Koreans and the Taiwanese have even more ambitious civilian nuclear power programmes in implementation than the Indians. The Brazilian nuclear power production plans have gone through a hiatus due to the general political and economic problems currently beset-ting the country. The same appears to be the case with regard to Argentina. In both cases, however, the assumption is that the national nuclear programmes will be resumed once the economic and finan-cial conditions are stabilised.

In the case of Pakistan, current headlines clearly indicate that the country is proceeding steadily towards the acquisition of a nuclear weapon capability. It is, none the less, appropriate to mention that the drive to acquire nuclear weapons was initiated by the Pakistanis only in the early seventies. Until then, Pakistan also appeared to be intent upon adhering to a civilian nuclear programme, with an operat-ing Canadian-supplied power plant at Karachi and a second one planned at Chashma.

According to the preceding analysis and historical evidence, weapons proliferation did not provide the genesis of the nuclear pro-grammes of any of the NNWS other than Israel and South Africa (and China, if it also is viewed as an NNWS prior to 1964). Despite bombastic claims to possess a weapons-making capability (Argen-tina) or portentous statements to acquiring the potential 'within eighteen months of a decision to do so' (India), the fact remains that none of the NNWS – other than Israel and South Africa – appear to have done anything in a focused and deliberate manner to acquire nuclear weapons during the first 20 years of their entries into the nuclear field. At least to the mid-sixties, and perhaps to the early seventies, the nuclear policies of six of the main NNWS adhered to the objective of the non-proliferation of nuclear weapons.

It is true, of course, that in the process of grafting the infrastructure for a nuclear power programme to their nascent industrial activities, one or another of the NNWS also acquired some of the building blocks of a weapons programme – a reprocessing plant (India), laboratory-scale reprocessing facilities (Argentina, Pakistan, Taiwan and South Korea), fuelling and machining skills, a cadre of experienced scientists and technical personnel. None of these acquisitions could be viewed as secret plans from the inception stage to proliferate weapons at some opportune date in the future. Had the Indians, Argentinians, Brazilians or Pakistanis been half-way as deliberate towards the acquisition of nuclear weapons as the Chinese, the Israelis and the South Africans, then the evidence of their activities would have been more deterministic and less erratic, the results more efficient and the objective achievements swifter in realisation[4].

In summary, the nuclear policies of the major NNWS may be categorised as follows, at least to the mid-sixties: Type I – military-oriented, with civilian by-product (Israel, South Africa (China)); Type II – civilian-oriented, with military by-product (Argentina, Brazil, India, Pakistan, South Korea, Taiwan); Type III – acquiring a nuclear power plant (all other NNWS that have or plan to have a nuclear power generating plant).[5]

In the period after the mid-sixties, and especially after the Indian nuclear explosion of 1974, the situation with respect to the nuclear programmes of the NNWS became more murky and diverse. The Israeli and South African programmes, then as now, have remained under wraps and have proceeded along their quietly determined, unheralded and unpublicised military objectives. The Indians refused to sign the NPT in 1968, and then steadily introduced – or re-introduced, since the Americans and the Soviets had conceived of them earlier – the possibility of 'peaceful nuclear explosions', culminating in the Pokharan test of 1974. The Brazilians and Argentinians also claimed the right to conduct peaceful nuclear explosions, although they have not yet exercised the option. There were reports that both the South Koreans and the Taiwanese had been discovered conducting activities that could lead to the fabrication of a nuclear bomb, and had been persuaded to desist from such work by the United States government. And it is now known that Pakistan initiated its world-wide clandestine search for equipment and technology to make the bomb in 1972, soon after its defeat in the Bangladesh War of 1971 but two years before the Indian nuclear explosion at Pokharan.[6]

The reasons for the preceding changes in NNWS's nuclear policies are as individual and varied as the states involved. Some of these will be discussed in the following section. In the meantime, it is noteworthy that the 'nuclear chain reaction' whereby the nuclearisation of one state was to be followed by a spate of proliferation simply has not taken place. While the Pakistanis may follow the Indians or the Indians the Pakistanis, as the case may be, there appears to be no causal link between them and the Brazilians, Argentinians, South Koreans or Taiwanese, or any other putative, suspect NNWS. As for the Israelis and the South Africans, the nuclear activities of other NNWS have never intervened in any manner to help or hinder their weapons-making plans. These were instituted earlier, and pursued in silent isolation, but with the probable connivance of powerful Western states. It is possible that the Indian nuclear test of 1974 did spur the nuclear ambitions of states such as Iran, Iraq or Libya. The latter states' activities were, however, haphazard, sporadic and easily aborted by a combination of natural, forceful and diplomatic means.

For any other NNWS with dreams of a nuclear weapons future, the situation, then as now, seems quite impractical. The international and organisational restraints embodied in the agreements and 'trigger lists' compiled by the Nuclear Suppliers Group (NSG), comprising nuclear technology and materials providers of both the NATO and the Warsaw Pact states, makes it quite impossible for an aspirant to undertake clandestine activity towards a nuclear weapon capability without discovery; or without the connivance of a powerful patron state. Indeed, any NNWS, such as Pakistan which is in the mode of acquiring a weapon capability, is able to do so only because of the Nelson's eye turned upon such activities by powerful supplier states, despite their own laws to the contrary and despite agreed-upon international restraints in such matters.

Policies Urged Upon NNWS by the NWS

Among the five nuclear weapon powers, only the United States, the

United Kingdom and the Soviet Union have actively participated in devising measures to control the horizontal spread of nuclear weapons-making capabilities. Except in recent years, both France and China vociferously rejected international nuclear control measures as a sham perpetrated by the two superpowers upon the rest of the world; or, variously, as a plot to create a condominium division of the world into their respective spheres of hegemonic influence. It is, therefore, not entirely surprising that some of the NNWS in our example – especially the larger ones such as Argéntina, Brazil and India – have reacted, likewise, with suspicion to control measures that, in appearance and substance, seek to impose and freeze an inequality of obligations and status upon them.

The essence of the bargain sought but never achieved between the NWS and the NNWS is the call by the latter for a freeze and then a roll-back in the vertical proliferation of the former's nuclear weapon arsenals. That was, and remains, the price asked by the NNWS for abjuring from the production of the weapons. Additionally, the NWS have been asked to provide unconditional joint guarantees against the threat or the use of nuclear weapons against the NNWS. It also has been stated by the NNWS that their refusal to sign the NPT did not automatically imply a resort to the production of nuclear weapons. Their position has been that the weapons option would not be surrendered for nothing in return, especially in a world where unilateral messianic drives and obstreperous behaviour by the superpowers remain a fact of everyday life.

The response of the NWS has been to assess the preceding position of the NNWS as disingenuous, since the demands ignore the existing realities and divisions of the world, and ask for changes in policies which are impossible to concede. Further, a generous interpretation of the NWS nuclear control measures would indicate that they are not narrowly conceived but based on the wider concerns of stabilising the general conditions of international security despite their own disputes. The argument is advanced also that states such as India or Brazil harbour autonomous great power pretensions that cannot be reconciled with controls on their secular acquisition of power.[7]

In point of logic, it is impossible to falsify either the professions of the NWS or those of the NNWS. Since interpretations of national intent ultimately rest on perceptions, enough evidence can be led either way to support either the NNWS's or the NWS's side of the debate. A choice between them must lie, ultimately, not on the 'facts'

– which can be doctored and transposed to suit one's purpose – but through other yardsticks. The real situation is that, beyond interpretations of intent, the NWS remain the 'haves' against the NNWS 'have-nots'. The NNWS have nothing to surrender but their intentions. Meanwhile, the NWS assuredly possess thousands of nuclear weapons, some of which presumably could be surrendered without reductions in their own rivalrous security needs. Again, it seems to be a fundamental contradiction in the NWS-NNWS debate to demand weapons abjuration from the NNWS, yet not insulate them from the use or threat of use of nuclear weapons.

The reality appears to be that neither the NWS nor the NNWS are willing to tie themselves down on future courses of action in matters which both view as imperative to their own survival, whatever the latter term means. The attempt by the NWS to give teeth to their control objectives through physical restraints on the international availability of nuclear technology and materials will undoubtedly delay or impede the nuclear activities of some of the NNWS, but probably none of the eight considered in this chapter. The NNWS note that in a remarkable mutuality of interests despite their own grave disputes, both the NATO and the Warsaw Pact states have come together in the NSG to 'control' others. It is further seen that, irrespective of the NSG restraints and enabling national legislation such as the United States Nuclear Non-Proliferation Act (NNPA) of 1978, waivers are continually given to strategically favoured states. For instance, Pakistan's undercover purchase agents, apprehended while taking delivery of sensitive nuclear equipment, are routinely released (in the United States, Canada and the Netherlands).[8] Congressional testimony also suggests that China has aided the Pakistanis in nuclear weapon design and possibly in the construction of the trigger mechanism for nuclear explosive devices.[9] Recent testimony suggests that the Chinese may have provided sensitive nuclear aid to the Iranians, and even to the South Africans.[10]

NNWS are prone to distinguish between the rhetoric and the reality of NWS non-proliferation activities and the exigent choices which often subtract from what belongs to God to add to that which goes to Caesar. It is apparent that the benign neglect accorded to Pakistan's world-wide hunt for nuclear weapons-making equipment – widely chronicled by official agencies in the advanced countries – devolves from that country's crucial role in Western strategy against the Soviet presence in Afghanistan. That Pakistan basks in temporary and perhaps contradictory favour within Western strategy is revealed by another intriguing revelation: soon after the Israeli raid on Iraq's Osiraq reactor in 1981, India was apparently approached by responsible elements of Western states to undertake a similar pre-emptive strike on Pakistan's centrifuge enrichment plant at Kahuta.[11] The Pakistanis, as well as other NNWS, are aware of such ambivalence in the superpowers' policies enjoined by their own and their allies' conflicting strategic needs. A persuasive argument is now being made that, over time, a Pakistani nuclear capability may complicate Israeli strategy in the Middle East at least as much as Indian strategy in South Asia.

Not much is heard now of the Partial Test Ban Treaty of 1963, but it is worth recalling that most of the suspect NNWS – such as Argentina, Brazil, India and Pakistan – unhesitatingly signed that treaty. The implication is that these states were quite willing at the time to accept the good-faith professions of the NWS and participate in the equal act of self-abnegation enjoined upon all by the clauses of that treaty. It was then felt that the 'partial' restraints would soon be followed by comprehensive controls on nuclear weapon testing and use, with obligations equally shared by the NWS and the NNWS. As we now know, the discussions leading up to and later enshrined in the clauses of the NPT belied such expectations. In the aftermath, a number of the significant NNWS tended to move away from their simpler and perhaps naive advocacy of international nuclear arms control measures. While the stance did not change, its manifestation became increasingly sceptical of NWS negotiating positions and more strident in demanding an equal sharing of obligations. Those positions have become quite rigid in the intervening years and it is unlikely that they will be modified in the future.

Individual NNWS now assess the changed environment for the international control of nuclear weapons in different ways. Argentina and Brazil, geographically distant from the cockpits of world tensions, maintain their refusals in the nuclear field, but otherwise have had few overt differences with the NWS. The same is true of states such as South Korea and Taiwan, whose special relations with the United States engender a special measure of caution in their contributions to the world-wide debate on nuclear matters. Likewise, South Africa and Israel withhold themselves from any public controversy over nuclear issues – their own, or those of others. Pakistan's positions are both easily and consistently stated: it will do as the Indians do. India was, at least in the early years, the prime candidate among the suspect NNWS to be singled out for the application of pressure, persuasion and sanctions to get it to conform to the un-equal provisions of the NPT. It was also the ideal candidate. As a non-aligned state, it was owed no special favours by either the West or the East while it remained dependent on both for economic aid. The volubility of its open system and free press – wherein all strategic issues were and are hotly debated – allied with its developed atomic energy establishment made it the most obvious 'Nth' country seek-ing nuclear weapons. That the country was also poor in per capita terms enhanced the moral fervour of those who questioned nuclear weapons in the hands of a starving nation.

Viewed generically, India's responses to the pressures and blan-dishments were really no different to those of the other NNWS in the post-test ban phase. The responses are likely to be emulated by the NNWS in succeeding years, given individual circumstance to that effect. Thus, while chagrined at the respect and status accorded by the NWS to China's Soviet-aided nuclear capability after 1964, India did not plunge into an immediate weapons drive of its own. It, none the less, refused to accept in exchange the weak and hedging assurances of support offered by the NWS for surrendering its weapons options for the future. The occasion for the Indian nuclear test in 1974 – ten years after China's – was not, as is frequently sug-gested by some observers, Madame Gandhi's political problems or a sudden national desire to garner prestige. The decision to undertake the nuclear test was a direct consequence of the appearance of United States Task Force 74, lead by the nuclear-armed aircraft carrier *Enterprise* in the Bay of Bengal in the closing stages of the 1971 Indo-Pakistani War. The test indicated a demand for according credibility to India's regional interests on the part of NWS. Having carried out the explosion, India denied that it was going to engage in the production of nuclear weapons.

More than ten years after the event, the situation is that India can probably make the bomb, but has not proceeded to a nuclear-weapon system. It would also be incorrect to assume that Indian decision-making in 1974 began and ended with a bombs-in-the-basement strategy. A few crude bombs in Indian hands would serve no purpose since against Pakistan India possesses an overwhelming conven-tional capability, and against others India would need to deliver bombs over long distances. India is likely to have the requisite delivery and command and control systems in the coming years, but while the option is maintained and updated, none of these capabilities have so far been converted into a nuclear-weapons-and-delivery system. Nor are there any moves to do so.[12]

In the continuing dialogue between the NWS and the NNWS on the control of nuclear weapons, India's behaviour may be compared and contrasted with the attitudes of the other suspect NNWS, but as modified in its own context. In relation to the past, India has not, so far, felt that its survival is at stake – as have the Israelis and the South Africans. Therefore, unlike Israel it has not devoted or developed its nuclear establishment for solely military outcomes. Nor, unlike South Africa has it focused on nuclear weapons and thereafter on civilian nuclear power plants. Unlike both Israel and South Africa, India has been an active participant in the NWS-NNWS dialogue: while rejecting one-way applications of nuclear restraints, it has nevertheless expressed its continued willingness to assume burdens in a system of shared and balanced obligations between the NNWS and the NWS.

Engaged in close military or quasi-military relationships with the United States, both South Korea and Taiwan fall in a special category of NNWS. Being outside the United Nations system, both states have had few incentives to express themselves openly within the framework of the NWS-NNWS dialogue on nuclear restraints. While survival perceptions may have encouraged South Korea and Taiwan to acquire the means to nuclear weapon capabilities, the effort has been aborted, ostensibly on United States advice.

Brazil and Argentina, like India, have not as yet felt that international events threaten their survival. It remains to be seen how the Argentinians will interpret the United Kingdom's deployment of the nuclear-armed submarine *HMS Invincible* in the Falklands/Malvinas War. For the moment, however, it is likely that, as with the Indians, Argentina and Brazil will continue to develop sophisticated nuclear facilities with the option, but not a straight conversion into, the production of nuclear weapons.

The situation with respect to Pakistan appears to be clearly one where a civilian-oriented nuclear programme was forcefully directed towards a military purpose. The change of purpose was initiated in the aftermath of the 1971 Indo-Pakistan War when half of Pakistan became Bangladesh and the Pakistani leadership feared for the survival of the rest of Pakistan. The Indian nuclear test of 1974 probably enlarged these fears and spurred the Pakistanis to acquire a nuclear weapon capability as speedily as possible.

Future Evolution of NNWS Policies

The positions of both the NWS and the NNWS in relation to the NPT and the equal-obligations demand are well defined and unlikely to be changed. The NPT framework of one-way restraints will probably not be acceptable to any of the suspect NNWS, or most of the others that have not signed the NPT. In that sense, the NPT should be viewed as having run its substantive course. However, the treaty's signatories may continue to maintain their adherence to it in formal terms.

The spate of institutional, organisational and physical controls deployed by the NSG in the aftermath of the Indian nuclear explosion of 1974 to restrict the availability of nuclear technology and materials will, in the short term, effectively deter those NNWS that would have sought to cover weapons drives behind a facade of civilian nuclear activities. Full-scope safeguards, with the pursuant clause enjoining inspection on all nuclear facilities, restrictions on the export of sensitive materials in the Zangger and NSG lists, and the operation of the United States NNPA Act, have cumulatively created a web of hurdles for would-be proliferators beyond the limited number of suspect NNWS.

Autonomous of the formal restraints, a new awareness of the risks associated with nuclear power generation and the escalating costs of power plant construction also have dampened the civilian market for nuclear technology world-wide. It is unlikely, therefore, that other nations seeking nuclear weapons would adopt the civilian power plant route to a weapons option.

The future policies of the majority of NNWS will not, however, change appreciably over past patterns, assuming that most of them have never been potential weapons proliferators. For those that still seek nuclear weapons, the choices will be made from the following means.

The most attractive option for an aspiring nuclear proliferator would be to adopt the Israeli path. A small plutonium-producing reactor is not a particularly complicated piece of engineering. A reprocessing plant is somewhat more complex and perhaps more dangerous, but a modest core of scientific and engineering personnel would be capable of constructing and operating it. Such skilled individuals, if not available at home, could be hired from abroad – and not necessarily from the advanced countries. The activities would have to be surreptitious and may be possible for many NNWS, as witness the recent Argentinian revelation of having constructed their own reprocessing plant.

The second method would be to emulate the Pakistanis, with clandestine purchases, preferably over a long time through layers of dummy business corporations and the co-operation of friendly countries. Admittedly, this would be a difficult operation, especially after the wide publicity given to the Pakistani effort. The Pakistani example probably could be replicated since the search would be for items less complex than those needed for a centrifuge enrichment plant; and if the prices offered are sufficiently remunerative to the seller. Despite the NSG restrictions – or because of them – brokers and middlemen are bound to come into existence to create a clandestine market for such items, given the forces of supply and demand. Just as there exists a thriving market for the secret international supply of arms, so a trade in nuclear-related items can be envisaged to arise at the appropriate stage.

The third avenue to proliferation would lie in legitimately acquiring nuclear technology and materials, as well as training, under the international safeguards restrictions. Indeed, this may well be the safest and most economical way of arranging the transfer of the essence of nuclear exchanges in this field – which is knowledge and not equipment.

Conclusion

It is reasonable to assess the current level of international restraints on the availability of nuclear technology and materials as buying time and delaying the onset of some would-be proliferators. That would remain a useful but not a sufficient measure of success in deterring other states from acquiring nuclear weapons. Yet the means to construct nuclear weapons are becoming easier and their availability more wide-spread in the form of accessible knowledge. While the steps to such a capability are not trivial, they are no longer a part of the awe-inspiring mystery and wonder of 20 years ago.

It does not follow that ease of access by open or surreptitious means to the acquisition of nuclear weapon capability will lead to nuclear proliferation among the NNWS. Even in the past, the only two real proliferators have been Israel and South Africa, and now there may be two more in South Asia. That rate of nuclear proliferation is far removed from the 'world of nuclear powers' envisioned by many analysts in the sixties and the seventies. There is no evidence to suggest that the pace will quicken in the future. The prognosis might well be that the pace of nuclear proliferation will be slower, since the most obvious proliferators have already 'gone nuclear'.

End Notes

1. Richard K. Betts, 'South Africa', in Joseph A. Yager (ed.), *Nonproliferation and US Foreign Policy* (The Brookings Institute, Washington, D.C., 1980), Ch. 3, pp. 283-308.
2. Peter Pringle and James Spigelman, *The Nuclear Barons* (Avon Books, New York, 1981), pp. 293-9.
3. M.R. Srinivasan, 'Kalpakkam and its Promise', *Mainstream* (New Delhi), 30 July 1983, pp. 7-9; and '15-year nuclear power profile drawn up', *Times of India*, 18 Apr. 1985.
4. For a good example of the meandering of NNWS nuclear decision-making policies, see James Everett Katz and Onkar S. Marwah, *Nuclear Power in Developing Countries, An Analysis of Decision Making* (D.C. Heath and Co., Cambridge, Massachusetts, 1982).
5. Note: depending on supply or organisational restraints, these plants may or may not provide a weapons option.
6. Zulfikar Ali Bhutto, *My Last Will and Testament* (Vikas Publications, New Delhi, 1980).
7. For a sceptical assessment of all Indian nuclear activities and professions, see Roberta Wholstetter, 'US Peaceful Aid and the Indian Bomb', in Albert Wholstetter, Victor Gilinsky, Robert Gillette and Roberta Wohlstetter, *Nuclear Policies: Fuel Without the Bomb* (Ballinger Publishing Co., Cambridge, Massachusetts, 1978), pp. 57-72.
8. 'Zia supervised supply of N-goods from Canada', *Times of India*, 30 Mar. 1985; and 'Suspicions on Pak nuclear intentions', *Times of India*, 29 Mar. 1985.
9. Ibid.
10. 'China's "secret" nuclear exports', *The Sunday Times* (London), 10 Nov. 1985, p. 1; and 'Panels Back Nuclear Pact with China, But Link US Nuclear Sales to Nonproliferation', *International Herald Tribune*, 15 Nov. 1985, p. 4.
11. From interviews with senior Indian government officials.
12. India's nuclear and space programmes probably would be militarised if Pakistan's nuclear activities became an overt weapon capability.

EMERGENT SUPPLIERS, THE NON-PROLIFERATION REGIME AND REGIONAL SECURITY

Stanley Ing

The current non-proliferation regime, as embodied in the Treaty on the Non-Proliferation of Nuclear Weapons (NPT) and the International Atomic Energy Agency (IAEA), has been relatively successful despite growing criticism that it has not fulfilled some important mandates. Aside from India, with its nuclear explosion in 1974, no other country has visibly joined the nuclear club. While the NPT/IAEA regime has helped to impede the development of a nuclear weapon capability by some countries, the policies of the supplier nations have been no less an inhibiting factor. Through unilateral actions and co-ordination of policies by member states, the nuclear suppliers have been able to maintain some control over the dissemination of nuclear technology and material.

In the view of the supplier countries, this control is necessary, particularly with regard to the transfer of proliferation-prone material such as enriched uranium, plutonium and related technologies. The fact that the NPT/IAEA regime lacks any provisions that might restrict such transfers is of critical concern to the supplier nations, especially the United States. Indeed, the NPT legally sanctions the transfer of so-called 'sensitive technologies' under Article IV. Yet so long as the supplier countries retain some control over nuclear transfers, the pace of weapons development can be constrained.

The ability to control weapons proliferation through the nuclear market is effective so long as there is only a limited number of suppliers and they are willing to co-ordinate their export policies. With the emergence of more nuclear suppliers, or suppliers which are reaching beyond their traditional market, this ability to restrain the rush towards acquiring proliferation-prone technologies is also being eroded. This chapter focuses on the emergence of new suppliers, their impact on the current non-proliferation regime and, more narrowly, the strategic implications this may occasion. However,

119

because the new suppliers are just entering the nuclear market and are not likely to make a significant impact until the 1990s, many of the arguments presented in this chapter are speculative.

The Emergent Nuclear Suppliers

Traditionally, the supply of nuclear technology comes from the industrialised nations, with a few countries dominating the world market. Near monopoly by the United States only gave way to French and West German entries in the early 1970s.[1] The Soviet Union also has a large share of the nuclear market, but mostly within Eastern Europe. However, the transition from a virtual monopoly of the nuclear market by the United States to a more oligopolistic situation is far from over.

This oligopolistic pattern of nuclear sales is now changing as former recipients become capable of developing their own technology, as well as producing their own reactor fuel. These emergent suppliers, most of which are from the Third World, in turn become exporters. Admittedly, their share of the market is relatively small, and the components they supply are not state-of-the-art materials. Nevertheless, these emergent suppliers do provide an alternative for countries which may find the commercial or non-proliferation policies of the industrialised countries too restrictive.

Nuclear trade among Third World countries is partly centred in South America with Argentina and Brazil being the major exporters. Already Brazil has nuclear relations with Paraguay and India. Argentina is also very active in the nuclear market, having sold enriched uranium to Iraq in 1980, and more recently having designed and constructed a small research reactor for Peru. Both South American suppliers appear to be developing strong connections with Spain. In South Asia India is emerging as a potentially major nuclear supplier. As the first Third World country to invest significantly in nuclear energy, India is able to convert its experience in this area into an exportable commodity. For a brief period there was a possibility that India might even form a partnership with an industrialised country in order to penetrate the world nuclear market. This has not materialised, but India has gone on to conclude nuclear agreements with some Third World countries. Among these are countries which are in the midst of a war, or are located in a region of some instability. These include Iraq, Syria and Libya. It is rumoured that Libya has attempted to trade oil for sensitive nuclear technology from India.[2]

China also is reported to have exported nuclear technology and fuel, but has done so in a very circumscribed manner. This is understandable, given the fact that two of the countries that China has aided are considered likely candidates to join the nuclear club. According to one report, China is providing Pakistan with centrifuge technology that would enable Islamabad eventually to develop an indigenous fuel fabrication capability.[3] In addition, China is said to have provided South Africa with a modest amount of enriched uranium.

Nuclear trade within the Third World is thus quite extensive, but how active it is, in terms of volume, is difficult to ascertain. Part of the problem is that some nuclear transfers are conducted in a clandestine manner and are not subject to IAEA safeguards or other forms of international verification.

While most of the emergent nuclear suppliers are from the Third World, the number of nuclear suppliers also is increased by the addition of countries which have decided to expand their sales beyond their traditional markets. The Soviet Union, for instance, is slowly beginning to export nuclear technology beyond its traditional market in Eastern Europe. In the Middle East the Soviet Union already has supplied Iraq with an IRT2000 reactor and Libya with a large research reactor at Tajoura.[4] Both are safeguarded. During negotiations for the supply of United States enriched uranium to India's Tarapur reactor, the Soviet Union also offered New Delhi the necessary fuel to maintain operations at the Indian power plant. In the end a compromise was reached whereby France replaced the United States as the major supplier of enriched uranium to India's Tarapur reactor.

The increase in the number of nuclear suppliers need not have any significant detrimental impact on the existing non-proliferation regime. Although the entry of new suppliers does provide some alternatives, most transactions still are safeguarded. For example, with the exception of Chile, all Latin American countries which have some form of nuclear co-operation with Argentina or Brazil are covered by full-scope safeguards. This safeguards coverage is extended either through the NPT or the 1967 Treaty of Tlatelolco.[5] In transferring nuclear technology, the Soviet Union is perhaps even more stringent in applying safeguards than most other supplier nations, such as France and the Federal Republic of Germany.

The potential increase in nuclear suppliers does not automatically mean that the current NPT/IAEA regime will diminish in importance. If anything, the transfer of nuclear technology to NPT signatories could draw into the regime, however loosely, those nuclear suppliers which have chosen to remain outside of the NPT. Yet, if there is an increase in the number of nuclear suppliers, and if their share of the nuclear market is increased, the NPT/IAEA regime could have difficulties in safeguarding these transactions. The inability to regulate this new pattern of nuclear trade, either because of technical problems or because such transfers are beyond the reach of the IAEA, could result in some erosion of confidence in the current non-proliferation regime.

Impact on the Non-Proliferation Regime

In order to be effective, the current NPT/IAEA regime needs to maintain the confidence of member states and even some of those which have declared adherence to its principles but have remained outside of the regime. In turn, this requires the regime to extend as widely as possible the treaty obligations contained in the NPT and the safeguards network of the IAEA. It is particularly important for the regime to include among its members as many threshold nations as possible. Confidence in the NPT/IAEA regime is tied to its perceived ability to account for, and to some degree regulate, the nuclear development of threshold states. To date, the regime has achieved limited success in persuading threshold states to subscribe to the terms of the NPT. Most of the countries that are considered to have strong incentives to acquire a nuclear capability are non-signatories. In itself, this is not a critical problem in that most of the important threshold nations are recipients of nuclear aid. In accepting nuclear technology or material from the industrialised supplier nations, they also accept some form of international safeguards. Although these safeguards are applied specifically to the transferred technology or material, there is some accounting of their end use.

As the number of nuclear suppliers increases to include exporters which remain outside the NPT, surveillance of nuclear developments in certain countries may become more difficult. The IAEA could find itself with no legal basis to inspect the nuclear technologies between two non-signatories. The nature of the nuclear technology and the proliferation risk involved between, say, Brazil and India may not contribute to weapons development, but the critical problem is that the NPT/IAEA regime is not in a position to verify these nuclear transfers.

Thus as the number and volume of nuclear trade among non-signatories increase, there is also a large network of nuclear transfers that the NPT/IAEA regime is excluded from safeguarding. Consequently, the international community is kept in the dark regarding the nature and pace of nuclear developments within perceived threshold countries. The nuclear programmes of these countries, in effect, operate free from international or NPT/IAEA scrutiny. There is little accounting of their nuclear programmes.

For the IAEA this lack of information and surveillance could greatly complicate its task of providing detection of military diversions and timely warning. IAEA safeguards coverage may extend to only parts of a country's nuclear programme, but not necessarily to those parts which have been gained from certain emergent suppliers which continue to be non-NPT signatories. Without access to the entire nuclear programme, detection time could be reduced. For example, according to one source, the development of Pakistan's Kahuta enrichment plant had gone unnoticed until 1978.[6] Argentina, too, has been developing an enrichment facility at Pilcaniyeu. Little was known about the facility until Argentina revealed its development in 1983.[7] As these emergent suppliers developed their own expertise in nuclear technology, their ties with the traditional suppliers were reduced. Since many of the emergent suppliers are also non-signatories to the NPT, a domestic capability in nuclear energy means increasingly less IAEA intrusions.

Admittedly, countries such as Pakistan and Argentina are beyond full-scope safeguards and are unlikely to become members of the NPT. However, even for NPT signatories there is difficulty in ascertaining the exact nature of a country's nuclear programme and its potential for nuclear weapon proliferation. Both Iraq and Libya are signatories to the NPT, but despite full-scope safeguards there is some concern that a nuclear weapon capability is not beyond the reach of either country. This is partly made possible by the entry of alternative suppliers which are not as demanding in the application of safeguards. Even the Soviet Union, which is just now attempting to expand its market, and which strictly adheres to the NPT, does not require full-scope safeguards as a condition for transferring nuclear technology.

The advantages of purchasing nuclear technology with less stringent safeguards and conditions could attract buyers who may have

incentives to develop a nuclear weapon capability or just those who
have reservations about the imposition of new export rules by certain suppliers. Should the emergent suppliers gain a larger share of
the nuclear market, the NPT/IAEA regime's global safeguards
coverage also may be reduced.

It is still too early to predict whether the increased volume of
nuclear transfers that is likely to remain beyond IAEA inspection
will bring into question the legitimacy of the NPT/IAEA regime.
However, one may begin to wonder about the relevance of a regime
that is being partly circumvented by emergent suppliers which do not
necessarily share the non-proliferation perspectives contained within
the current regime. In some respects, these emergent suppliers never
did fully share the views of the NPT/IAEA regime. But not having
developed their own nuclear capability, these differences of view did
not have a significant impact on the NPT/IAEA regime. With a
more developed export capability, this could change.

While the addition of more suppliers could loosen the controls
over horizontal proliferation, it does not mean that nuclear transfers
among non-signatories would be totally unsafeguarded. Despite
remaining outside the NPT framework, the emergent suppliers from
the Third World appear to have been cautious in exporting their
nuclear technology. For most nuclear transfers some safeguards
provisions are imposed. In regions where international safeguards
are not applicable, there are efforts to conclude regional agreements
on the peaceful uses of nuclear energy. Most recently, Argentina and
Brazil discussed plans to open both countries' nuclear facilities for
mutual inspection. Such a plan, if fully implemented, would not only
defuse the nuclear competition between the two countries, but also
would open nuclear facilities for future safeguards inspections.[8]

In itself this should be a welcome development, and for the NPT/
IAEA regime this arrangement could be the first of other regional
non-proliferation accords. Regional regimes could make a positive
contribution in preventing horizontal proliferation, but their possible negative impacts should not be overlooked.

While regional regimes could supplement the work of the NPT/
IAEA regime, they also could serve as rivals to the latter. Regional
regimes may be formed because the NPT is viewed as being too
unequal and restrictive, or as a result of requirements imposed by
regional politics. Whatever the rationale for a separate regime, the
end-product undoubtedly would be at variance with the NPT/IAEA
regime. Aside from the problem of undermining attempts to achieve

a uniform system of safeguards, regional regimes also could be less demanding in their non-proliferation standards. The 1967 Treaty of Tlatelolco, for instance, still permits peaceful nuclear explosions, while the NPT does not. The lack of uniform safeguards procedures and standards could create problems for the inspection of transferred technology. The case of the European Atomic Energy Community safeguards system already has shown how in the 1976 Canadian uranium embargo of Europe, such differences of view could disrupt commerce even between friendly countries.

The creation of new regional regimes also could give political legitimacy to nuclear transfers that are governed by less stringent safeguards. For some threshold countries, joining a new regional regime could eliminate the need to justify continually their refusal to sign the NPT. Some South American countries are pointing to the Treaty of Tlatelolco as sufficient evidence of their peaceful intentions. As a result, the NPT could cease to be the standard by which a country's non-proliferation concern is measured. This may be overstating the argument, but if regional regimes are created, there is a possibility that the NPT could become just another regime among a few others, and it may not be viewed further as the cornerstone of international non-proliferation efforts. However, the Third Review of the NPT in September 1985 revealed that, at least for Canada, the NPT remains the critical basis of its non-proliferation efforts. According to Ambassador D.C. Roche, 'Canada's own objectives in the review conference were already met.' This included 'the maintenance of the NPT as a basic element of the non-proliferation regime and a reaffirmation of the purpose and provisions of the NPT'.[9]

In addition to the NPT/IAEA regime, further increase of the market share by the emergent suppliers also could have adverse effects on the policies and unity of the Nuclear Suppliers Group (NSG). Co-ordination of policies within the NSG is already difficult, and the need to be more competitive as a result of more supplier alternatives could lead to a looser interpretation of suppliers' guidelines. This is only a possibility; a more likely result is that members of the NSG would not accept a significantly tighter safeguards system than that already agreed to. Thus, full-scope safeguards are not likely to become a condition of export for NSG members as countries such as Canada are urging.

These past difficulties show that as the supplier condition moves from a monopolistic situation to more of a multi-centred market,

[e]ach phase in the transition has increased the risks of political discord over the handling of nuclear trade and has brought fewer opportunities for the cartel-like fixing of trade policy, or for coercing imports into renouncing nuclear weaponry in exchange for trade.[10]

The entry of the new emergent suppliers into the nuclear market could create even more discord among the old suppliers, especially if global nuclear export remains fairly static. Moreover, if the emergent suppliers further develop their export capabilities, the option of co-ordinating nuclear guidelines may be taken away from the NSG. Certain NSG countries have argued that some safeguards need to be relaxed in order to compete with the emergent nations which demand less stringent safeguards. In this respect, the greatest immediate danger comes not from the emergent suppliers but from the NSG members who are using the entry of new suppliers to lower existing nuclear safeguards for the purpose of facilitating nuclear export.

Co-ordination of supplier export policies has not been too effective and in the past has driven the United States and Canada to seek unilateral measures. The United States, with its 1978 Nuclear Non-Proliferation Act, and Canada, with its 1974 and 1976 policy changes, were attempting to use domestic legislation to impose tighter safeguards than possible in the multilateral arena. This resort to national legislation was in part a response to domestic public opinion and in part a genuine effort to ensure that transferred technology would be used solely for peaceful purposes. Initially, this national legislation had some effect, forcing the recipient countries either to comply with the new regulations or to terminate their nuclear assistance. In the latter case, the recipient nations could have turned to only a few other suppliers whose export policies also were fairly vigorous, but these also could be pressured by the United States into refusing to transfer the required technology.

In not sharing the same views on non-proliferation as the United States, the emergent suppliers are in some ways less susceptible to United States pressure. This broadens the list of alternative suppliers and reduces the negative impact which national legislation could have on a country's nuclear programme.

The Emergent Suppliers and Some Strategic Implications

It is commonly argued that the decision to develop nuclear weapons is politically and strategically motivated. Consequently, the increase in the number of nuclear suppliers is not likely to have an appreciable effect on a country's nuclear arms policy. The decision to acquire nuclear weapons would have been made according to other priorities and concerns and is not likely to be based on supplier conditions.

However, once a country has decided to develop a nuclear weapons programme, the increased number of exporters becomes an important factor. In addition, the diffusion of sources could provide some cover for a clandestine attempt at developing nuclear weapons. Certainly, Pakistan has benefited from the entry of China into the nuclear market, as has Iraq.

More importantly, the emergent suppliers tend to concentrate not on the export of large nuclear power plants, except perhaps the Soviet Union, but on fuel fabrication and research reactors. This has implications for horizontal proliferation in that previously the major barrier to weapons development was the difficulty in obtaining weapons-grade fissile material. Uranium enrichment was not only cost prohibitive, but such technologies were not widely disseminated because of the proliferation risk. Plutonium was thought to be the most likely route towards horizontal proliferation. With new technologies, such as the gas centrifuge method, uranium enrichment is now becoming the preferred route to weapons development. Uranium enrichment facilities offer two advantages. The facilities can be small in scale and the cost of operating them not prohibitively costly. Furthermore, many emergent suppliers have established domestic enrichment facilities, and some are willing to transfer their expertise in this area. This helps to lower the barriers against non-proliferation and to create opportunities for countries which have been unable to establish fuel fabrication facilities. However, it should be noted that such fuel fabrication facilities are of the research variety. Most emergent suppliers have yet to develop fully operational 'sensitive technologies' such as fuel fabrication plants.

The increased number of nuclear suppliers could help create a situation where components for nuclear development could be bought in an off-the-shelf fashion from various supplier countries. This is not to suggest that a nuclear device could be assembled easily. The availability of nuclear technology and fissile materials means that a country no longer has to spend years developing a nuclear technological infrastructure before proceeding with a nuclear weapons programme. This opens the way for many countries which have had little expertise in nuclear technology to contemplate the strategic advantages of acquiring a nuclear weapon capability. With a minimal level of technological sophistication, a threshold country could attempt to develop a nuclear option with the help of imported components. This route already has been taken by Pakistan, which is attempting to supplement its nuclear weapons programme with imported components from the Netherlands, the United States, China and even Canada. It also is reported that Libya made attempts to secure from Argentina nuclear components as partial payment for a $100 million arms transfer to Buenos Aires during the 1982 Falklands War.[11] If this is indeed true, then Libya would be one step closer to obtaining a nuclear weapon capability without actually first establishing the necessary industrial infrastructure that is thought to be a prerequisite. In short, the increased availability of nuclear technology from the emergent suppliers could help quicken the pace of nuclear weapons development.

However, countries such as Libya and Iraq are not representative of the technological sophistication of most threshold countries. Those that are considered likely candidates to join the nuclear club have achieved a level of technological and industrial development that brings them very close to producing a nuclear capability. As Warren Donnelly writes, 'many non-nuclear weapons states today have more of a nuclear industrial base to produce atom bombs than the US had in the early days of the Manhattan Project'.[12] This high industrial base could be enhanced by the wider availability of nuclear suppliers and increased contact with them.

A move towards greater reliance on emergent suppliers also could dictate the course of nuclear weapons proliferation. In the future, because the emergent suppliers do not export complete power reactors, and because the nuclear components they do export are easier to obtain, certain threshold countries may be persuaded to establish facilities dedicated solely to nuclear weapons development. Such a route could incur political costs, but this, too, may be acceptable in view of the financial savings and the perceived strategic importance of quickly acquiring a nuclear capability. In this instance, the line between the peaceful and the military applications of nuclear energy is quite clear.

This is different from the current trend where weapons development usually proceeds parallel to the establishment of a nuclear reactor programme. The line between the military and peaceful applications of nuclear energy often is blurred. Reactors could produce electricity for peaceful use, while the spent fuel could be diverted for the manufacture of nuclear weapons. Consequently, the nuclear reactor programmes of most threshold countries contain some ambiguity regarding the level of weapons development.

Yet this, too, may be changing. The increased export capability of the emergent suppliers reduces this nuclear ambiguity in two ways. First, because emergent suppliers do not export complete nuclear power plants but mostly components, many of which are for research reactors and fuel fabrication facilities, there might be a tendency for regional rivals to view such transfers as military-related. Even if a recipient nation does have a civilian nuclear programme, there might be some concern as to whether this would justify importing fuel fabrication technologies. This is of particular concern when the suppliers are perceived to be less stringent in their safeguards applications.

Second, the ability to export means that the emergent suppliers have fully developed the technology involved. This removes another layer of ambiguity that has come to envelop the nuclear programme of so many threshold countries. As their export capability grows, the threshold countries reveal more clearly the level of their nuclear weapons development. The ability to export fuel-fabrication-related technology, and even enriched uranium, indicates that a number of threshold countries are very close to acquiring a nuclear weapon capability.

As the capabilities of a certain threshold country become clearer, a regional adversary may not wait for a nuclear test to conclude that the intentions of the threshold country are less than peaceful. This may not automatically drive the regional adversary to seek a nuclear option of its own. It may decide that it cannot compete at the nuclear level with the threshold country, or it may prefer to live with the nuclear ambiguity despite increasing evidence that the nuclear weapons programme of the threshold country is in an advanced state. Evidence of such nuclear capabilities does contribute to the instability of the regional strategic environment and it could serve as the final pretext for other countries to initiate nuclear weapons programmes of their own.

End Notes

1. By 1973 the United States share of the nuclear export market had slipped to 82 per cent from 100 per cent in 1966. Over the span of three years the United States share fell to 16 per cent. See 'Westinghouse Gets Korea Electric Order for Two Nuclear Plants', *Wall Street Journal*, 4 Apr. 1978, p. 13.

2. Robert F. Goheen,'Problems of Proliferation: US Policy and the Third World', *World Politics*, vol. 35, no. 2 (January 1983), p. 199.
3. Robert Manning, 'A backyard bomb?', *Far Eastern Economic Review*, 2 Aug. 1984, p. 10.
4. Canada, House of Commons, Standing Committee on External Affairs and National Defence (SCEAND), no. 31 (1 October 1985), p. 31:5.
5. John R. Redick, 'The Tlatelolco Regime and Nonproliferation in Latin America', *International Organization*, vol. 35, no. 1 (Winter 1981), p. 129.
6. Goheen, 'Problems of Proliferation: US Policy and the Third World', p. 203.
7. Leonard S. Spector, 'Nuclear proliferation: the pace quickens', *Bulletin of the Atomic Scientists*, vol. 41, no. 1 (January 1985), p. 13.
8. 'Argentina and Brazil reportedly agree to major A-plant pact', *Christian Science Monitor*, vol. 77, no. 79, 18 Mar. 1985, p. 3.
9. William Walker and Mans Lonnroth, 'Proliferation and Nuclear Trade: A Look Ahead', *Bulletin of the Atomic Scientist*, vol. 40, no. 4 (April 1984), p. 32.
10. Spector, 'Nuclear proliferation: the pace quickens', p. 12.
11. Warren Donnelly, 'Assessment of the Proliferation Threat of Today and Tomorrow', Congressional Research Service, Library of Congress, cited in *Nuclear News*, vol. 27, no. 15 (December 1984), p. 96.
12. Ashok Kapur, *International Nuclear Proliferation. Multilateral Diplomacy and Regional Aspects* (Praeger, New York, 1979), p. 187.

THE NUCLEAR INDUSTRY AND THE NPT: A PERSPECTIVE FROM WASHINGTON

Dwight J. Porter

Overview

Any linkage between the nuclear industry and the Treaty on the Non-Proliferation of Nuclear Weapons (NPT) is not clear, even though industry often transfers a great deal of non-sensitive nuclear technology to its nuclear customers. The NPT is, of course, largely a matter concerning governments and the interaction of international policies and politics which, in some countries, are beyond the influence of industry. The capability of the United States nuclear industry to affect its government's nuclear export policies has, in the last decade, been at best marginal. In other countries industry perhaps fared better.

However, the nuclear industries of the world would suffer greatly without the NPT. Today's nuclear reactor business is based largely on the export market. The twin bases for the world non-proliferation regime – the NPT and the International Atomic Energy Agency (IAEA) – are the keys to the continuation of orderly world nuclear trade. Most of the world's nuclear industrial establishments understand this and support the IAEA and the NPT.

Granted, there have been instances in the past when national nuclear industries urged their governments to support technology and hardware transfers of sensitive nuclear technologies such as reprocessing plants, transfers which did not meet with universal approbation in other nations. Even in these instances, however, the exporting nation demanded the application of international safeguards to the facility or nuclear material that it sold abroad, which is the minimum requirement specified in the NPT.

While nuclear industry has a major – indeed vital – stake in the continued viability of the non-proliferation regime and the institutions which sustain it, the capacity of industry to influence events is not always evident. It is important to remember that we are dealing with the most politicised and government-regulated industry in the

131

world. The United States, for instance, unilaterally altered solemn commitments to other nations when it passed its Nuclear Non-Proliferation Act (NNPA). So did some other supplier nations, even though the majority of advanced nations did not accept or apply the new goals of United States export requirements (primarily full-scope safeguards). The subject of nuclear non-proliferation, in some countries such as the United States, generates heated emotion. This often leads to legislative excess and to formulation of puzzling laws and regulations which unilaterally have revised some of the earlier (basically sensible and universally accepted) ground rules under which United States nuclear exports took place. (The phenomenon was also observed in Canada which had a much more specific reason for its concerns.)

It also is important to emphasise that the nuclear industry is a buyer's market, as domestic orders fail to utilise the productive capacity of existing reactor and component factories. This leads to fierce competition for export business, and governments have moved in to protect, support and often subsidise their industries in a variety of ways. It is not surprising that many governments follow this pattern of action. However, sometimes differing nuclear export policies will provide disadvantage to exporters in the nation with the most constraints on exports. A recent case in point is China, with which the United States government, with its stringent legal requirements, is still trying to conclude a nuclear agreement.[1] This is the same China to which United States allies for years have been eager to sell reactors and nuclear technology with the full and active support of their governments. China is not, of course, an NPT party, and lack of consistency in national nuclear export policies has led to the feeling among many nuclear importing states which are adherents to the NPT that the obligations of Article IV are not taken seriously by some exporters, thereby compromising the energy supply security that they feel the NPT Article IV bargain was designed to provide.

In the provisions of the NPT, Article IV deals with technological co-operation and exports. The pertinent language is: 'Parties to the Treaty undertake to facilitate and have the right to participate in the fullest possible exchange of equipment, materials and scientific and technological information on the peaceful uses of nuclear energy.' This article has particular relevance to the needs of the developing areas of the world.

The developing countries, often referred to as the Group of 77, have been vocal in their contentions that the industrially developed nations – and, particularly, the nuclear-weapon states – have not fulfilled this part of the 'bargain'. Although not a justifiable criticism, this is a complex issue which must be examined from several viewpoints, including that of the transfer of technology commercially developed by the nuclear industry. Note also that nuclear power (indeed, any power generation facility) requires major capital investment. The Third World's real frustrations come more from lack of ability to pay than from failure to gain access to nuclear technology.

Before discussing materials, equipment and technology related to nuclear power, it should be pointed out that there are many other uses of nuclear energy, such as those in industry, hydrology, biology, medicine and agriculture, which at the present time are of far greater significance to most of the Group of 77 nations than nuclear power. For example, in 1982 about 80 per cent of the IAEA's technical co-operation budget of approximately $23 million was spent on these and similar activities. One does not recall hearing allegations of restrictions on transfers of this type of nuclear technology. The only limitations appear to be financial, plus the ability of the recipient nation to utilise such specialised technology.

Nuclear Industry and Technology Transfer

In recent years the term 'appropriate technology' has come into vogue. Is nuclear power an appropriate technology for developing nations? Anti-nuclear groups in the advanced world often use this argument to oppose nuclear exports to the developing world. This serves to add to the frustrations of the poor countries which are desperately striving to modernise by developing electric power generation facilities. There are many nations for which nuclear power is not, or not yet, 'appropriate'; for example, those for which the capital cost is too great, demand for electrical energy too low, the distribution system insufficiently developed, or the infrastructure (including a cadre of trained specialists) clearly inadequate. There are, however, a number of the 'industrially developing countries' where nuclear power is being introduced. In these countries which are party to the NPT, is there participation 'in the fullest possible exchange' of nuclear power equipment, materials and technology?

With respect to the nuclear power fuel cycle, one of the major criticisms by these developing countries has related to non-transfer of the so-called 'sensitive technologies' – primarily uranium enrichment and chemical reprocessing. These are the technologies at which the nuclear power fuel cycle (particularly in the case of enrichment) and the production of weapons-usable materials are most similar. This criticism is heard less frequently today than it once was, since there appears to be general acceptance of the reality that such technology should be provided only when the recipient has a reasonable 'need to know'. Working Group 3 of the International Fuel Cycle Evaluation (INFCE) found, for example, that the large investments and economies of scale inherent in these technologies favour the purchase of materials or services rather than the construction of indigenous facilities, except for those countries having major nuclear power programmes. Increasingly, as well, greater attention is being given to long-term storage of spent fuel rather than its reprocessing; technologies for storage are non-sensitive and readily available from a number of nations.

In the United States, enrichment technologies, which always have been classified, are not exported. Although chemical reprocessing technology was declassified early in the Atoms for Peace programme, its export has been embargoed for over a decade as a matter of non-proliferation policy. Furthermore, in the absence of a commercial reprocessing industry, the United States no longer is considered as a leader in or a commercial supplier of such technology and equipment. Although their policies are not as restrictive as those of the United States, other potential supplier nations which are members of the Nuclear Suppliers Group are pledged to use 'restraint' in the transfers of both enrichment and reprocessing technology. What this really means is that 'restraint' will be exercised when the nuclear intentions of the importing country are suspect or ambiguous.

In so far as the availability of materials and services at the front end of the fuel cycle is concerned, the supply of these is more than adequate. For light-water reactor fuel, the supply of enrichment services is about double the current demand, not to mention inventories of slightly-enriched uranium fuel which are available, often at 'bargain prices', from utilities with deferred or cancelled nuclear power projects. Substantial excess capacity also exists for the conversion of uranium concentrates and the fabrication of fuel. All of this means not only adequate supplies but a highly competitive market-place favouring the buyer.

Enrichment, reprocessing and spent fuel storage are largely

governmental or quasi-governmental activities; thus policies in these areas on technology transfer, licensing, pricing, etc., are not basically within the purview of the 'commercial' nuclear industry. In so far as uranium production is concerned, while this is largely a private activity, the minerals extraction technology is relatively conventional and readily available. Technology for uranium ore exploration, as well as estimates of reserves, information on geologically favourable areas and so forth have been widely disseminated by individual nations as well as by such international organisations as the IAEA and the Organisation for Economic Co-operation and Development (OECD).

This leaves uranium conversion, fuel fabrication and reactors as the only major nuclear power technologies which are basically the responsibility of the private industrial sector. Since there is more than adequate capacity for uranium conversion available in the international market, and since the technology has been widely disseminated and can be obtained under licensing arrangements, conversion will receive minimal attention below.

Where nuclear equipment, materials or technology are within control of the private sector, most governments have neither a policy nor a legal basis for controlling the conditions under which they will be made available to another government or private entity in an NPT-adherent state, the language of Article IV notwithstanding. The private sector has been willing to make nuclear power technology available. The licensing fees and commercial terms and conditions which have been charged are reasonable in relation to the investment made in development of the technology. Candidly, this has not been primarily a matter of altruism – except in the early days of the atom when it was done by the United States government – but has resulted from the pressure of competition and the recognition that there is almost no nuclear power technology which is beyond the ability of an industrialised nation – or probably even an industrially developing nation – to master if it is prepared to give it a sufficiently high manpower and economic priority.

To illustrate how the industry has made available to other countries' nuclear fuel fabrication and power reactor equipment and technology, let us examine the case most familiar to this author: Westinghouse. In the fuel fabrication area, for example, Westinghouse currently is competing with four other companies, two American and two European, for the construction of a nuclear fuel fabrication facility in Korea. This facility would be capable of supplying all of the fuel reloads needed for the first ten Korean nuclear power plants. The company that wins the award will license and supply the technology, as well as some of the equipment and adequate engineering and supervision during construction and initial operation to ensure such aspects as plant safety, quality of product and plant production capability. Prior to this Korean proposal, Westinghouse already had licensed seven organisations outside of the United States to produce its pressurised-water reactor fuel.

In so far as nuclear power reactors are concerned, Westinghouse has supplied 37 pressurised-water reactors to twelve countries, beginning with the 1956 order for the 11-megawatt BR-3 reactor in Belgium, the second commercial pressurised-water reactor in the world. Westinghouse currently has nuclear licensees and international operations in nine countries, involving 27 associates, covering such operations as nuclear system design, component manufacture, system management and services. To illustrate the extensive scope of these activities, in Spain, when Westinghouse first entered into a licensing arrangement for components in 1972, Spanish industry was capable of supplying about 20 to 25 per cent of the nuclear components on a monetary value basis for its evolving nuclear power programme. Today, Westinghouse's wholly owned subsidiary, Westinghouse Nuclear-Espanola, has a work force composed of 75 per cent Spanish nationals, including essentially all of its top management; initially, this staff was 70 per cent non-Spanish.

Another illustration would be that of Belgium. In the early 1970s, Westinghouse chartered a company, Westinghouse Nuclear-Europe, which quickly grew to employ more than 400 people. At one time its staff included over 30 nationalities, making it a truly international effort. One of Westinghouse's Belgian licensees is the Ateliers de Constructions de Charleroi, in which Westinghouse at various times has been both a minority and majority owner. Westinghouse also has held an equity position in its fuel fabrication licensee, Société Franco-Belge de Fabrication de Combustibles, but has since withdrawn from financial participation.

Similar experiences could be cited for other nations, including France, Italy, Japan and Korea. Although Westinghouse had an earlier start and has had more extensive experience in nuclear power technology transfers and related assistance to foreign nations than have other nuclear reactor suppliers, it is likely that they could present similar examples. Thus it is difficult to make a case to meet the obligations of Article IV regarding the right of parties to the NPT to 'participate in the fullest possible exchange' of peaceful nuclear equipment and technology.

Another important area of international participation is that of assistance and co-operation in nuclear reactor safety and regulatory matters. The nuclear industry plays a significant role in ensuring the safety of power reactors and their technology. However, governmental and international organisations also have a major role. The United States Nuclear Regulatory Commission (NRC), for example, has bilateral exchange agreements with a number of nations. One category of agreements, of which there are 21, provides a mechanism for the timely exchange of information on reactor safety. The second category generally covers the direct participation of other nations in NRC's ongoing safety research programmes; there are 37 of these arrangements involving 16 countries. The Department of Energy also has several co-operative international agreements related to nuclear safety and environmental matters, including the management of radioactive wastes.

In the area of multilateral co-operation, the IAEA, OECD, United Nations Environment Programme and International Maritime Organisation all are actively concerned with the environmental aspects of nuclear energy. Of these agencies, the IAEA undoubtedly is the major player. For example, in early 1984 technical officers of its Division of Nuclear Safety were involved in 150 technical co-operation projects. Activities range from assisting in the establishment of regulatory regimes for radiation protection to the strengthening of specific technical capabilities. In projecting future needs for assistance in nuclear reactor safety, the IAEA has estimated that there will be 37 power reactors operating in 15 developing countries by 1986. Between 1975 and 1984 the IAEA has been responsible for 39 safety-related missions covering such major areas as siting, safety report review and regulatory body and nuclear legislation advisories. It also has provided both long- and short-term expert assistance in the safety field to 14 countries.

In the training area, the IAEA conducted 21 inter-regional safety-related courses between 1978 and 1983, varying in length from three to nine weeks. Most of these programmes were not repetitive, covering such diverse topics as quality assurance and probabilistic risk assessment. Twelve of these courses were given in the United States and the remainder in Argentina, Spain, the Federal Republic of Germany and France. The IAEA also has begun a programme of Operational Safety Review Team (OSART) missions.

These teams, comprised of experts with extensive nuclear plant operating experience, review the status of nuclear power plants and assess their ability to operate safely.

In addition, the IAEA has set up an Incident Reporting System (IRS) to collect information on unusual and significant occurrences at operating nuclear power reactors and to provide this information to plant operators and regulatory bodies within the nuclear community. Early in 1985 the agency's director general named a 13-member International Safety Advisory Group (INSAG) to discuss 'general nuclear safety issues of international significance' and to 'formulate, where possible, commonly shared safety concepts'.

This rather formidable enumeration of co-operative safety activities has been given to show the extensive opportunities for international participation in nuclear energy technology which are available from industry, individual governments and international organisations, as well as the complementary nature of the various programmes. Most of the financial resources of the international organisations come from the advanced industrialised world. This monetary support serves to keep the bargain in the Article IV trade-off between nuclear-weapon states and non-nuclear weapon states.

The Nuclear Industry and the Future of the NPT Regime

What may the future may hold? Restricting this narrowly to the relationship between the NPT and the nuclear industry, one could dismiss the subject rather quickly. It is probable that the nuclear industry will continue to be willing to make essentially all of its non-sensitive products and technology available to NPT parties under reasonable economic terms and conditions. In fact, the large present excess of supply over demand – which is likely to continue well into the 1990s – should virtually ensure this.

But, broadening this subject somewhat, will the competitive conditions which this oversupply engenders create a situation under which some supplier nations will be willing to provide nuclear materials, equipment and technology under conditions which may not fully support the objectives of the NPT? Furthermore, will the growing number of nuclear suppliers, including some such as India, Argentina and Brazil which are not party to the NPT, tend to weaken the rather broad consensus on non-proliferation conditions for supply which has been painstakingly built up over several decades? And what might be the non-proliferation policy of China should it become a major nuclear supplier in the future?

With regard to the present major suppliers, there is no tendency to break away from the guidelines of the Nuclear Suppliers Group (NSG), even in the face of serious economic threats to their nuclear industries. To the contrary, the recent agreement among Western suppliers on a detailed trigger list of components and materials for gas centrifuge enrichment plants and the reported near agreement on a similar list for chemical reprocessing must be viewed as encouraging signs.

Probably the most contentious issue now and for the foreseeable future is that of 'full-scope' or 'comprehensive' safeguards. There are only four supplier nations which currently require such safeguards on exports of source and special nuclear materials and major components of reactors and fuel cycle facilities: Australia, Canada, Sweden and the United States. Most other supplier nations appear to be convinced that this requirement is unnecessary, at least for technologies other than enrichment and reprocessing, although some have indicated their willingness to adopt a full-scope safeguards policy if all major suppliers would do so. This disparity in safeguards policies on occasion has cost the nuclear industry, in both Canada and the United States, opportunities to compete for nuclear export business. On the other side of the coin are those who take the position that only by requiring such safeguards can NPT parties be 'rewarded' relative to those nations which are unwilling to adhere to the treaty. In the United States legislative proposals have been introduced during the past several years to make comprehensive safeguards a requirement for all exports of nuclear materials, equipment and technology. This would have the effect of making 'pariah nations' out of non-NPT adherents in so far as nuclear co-operation with the United States is concerned. Passage of such legislation would be a highly undesirable development, not so much for the nuclear industry, which currently has only minor commerce with these countries in any event, but from the standpoint of the United States government's efforts to inhibit proliferation. Even a limited exchange of non-sensitive nuclear technology or export of parts for the repair or safety upgrading of an existing reactor permits a continuing dialogue with these countries. This could lead to favourable changes in attitudes or policies.

The question of how the emerging supplier states are likely to act with regard to conditions which they place on international transfer of nuclear materials, equipment and technology is, quite frankly, more difficult to answer. On the positive side, to date these states seem on the whole to have acted in a responsible manner. Continuing efforts must be made to encourage them to adopt policies reasonably consistent with the present consensus of the major nuclear supplier states. These efforts are most likely to succeed if they are carried out on a low-key, diplomatic basis – not by attempts at coercion, through the levelling of highly public charges and counter-charges, or through legislative fiat. Only a negative impact would result from attempts to isolate such states from the main stream of nuclear commerce; this would most likely lead to a 'sub-tier' of nuclear supplier states willing to provide their technology under less effective safeguards and controls against possible nuclear-weapon proliferation.

A major factor for speculation is the eventual entry of China into the international nuclear market-place. As a direct supplier, its influence probably will be small for the immediate future unless it should decide to market nuclear fuel, either enriched uranium or plutonium, or the technology for producing these materials. Twenty years after detonating its first nuclear explosive device, China is just beginning to introduce nuclear power. It will have to create or otherwise obtain a considerable body of technology and acquire manufacturing and other infrastructure and marketing expertise before it can become a major supplier. None the less, as a nuclear-weapon state, its policies and attitudes towards nuclear proliferation are significant.

In the 1960s and 1970s China's policy on the spread of nuclear weapons appeared, to outside observers, to be basically contrary to majority world views. Reportedly, it was based on the philosophy that any decision to acquire nuclear weapons was the sovereign prerogative of each individual nation. Beginning in the early 1980s, however, China took a number of steps which have brought its policies into much closer harmony with the international consensus. For example, it applied for membership in the International Atomic Energy Agency and was admitted in January 1984; in September 1984 China was elected as a permanent member of the agency's Board of Governors.

During Premier Zhao's January 1984 visit to the United States, he stated during a White House dinner that 'we do not advocate or encourage nuclear proliferation'. This policy subsequently was adopted by the Sixth National People's Congress, giving it the effect of a directive to all organs of the Chinese government. In January

1985 Vice Premier Li Peng made an even more definitive statement, as follows:

On China's nuclear policy, Premier Zhao Ziyang solemnly declared at the second session of the Sixth National People's Congress held in May 1984 that China was critical of the discriminatory 'Treaty on the Non-Proliferation of Nuclear Weapons' and had declined to accede to it, and that, on the other hand, China by no means favored nuclear proliferation, nor did it engage in such proliferation by helping other countries develop nuclear weapons. I would like to reiterate here that we have no intention, either at present or in the future, to help non-nuclear countries develop nuclear weapons. Last year China joined the International Atomic Energy Agency and was appointed a council member country. China will maintain good relations of cooperation with the Agency and commit itself to its due obligations and abide by the Agency's stipulations. Co-operation in the field of nuclear energy China is having or discussing with other countries, including France, the Federal Republic of Germany, the United States, Brazil, Pakistan and Japan, is and will be conducted for peaceful purposes only and not for not-peaceful purposes.

While one would hope for eventual change in China's attitude towards accession to the NPT, Li Peng's statement with regard to the treaty is consistent with China's past attitudes and views on other international matters. This position is not surprising, given China's perceived role of leadership in the Third World; many Third World nations also feel that the NPT is discriminatory. China also has indicated in the past that it considers the NPT as a United States-Soviet Union attempt at hegemony. Despite this, the balance of the Li Peng statement puts China in much the same position as France – namely, that it will not become a party to the NPT, but will conduct its nuclear export policy as if it were. What this may mean in detailed terms is not yet clear. There is no clear indication that China is, for example, following the principles of the NSG Guidelines as a basis for its export control policy. The trend, however, seems to be in that direction.

The recently concluded nuclear co-operation agreement between China and Brazil provides for the application of IAEA safeguards to assistance, equipment and materials provided by either party. This is the first instance in which China has either agreed to accept such safeguards within its own territory or required the recipient of its aid to accept them. As such, this agreement must be regarded as a rather substantial breakthrough. It also should be noted that the agreement does *not* provide for any exchange involving 'sensitive technology'. China plans to follow this pattern in all of its future nuclear co-operation agreements with non-nuclear-weapon states, but it seems to prefer the equivalent of bilateral control arrangements (and 'peaceful assurances') in its agreements with nuclear-weapon states.

Despite its willingness to accept IAEA safeguards in its bilateral agreements with non-nuclear-weapon states, to date China has not indicated a willingness generally to open its civil nuclear facilities to IAEA inspections through a 'voluntary offer'. This leaves it as the only nuclear-weapon state which has not made such an offer – a fact which was underlined by Andronik Petrosyants, Chairman of the Soviet Union's State Committee for the Utilisation of Atomic Energy, when the Soviet Union signed its agreement with the IAEA for such inspections in February 1985. It is likely that the Chinese ultimately will decide to make a 'voluntary offer' – perhaps in the near future. As China continues to move into this new and, until recently, unknown area of international relations, it has moved thus far with a speed which clearly indicates a major policy shift. A motivating factor certainly has been its desire to obtain nuclear power technology from other nations and to look forward to a gradually increasing role as a nuclear exporter.

Another interesting area of speculation is on the possible impact of China's offer to accept spent nuclear fuel from other nations for storage in the Gobi Desert. According to published reports, a consortium of three private organisations in the Federal Republic of Germany and the China Nuclear Energy Industry Group (a governmental entity) recently have entered into an agreement to take such fuel through the year 2000. China apparently would obtain title to the fuel and ultimately would reprocess it, utilising the recovered slightly-enriched uranium and plutonium for fuelling civil power reactors. It also has been reported that China might be willing to return the equivalent fuel value to the sending country in the form of slightly-enriched uranium or even as fabricated fuel.

Reportedly, China is prepared to accept IAEA safeguards and re-export controls on the special nuclear material involved. Of course, any spent fuel over which the United States has retransfer approval rights could not be retransferred to China under United States law in the absence of the United States-China agreement for co-operation; even if one existed, it is unclear what United States policy might be towards such transfers. China is, however, setting a very valuable precedent by becoming the first nation to offer spent fuel disposal services which are not tied to other commercial considerations.

This may open the 'nuclear power option' to some nations requiring a solution to the back-end of the fuel cycle before initiating a nuclear programme. On the other hand, the relatively high charge (reported to be over $1,500 per kilogram, or almost twice that now being asked for reprocessing) may inhibit many from considering this as a viable option.

Concluding Comment

Although the nuclear power industry plays only a subsidiary role in supporting the objectives of the Nuclear Non-Proliferation Treaty, it is still an important role. The industry needs trade to survive; the NPT and the IAEA provide the rational framework which makes orderly trade possible. The commercial nuclear industry, for its own purposes, to date has done almost everything reasonably possible in making available non-sensitive equipment, materials and technology to those nations which adhere to the NPT. There is every reason to believe that this supportive role will continue unabated in the future. It will be up to governments to provide the financial support and favourable export policies which can bring nuclear-generated electricity to the Third World.

End Note

1. Editor's note: 'Senate Approves Nuclear Accord With China – The Senate approved November 21 the nuclear cooperation agreement which allows the United States to send nuclear technology and equipment to the People's Republic of China. . . . No transfers will take place until the agreement takes effect December 11. The agreement has yet to be approved by the House of Representatives. It would fail to take effect only if both the House and the Senate disapproved it.' *Congressional Report*, Washington, D.C., 22 November 1985.

THE NUCLEAR INDUSTRY AND THE NPT: A CANADIAN VIEW

W. MacOwan

This chapter examines the effect of Canada's safeguards policy upon Canadian industry and on the conduct of Canada's international nuclear trade.

Trade of any kind, be it in goods, services or ideas, is the source of all national revenues and provides the strength from which any nation or person can exercise influence on the affairs of humanity for good or for bad. The views of the nuclear industry on the effect of non-proliferation policies on trade are therefore pertinent.

From a businessman's perspective, free trade is positive, provided it is conducted in a fair manner according to universal rules of accounting and economics, and not made a vehicle for national policies through subsidies. At this time there is no such thing as 'fair free trade' in the international nuclear electric power generating business. The situation is more like a 'free-for-all' where some contestants have their hands tied behind their backs.

India paid a high price for the 1974 nuclear explosion when its nuclear electric development was slowed considerably by Canada's unilateral decision to terminate all nuclear collaboration. Canada paid a still higher price in this voluntary exclusion from the potentially large Indian market for nuclear electric power systems. This declaration of nuclear purity was not enough for the government of that time. To the amazement and consternation of the Canadian nuclear industry, Canada proceeded to flagellate itself and punish all of its nuclear customers for this one transgression by India. The punishment extended even to such traditional neutralists as Sweden and Switzerland. All Canada's existing nuclear trading partners were told that they must renegotiate existing contracts to encompass more stringent new safeguards requirements. Despite lengthy negotiations, these countries had to sign as required by Canada or be cut off from Canadian uranium supplies – quite a penalty at that time. Canada had imposed, essentially without consultation, a retroactive change in the terms of existing trade agreements.

The Nuclear Industry: A Canadian View

By this action Canada severely damaged its reputation as a reliable nuclear trading partner and, in addition, undoubtedly caused misgivings around the world concerning the possibility of similar arbitrary action with regard to other long-term trade agreements not pertaining to nuclear matters.

Not satisfied with the 1974 revision of safeguards policy, Canada unilaterally again escalated its safeguards requirements by a further policy statement in December 1976. This statement required that Canada would deal only with those non-nuclear-weapon states which had ratified the Treaty on the Non-Proliferation of Nuclear Weapons (NPT) or would accept international safeguards on their entire nuclear programme: full-scope safeguards. The Canadian government also stated at that time:

> As in the past, we are prepared to accept the commercial consequences of being clearly ahead of other suppliers. This is the price we are prepared to pay to curb the threat to mankind of nuclear proliferation. We recognize that for this policy to be fully effective we must persuade other nuclear suppliers to adopt similar export policies.

Now, almost a decade later, the principal nuclear electric power plant exporters have yet to be persuaded to follow the Canadian example.

While all nuclear power supplier nations profess to work under a set of international rules, the reality is that each supplier country behaves differently in the market-place. In 1979 when Argentina bought the second unit for its Embalse nuclear plant, Canada was not really in the game, even though the first unit in that station was Canadian. Another supplier country sold an untried plant over a repeat of the well-researched Canadian unit. Obviously, these two nuclear suppliers had different inhibitions; they also had totally different support from their governments. This was not a unique case; these things still happen. Some supplier nations appear to apply safeguards requirements in the manner most likely to gain an advantage in the market-place.

The Canadian nuclear industry is just as concerned by the possibility of proliferation of nuclear weapons as anyone. However, it seems obvious that Canada's safeguards policies serve only to nudge international nuclear trade into the hands of others who may not differentiate quite so clearly between nuclear developments beneficial to humanity and those having the potential for disaster.

A policy denying the beneficial use of nuclear energy to certain countries must inevitably result in those countries finding some way to obtain the required nuclear supplies from a competitor supplier or through the determined work of their own experts. Neither of these events do anything to limit the possibilities for proliferation of nuclear weapons, but are more likely to encourage proliferation. Additionally, a prospective customer nation which has been denied nuclear supplies will harbour resentment which may spread into other areas of trade or international relationship. The anthems of praise being sung for the NPT relate more to what the NPT might be rather than to what it is. These questions concerning Canada's safeguards policies should be answered honestly: Did they limit nuclear weapons proliferation? Did they improve international relationships? Did they foster the development and use of nuclear energy for the benefit of humanity? Did they put one of Canada's unique talents to good use in the betterment of living conditions and the lessening of causes for war? They certainly did take Canada out of circulation as a world leader in the peaceful uses of nuclear energy and they did encourage Canada's nuclear customers to diversify their sources of supply in order to gain a perceived increase in security of supply. Are these new supply sources more likely than Canada to take a lead in the struggle to prevent proliferation of nuclear weapons? The safeguards policies initiated by Canada may in fact have weakened Canada's ability to influence the very outcome most desired.

In international nuclear trade Canada may not be the 'good guy' it would like to think it is. Canada has buried its peaceful, beneficial nuclear talents in the sand and is afraid to use them in case this might permit other countries easier access into the nuclear weapons business. Canada does not seem to comprehend that it has neither the power nor the credibility to stop other nations from doing whatever they think necessary to protect their national interests. Canada no longer holds any monopoly in nuclear supplies, so its edicts are not good international coinage.

Canada could do more to limit the proliferation of nuclear weapons if it gave the world a lead in the peaceful uses of nuclear energy, uses that benefit all of humanity. Canada already has an edge in that field – in nuclear medicine, food processing, plant genetics and the integration of reliable nuclear electric power producing plants with industrial and agricultural centres. The Bruce Nuclear Power Centre, for instance, is unique in the world, and yet Canada does very little to promote this concept beyond its own shores.

What are Canada's options for the future in terms of safeguards policy? Canada must work for a new beginning in the international forum. A nuclear electric power plant is not necessarily a precursor to the manufacture of nuclear weapons. It is certainly neither the fastest nor the cheapest avenue to that objective. The more wide-spread use of Canada's benevolent nuclear supplies would, however, be an influence against the need for weapons of any kind. Canada's priority objective of preventing the spread of instruments of destruction does not require that it restrict its trade in nuclear items designed to benefit humanity. Canada should work even harder for international agreement on some practicable and comprehensive ground rules for international trade in these items, which can be enforced on a global basis. Without such world acceptance, Canada's naive idealism serves only to penalise the sincere and defeat the very cause which Canadians wish to champion.

Pending universal acceptance, Canada must not put impediments that are unique to itself in the way of benevolent nuclear trade. The more wide-spread availability of low-cost nuclear electric power could do more to lessen the causes for war than all of our zealous anti-proliferation talk. It would also greatly reduce the environmental damage now resulting from the combustion of fossil fuels.

III.
THE TREATY ON THE NON-PROLIFERATION OF NUCLEAR WEAPONS IN REVIEW

THE NPT REGIME, PRESENT AND FUTURE GLOBAL SECURITY: AN AMERICAN VIEW

Sam Thompson

Evolution of the Non-Proliferation Regime

Over the last three decades, the non-proliferation policy of the United States has benefited from a remarkable continuity and steadfastness of purpose. In 1953, soon after he was elected, President Eisenhower took an historic step in inaugurating the 'Atoms for Peace' programme. By this act the United States volunteered to share its peaceful nuclear technologies for the good of mankind.

The International Atomic Energy Agency (IAEA), also proposed by President Eisenhower, was established in 1957 as an international institution through which to pursue those same goals. The IAEA was given a dual mission: to promote the peaceful use of nuclear energy, and to establish a system of international safeguards against diversion of nuclear materials for non-peaceful purposes. Through the intervening years, the IAEA has assumed even greater importance as a key instrument in the non-proliferation regime. It is an agency the United States ranks among the most important of international institutions.

The Treaty of the Non-Proliferation of Nuclear Weapons (NPT), which entered into force in 1970, provided a juridical framework for the evolving non-proliferation regime effort. The NPT is supplemented by the Treaty for the Prohibition of Nuclear Weapons in Latin America (Treaty of Tlatelolco), which was entered into force in 1968.

The non-proliferation regime appeared sound in the early 1970s, but confidence in the regime was shaken when India exploded a nuclear device in 1974. Even before the Indian explosion, there had been a growing realisation that variations in export policies of the different nuclear suppliers meant that the measures being applied to deter proliferation were far from uniform. To alleviate this problem, the major nuclear suppliers met in London in 1974 to discuss common multilateral export policies. This meeting was a major step in itself. Under the guidelines first adopted in 1976, members of the Nuclear Suppliers Group (NSG) agreed to transfer certain technology, equipment and material only if a customer nation agreed to apply IAEA safeguards to the item supplied and to ensure its peaceful use. Through the late 1970s there was increasing convergence among the advanced nuclear supplier countries, generally on sensitive nuclear exports and safeguards conditions.

In sum, an international non-proliferation regime is now in place which, while clearly not perfect, is functioning effectively. Institutions such as the IAEA have been established. Rules have been codified in important instruments such as the NPT, the Treaty of Tlatelolco and the NSG Guidelines. Norms of behaviour have evolved through a myriad of bilateral and multilateral contacts.

Before turning to the approach of the Reagan Administration, it is important to place current policy in the context in which it was formulated. The Carter Administration's policy had been fundamentally shaped by the view that nuclear energy development world-wide created significant proliferation risks. Decisions had been made to defer reprocessing and plutonium use in the United States, paralleled by unilateral attempts to curtail the supply of nuclear technology abroad and particularly to discourage the use of plutonium-based technologies by other major industrial nations. Rather than setting a good example, this unilateral approach and negative attitude towards nuclear power was perceived by some friends of the United States as a challenge to their desire for energy independence. The effect was to reduce United States influence in the international nuclear arena and erode trust in the United States as a predictable nuclear trading partner.

The enactment in the late 1970s of the Nuclear Non-Proliferation Act represented a serious effort to promote a more stringent and uniform set of international standards for nuclear exports. None the less, in part because of its retroactive provisions, it also precluded carrying out certain supply contracts and agreements to co-operate in the nuclear area, thus impairing the ability of the United States to provide incentives for countries to act consistently with non-proliferation goals. As a result, the United States was less able to win support of key nations on critical supply, safeguards and other non-proliferation issues.

The Reagan Administration Approach

The policy of the Reagan Administration and the specific steps it has taken reflect broad continuity with past administrations on non-proliferation goals. The fundamental point is that this administration is fully committed to a strong non-proliferation policy. In a policy statement made soon after he took office, President Reagan declared that preventing the spread of nuclear explosives is one of the most critical challenges facing the United States in international affairs. Further proliferation, he said, would pose a severe threat to international peace, regional and global stability, and the security interests of the United States and other countries. He pledged that the United States would seek to prevent the spread of nuclear explosives as a fundamental national security and foreign policy objective. In this connection, President Reagan has indicated that the United States would view a material violation of the NPT, the Treaty of Tlatelolco or an international safeguards agreement as having profound consequences for international order and United States bilateral relations, and also would view any nuclear explosion by a non-nuclear-weapon state with grave concern.

At the same time, President Reagan committed the United States to full co-operation with other nations in the peaceful uses of nuclear energy. Such uses include nuclear power programmes to meet energy security needs under a regime of adequate safeguards and controls. In pursuit of these twin goals, the Reagan Administration has sought to shape a realistic and common-sense approach designed to facilitate co-operation with friends and to ensure United States leadership in international nuclear affairs. At the same time, another fundamental tenet of United States policy remains unchanged. The United States is determined never to sacrifice its non-proliferation principles for commercial gain or political advantage and believes this standard should be the universal norm.

At the heart of the Reagan Administration's non-proliferation policy is the recognition that there is no single technical or political answer to the problem of nuclear proliferation. Technical measures, political security initiatives and institution-building are all needed. However, since it must be recognised that technical restraints cannot successfully prevent nations from acquiring the ability to develop nuclear explosives forever, political measures are more important in the long term than technical measures.

One important underlying aspect of current United States policy is that it seeks to reflect a realistic assessment of the legitimacy of nuclear power. For the Reagan Administration, the development of nuclear power is not an energy source of last resort, and it should not be viewed as automatically increasing the risk of nuclear proliferation. Nuclear energy is viewed as playing a major role in coming decades in providing safe and efficient electric power in the United States and as increasingly important for the economic development and energy security of many nations around the world, particularly countries in Western Europe and Japan.

Current United States policy emphasises the need to make rational distinctions between close friends and allies who pose no real proliferation risk, and those countries or areas of the world where there are real concerns about the spread of nuclear weapons. Accordingly, President Reagan has indicated the United States will continue to inhibit the transfer of sensitive nuclear material, equipment and technology to regions of instability such as the Middle East and South Asia. In certain cases of extreme concern the United States will oppose and seek to inhibit any nuclear-related co-operation.

At the same time, the Reagan Administration has sought to restore the image of the United States as a reliable nuclear partner. This policy is based on the view that trading partners such as Japan, which have committed themselves to firm non-proliferation policies of their own, should be able to rely on the United States as a predictable and assured source of supply. A policy of denial towards countries with excellent non-proliferation credentials is viewed as arbitrary and counter-productive.

President Reagan has stated that the United States will not inhibit the development of civil reprocessing and breeder reactors in countries with advanced nuclear programmes that do not constitute a proliferation risk. In keeping with this policy, the United States has been discussing with Japan and the European Atomic Energy Agency (EURATOM) long-term arrangements in reprocessing and plutonium use. The United States is of the view that such long-term arrangements will be beneficial and will enhance the global non-proliferation regime.

By adopting a policy based on co-operation and reliability, the United States expects to be better able to work with such countries to ensure that they apply the most stringent safeguards controls possible over the sensitive technology and materials they are using and, importantly, to be in a stronger position to enlist their active support in strengthening the global non-proliferation regime.

Although current United States policy reflects a change in approach with respect to the use of plutonium in limited circumstances, it still embodies a recognition of the dangers and risks associated with reprocessing and plutonium use. The United States appreciates the need for great caution and restraint in dealing with these risks and the importance of limiting sensitive activities to as few locations as possible and to places where no significant risk of proliferation exists.

The Reagan Administration also seeks to strengthen nuclear export controls. As part of this effort, the Reagan Administration carefully monitors nuclear-related exports from the United States. For example, the United States Department of Energy regulations regarding the export of nuclear technology have been tightened. Such restrictions have reduced the risk that foreign subsidiaries of United States firms could circumvent United States government nuclear export controls.

More importantly, the United States has worked closely with other countries to upgrade and strengthen international norms and procedures. In particular, new guidelines were adopted in January 1984 to control the export of sensitive centrifuge uranium enrichment technology. Similarly, as of mid-May 1985 controls have been upgraded on reprocessing technology. Future efforts will be made on other processes having proliferation relevance.

Another principal focus has been President Reagan's proposal for the adoption by all nuclear suppliers of a common policy to require comprehensive safeguards in a recipient state as a condition for all significant new nuclear supply commitments to that state. Such comprehensive safeguards would entail IAEA safeguards on all the nuclear activities in the non-nuclear-weapon recipient state, not just on the particular item being exported, as a condition for significant new supply commitments. Efforts to develop a supplier consensus in favour of this approach continue. An especially important component of the Reagan Administration's broad-based and multifaceted effort to prevent proliferation has been to strengthen existing political institutions. One of the most critical institutions is the NPT, which was designed to foster the security of all countries by preventing the spread of nuclear weapons, contributing to the peaceful uses of nuclear energy and encouraging negotiations to slow the arms race. Though there are strong differences of view regarding its relative success in achieving these goals, the NPT has been a vital contribution to ensuring global security.

By adhering to the NPT, more than 125 states have renounced the right to acquire nuclear weapons, demonstrating an increasing acceptance of the non-proliferation norm. The international perception that the acquisition of nuclear explosives is illegitimate is itself an important deterrent. Similarly, the pledge by the existing nuclear-weapon states not to assist any country in acquiring such weapons helps buttress the technical barriers to proliferation, as do the treaty's broader nuclear supply obligations. In addition, the treaty's safeguards article provides the basis for demonstrating that equipment and nuclear materials provided for peaceful purposes are not misused. This assurance is a key confidence-building measure which lessens suspicions among nations regarding the nuclear programmes of others.

The Reagan Administration also seeks to bolster other institutional barriers, including the Treaty of Tlatelolco and the IAEA. In the case of the former, the Reagan Administration in 1982 ratified Protocol I of the treaty applying certain non-proliferation provisions to United States territories in the treaty zone and has urged others to ratify the treaty to bring it fully into force. With respect to the IAEA, the United States is pursuing improvements in the agency's safeguards system, working with others to address the problem of safeguards in large reprocessing plants and in gas centrifuge facilities. In addition, the United States has contributed funds to develop and procure new safeguards equipment, has loaned technical experts to the IAEA to improve the effectiveness and efficiency of safeguards, and has worked with other countries to minimise extraneous political controversy within the agency.

Another important facet of the Reagan Administration's non-proliferation policy is its increased emphasis on reducing the motivation for acquiring nuclear explosives. One aspect of this approach is the preservation of strong and credible United States alliances abroad. Another is stabilisation of conflict-prone regions and resolution of local disputes. In some cases, United States economic and security assistance has served this purpose.

A further distinguishing aspect of the Reagan Administration's non-proliferation policy is the attempt to foster limited, non-sensitive nuclear co-operation as part of a dialogue on non-proliferation issues, even with countries that disagree with the United States. The Reagan Administration believes that it is better to promote dialogue with countries that have not adopted comprehensive safeguards than to introduce a simple policy of denial. This dialogue has been used to urge such states to broaden the application of safeguards on their peaceful nuclear programmes. The fact that some such states – Brazil, Argentina and South Africa, for example – are emerging as nuclear suppliers in their own right makes it all the more desirable that we maintain a dialogue with them in the nuclear field.

Another facet of the government's policy relates only indirectly to non-proliferation policy, but it does so in an important way: the Reagan Administration's arms reduction policies. Over the long-term, deep reductions in United States and Soviet Union stockpiles of nuclear weapons, such as those proposed by President Reagan, would strengthen the non-proliferation regime. Admittedly, such reductions would have little direct impact on countries seeking nuclear weapons because of local insecurities or fears of a traditional rival. However, by gradually de-emphasising the role of nuclear weapons in world politics, the reduction of United States and Soviet Union nuclear arsenals could strengthen broader political con-straints against acquiring nuclear weapons and reduce any 'prestige' factor associated with them. Moreover, such reductions would also bolster the NPT inasmuch as it is the alleged failure of the super-powers to live up to Article VI obligations that has proven to be the most divisive issue at the three review conferences.

The NPT Regime and Future Global Security – Probabilities and Possibilities[1]

Having examined the United States approach to preventing the spread of nuclear weapons in the world today, what are the trends and chal-lenges in the non-proliferation area that will affect future global security? Prediction in the nuclear field is a risky business due to the multiplicity of shifting forces that interact – developments in energy technology, domestic and international political alignments, refinements in inter-national law, and global economic and financial fluctuations. The record of past predictions – whether of projected growth of nuclear power or the likely spread of nuclear weapons – has been very poor indeed.

Nevertheless, with that cautionary note, it is possible to identify some probabilities and possibilities for the future. Some of these trends are already upon us. In all cases, it is not too soon to begin thinking about policies to meet the challenges they pose and to head them off or contain them. How well we do so will greatly influence global security in the decades that lie ahead.

Probabilities

At least for the coming decade, demand for nuclear power is likely to be limited. Reduced energy demand and financial constraints, along with public concern, already have retarded the addition of new nuclear plants in the industrial countries. Among developing countries, even when projected energy needs might justify nuclear development, the high front-end costs and long lead times before this investment can be recouped may place power reactors out of reach, particularly since most such countries already are burdened with heavy debt.

With opportunities for reactor sales very limited, pressures will grow on domestic nuclear industries and, in turn, on national officials to find a competitive edge. So far, the industrial countries have resisted the temptation to use non-proliferation concessions to obtain that edge. To ensure that this situation persists, nuclear suppliers must continue to maintain close contact and co-operation. It is only through continued, active sharing of information and views that potential competitors can be assured that everyone is playing by the same rules. Strong nuclear export norms are in the interest of all countries, since without them a key underpinning of peaceful nuclear co-operation would be lost.

Notwithstanding limited demand for nuclear power, many developing countries will initiate or expand nuclear research programmes. Historically, such nuclear research has not always been closely coupled to the commercial nuclear power sector. Rather, its objective has been to gain information and experience in a broad range of nuclear energy technologies. For some developing countries there also will be pressures to begin work on more advanced, if not sensitive, fuel cycle activities. Unsafeguarded research and development on sensitive fuel cycle technologies would be a cause of particular non-proliferation concern. Even pilot-scale facilities can support a nuclear explosives programme, and their presence can result in suspicion among neighbouring countries.

Restraint on the part of the major nuclear suppliers in the transfer of sensitive nuclear technologies, albeit necessary, is at best a partial answer. Also needed are first, closer co-operation with technicians in developing countries that are more advanced, with a view to development of technically feasible alternatives to sensitive activities and, second, new international approaches that would allow such countries to obtain a broad range of nuclear benefits without directly engaging in activities of proliferation concern.

Another trend that will test the NPT regime is the continued development of new nuclear technologies, particularly in the uranium enrichment field but also in advances in centrifuge, laser isotope separation and chemical separation processes, all of which raise potential problems. To meet this challenge, the major suppliers will need to continue to clarify and refine the international nuclear export guidelines that were developed in the 1970s to ensure that the control systems keep pace with technology. Similar efforts aimed at controlling so-called 'dual-use' items will be all the more necessary – and difficult.

Still another probability is the steady emergence of additional nuclear suppliers. Although such suppliers could not soon compete directly with existing suppliers for sales of fuel and nuclear power plants, their capability to supply other items could engender competition and increase pressures on the major suppliers to dilute their controls. Countries such as Argentina, Brazil, India, Israel, South Korea, Spain, South Africa and China will become increasingly capable of supplying research reactors, nuclear fuel, consulting services, heavy water, dual-use items or even sensitive technology. These nations could undermine the non-proliferation regime if they fail to condition their nuclear exports on reasonable non-proliferation assurances and controls. Their motivations for doing so could vary from the pursuit of hard currency or of scarce resources to the pursuit of political favours. Fortunately, there have been heartening signs that these new suppliers will take a responsible approach. For example, China has taken steps to participate in international non-proliferation efforts by requiring safeguards on its nuclear exports and by joining the IAEA, and both South Africa and Argentina have indicated that they will require IAEA safeguards on their nuclear exports. Nevertheless, continued special efforts are needed to encourage new suppliers to adopt the norms of nuclear commerce that have evolved over the last 30 years, and to convince them that narrow commercial and political interests should not be allowed to outweigh crucial global stability interests.

For the United States, there may be only limited opportunities to encourage acceptance of existing norms in some cases. Several of the most important emerging suppliers are not NPT parties and have not accepted safeguards on all their nuclear activities. While the United States works most closely and fully with those non-nuclear-weapon states that demonstrate a firm commitment to global non-proliferation efforts by accepting such safeguards, limited co-operation in non-sensitive areas with non-nuclear-weapon states not accepting such safeguards also serves non-proliferation goals. Establishment of limited ties and, in this context, a nuclear dialogue with such countries can help move them closer towards full adherence to international rules of nuclear behaviour. The alternative of severing all ties in the nuclear field eliminates the possibility of affecting their policies in the nuclear field.

Another relevant expectation is that certain countries with mature nuclear programmes will shift to more advanced fuel cycle activities involving the civil use of plutonium in breeders and light water reactors. It appears, though, that the eventual closure of the back end of the fuel cycle is being preceded, even in France and Japan, by a slowdown in advanced fuel cycle programmes. This hiatus provides a breathing space in the question of how to manage the proliferation risks associated with these technologies.

The processing, storage and use of plutonium should be restricted to as few sites as possible, although stubborn resistance to this goal can be expected from a number of countries wanting to maintain independent fuel cycles and the option of closing these fuel cycles. Co-ordinated planning among nations also must be strengthened to help ensure adequate physical protection, safeguards and transportation arrangements. A suitable international plutonium storage regime, perhaps evolving out of procedures to govern access to the plutonium already present at La Hague and Windscale, also could play its part. Another step would be wide-spread adherence to the International Convention on the Physical Protection of Nuclear Materials.

Ensuring the safe use of plutonium also will require more work to design and implement safeguards on large, commercial reprocessing plants. We have begun forging an international consensus on effective safeguards for these facilities, but this effort should be broadened. Lessons applicable to this exercise can be learned from the recent international project on safeguards for gas centrifuge enrichment facilities, the Hexapartite Safeguards Project. This project, completed in 1983, dealt successfully with both the technical and political aspects of safeguarding that new technology.

In all probability, a number of significant non-nuclear-weapon states will continue to have both safeguarded and unsafeguarded nuclear activities. Such mixed fuel cycles already are a cause of proliferation concern. Unsafeguarded activities heighten regional suspicions that can trigger regional nuclear competition and greatly complicate the safeguards task of the IAEA. The fact is that the principal proliferation risks today arise in countries that are not prepared to demonstrate the peaceful nature of their nuclear programme by accepting IAEA safeguards on all their nuclear activities.

Efforts are needed to convince such countries to place all their facilities under safeguards and to dissuade others from acquiring unsafeguarded facilities. Of special importance would be agreement among the major suppliers to require comprehensive safeguards as a condition for any significant new supply commitment. That objective continues to be a high-priority item on the United States non-proliferation agenda.

Still another probability is that as global economic development proceeds, and as the technology surrounding atomic energy becomes more widely available, more countries will approach the threshold of a technical capability to make nuclear explosives. Though a key part of a comprehensive non-proliferation strategy, efforts to strengthen technical constraints cannot forever prevent countries from acquiring the ability to develop nuclear explosives. In the coming decades a credible and effective strategy will depend even more than it does now on influencing the motivations of individual countries and strengthening global institutions and norms against acquiring nuclear explosives.

To meet this challenge, concerted diplomatic and political efforts are needed to foster stability in conflict-prone regions. In the first place, a dialogue among countries in such regions should be encouraged. In some situations prudent use of conventional arms transfers can meet legitimate needs for self-defence, enhance a sense of security and lessen the pressures to acquire nuclear explosives. In addition, the Treaty of Tlatelolco helps contain regional suspicions in Latin America that can lead to decisions to acquire nuclear explosives. The few nations that remain outside that treaty should be encouraged to accept its restrictions. Finally, the Reagan Administration recognises that steps to reduce the nuclear arsenals of the United States and the Soviet Union can contribute to creating, over the long run, a climate of global security and thereby bolster the NPT regime.

Possibilities

Turning now to some possibilities for the future, the NPT comes up for extension in 1995. Though it is likely that it will be extended, proposals could be offered to adopt weakening changes to the important commitments embodied in the treaty. Some countries might even threaten to withdraw. As we approach 1995 we should look for ways to strengthen the treaty. Strengthened peaceful nuclear co-operation with NPT parties will contribute to a climate conducive to such renewal. Similarly, the degree of success in achieving the type of deep reductions of strategic and tactical nuclear weapons sought by the Reagan Administration will further affect the long-term health of the treaty. Adding new members also will be important to demonstrate increasing universality, although this becomes increasingly difficult as we get down to the small but active group of NPT oppositionist states. Most of all, the ultimate vitality of the treaty will depend upon recognition by the parties that the treaty provides vital security benefits and that its erosion would leave them worse off.

In the shorter term, every effort should be made to prevent the 1990 Review Conference from resulting in what is perceived as a failure. This will require that the United States encourage other parties to focus on the vital security benefits of the treaty, that the United States administration puts forward its positions firmly and convincingly, and that both realism and restraint are encouraged, particularly on the part of those who might be tempted to place the NPT at risk by forcing Article VI issues as occurred at Geneva in both 1980 and 1985, or by introducing issues that are highly politicised and not really relevant to the treaty review, also evident at previous review conferences.

Another possible future development is an intensified and debilitating politicisation of the International Atomic Energy Agency. The NPT regime, itself, depends on a strong and effective agency. Without it, significant international nuclear commerce would come to a virtual standstill. In the years to come, United States administrations shall need to continue to resist a tendency for the agency's attention to be diverted to divisive issues that are best handled in other international forums.

Finally, the NPT regime faces the possibility of a dramatic proliferation event, whether another test, a safeguards violation, a decision by some country to withdraw from the NPT, or even an act of nuclear terrorism. Inadequate responses to such events may have as negative an impact on the NPT regime as the events themselves. Therefore, despite an understandable reluctance to consider these potential occurrences, it is only prudent to begin assessing how to contain their adverse consequences. This is partially a matter of contingency planning by individual states. But, in addition, those countries that support the non-proliferation regime must consider whether to seek prior agreement or understanding on possible sanctions beyond the very general commitments now contained in the NSG Guidelines and IAEA statute.

The problem is that few governments want to tie their hands by committing themselves to specific actions in advance of hypothetical contingencies. In fact, the lack of effective sanctions is a gap that the non-proliferation regime shares with international law generally. However, the potential impact of the nuclear field on global security makes it eminently important to find ways of deterring conduct that transgresses proliferation norms. Credible sanctions can help deter such conduct, and a readiness to support the regime firmly after a dramatic proliferation event may be needed to contain the damage and head off even more unrestrained actions. This is not to minimise the difficulties in establishing credible sanctions. Moreover, it is not feasible or desirable to establish in the abstract a precise and complete set of sanctions. Common sense suggests that responses by individual countries would always have to be tailored somewhat to the relationship with the country in question. But we should not let these difficulties prevent us from pursuing this area further.

Of less impact than a dramatic event, but of great concern none the less, is the possibility that an increasing number of near-nuclear states will adopt policies of ambiguity about their nuclear explosive capabilities and intentions. The threat to the non-proliferation regime posed by policies of nuclear ambiguity represents a different order of danger than the effects of outright proliferation, but in the long term it can be equally damaging to the regime. Every effort should be made to discourage such an approach by encouraging states to adhere to the NPT or Treaty of Tlatelolco or, as a minimum, by obtaining agreement to voluntary acceptance of IAEA safeguards on all nuclear facilities.

Conclusion – A Prognosis

In spite of the problems that lie ahead and that will continue to pose a proliferation threat to global security, we should not be pessimistic. Some experts outside of the United States government have proposed that the world begin thinking in terms of living with many nuclear-weapon powers, that extensive proliferation is inevitable. Some even go so far as to argue that the spread of nuclear weapons would not be so bad.

The Reagan Administration in no way shares this view, for it simply is not true that wide-spread proliferation is inevitable. Much has been done and can be done to prevent it. It is vital to recall that, in the early 1960s, President John F. Kennedy warned of a world of 15 to 20 nuclear-weapon states by 1975. Many predicted that by the mid-1980s there would be up to 25 nuclear-weapon states. Such predictions proved to be fallacious because of determined efforts undertaken by the international community to deter the spread of nuclear weapons through a strong set of technical, political and institutional barriers. Without these efforts, the nightmare of rampant proliferation might well have become reality.

These international efforts have been possible because in this enterprise there is common ground between industrialised and developing countries, between nuclear suppliers and nuclear consumers, and even between the United States and the Soviet Union. The NPT, as the most widely adhered-to arms control agreement in history, symbolises this wide-spread commonality of purpose and, in the view of the Reagan Administration, will remain the juridical and institutional focal point of the non-proliferation regime for many years to come. The United States will work with other countries, pursuing a non-proliferation strategy comprised of a broad range of measures, to buttress the components of the regime and to ensure that today's pessimists are proven wrong in the decades ahead.

End Note

1. This section draws upon a paper by Lewis Dunn entitled, 'Atoms for Peace – Probabilities and Possibilities in the Decades Ahead', presented at the Atoms for Peace Conference, Centre for Strategic and International Studies, Georgetown University, 7-8 December 1983.

CANADA AND THE NPT:
THE ENDURING RELATIONSHIP

Douglas Roche

Introduction

In the autumn of 1985 the Treaty on the Non-Proliferation of Nuclear Weapons (NPT) was reviewed for the third time. What is the meaning of this event? And why is the NPT important to Canada?

Although Canada participated together with the United Kingdom in helping the United States develop the world's first atomic weapons during World War II, it was the first country to consciously forgo the development of nuclear weapons despite clearly having the technology and capability to do so from the earliest days of the nuclear era. This was a deliberate policy decision taken at a time when the nuclear club was in its infancy. Canada declined to develop a nuclear weapon capability and has adhered firmly to that decision.

Of course, Canada participates in the NATO alliance, and at one time permitted nuclear weapons to be deployed on its territory. The last of these weapons were removed from Canada in 1984. It is the clearly stated policy of the Canadian government not to accept any nuclear weapons or permit them to be deployed in Canada. Any contingency plans that might be developed in the event of a crisis or an emergency could take effect only with the concurrence of Canada.

Canada has served, and has been well served, by the international non-proliferation and safeguards regime, which had its origins in the 1946 resolution creating the United Nations Atomic Energy Commission (UNAEC), later developed into the International Atomic Energy Association (IAEA) and culminated in the 1968 Nuclear Non-Proliferation Treaty.

Canada's record in its efforts to prevent the proliferation of nuclear weapons is indeed unique. Canada has a set of non-proliferation credentials which is shared by few other countries in the world. In non-proliferation – horizontal and vertical – Canada has led, and continues to lead, by example.

165

Moreover, the NPT has been of distinct commercial value to the country. Canada is the world's largest supplier of uranium, all of which is subject to a 'peaceful uses' provision. It is the world's largest supplier of bulk radio-isotopes for agricultural, medical and scientific applications. It is the fifth-largest vendor of power reactors with its world-renowned CANDU. It is the sixth-largest generator of nuclear power with an operating capacity of over 8,000 MW(E). And approximately 100,000 Canadians work directly or indirectly in the Canadian nuclear power programme, worth $1 billion to the Canadian economy.

Canada's nuclear programme is strictly for peaceful purposes and entirely subject to safeguards. In nuclear exports Canada imposes a rigorous set of requirements on its potential customers – both nuclear-weapon and non-nuclear-weapon states alike – requirements which go far beyond the full-scope safeguards of the IAEA. Canada will export nuclear materials, equipment and technology only to those countries that have accepted IAEA or equivalent safeguards over their entire nuclear programme and activities.

NPT Review

It is with this solid reputation as a country historically involved and committed to non-proliferation, as well as one on the leading edge in developing the peaceful uses of nuclear technology, that Canada came to the Third Review Conference of the NPT. Canada is a country which deeply respects and values the NPT as an invaluable international treaty embodying the objectives of Canada's arms control, non-proliferation and peaceful-uses policies: to encourage negotiations between the superpowers leading to a cessation of the nuclear arms race, with the long-term goal of general and complete disarmament; to prevent the further spread of nuclear weapons; and to promote and facilitate the peaceful uses of nuclear energy. The importance of the NPT as an essential instrument of international security cannot be over-emphasised. It is a vital security linchpin which benefits all countries by reducing the risk of nuclear proliferation. The NPT is also an instrument of regional security, since concern over the nuclear activities of some countries, particularly those not party to the NPT, can contribute to uncertainty, suspicion, fear and, consequently, increased regional tensions.

The NPT is the legal embodiment of a bargain made between the nuclear and non-nuclear states. The non-nuclear states agreed to

Canada and the NPT: The Enduring Relationship 167

forgo the acquisition of nuclear weapons (that is, horizontal proliferation) in exchange for an undertaking by the nuclear states to
halt the arms race in nuclear weapons (that is, vertical proliferation).
This agreement, the outcome of long negotiations, is clearly set out
in Article VI of the treaty:

> Each of the Parties to the Treaty undertakes to pursue negotia-
> tions in good faith on effective measures relating to cessation of the
> nuclear arms race at an early date and to nuclear disarmament.

This article defines the obligations of 'Each of the Parties' – both
nuclear-weapon and non-nuclear-weapon states – to pursue negotiations 'in good faith' with the goals, first of halting the nuclear arms
race, and then proceeding to disarmament. As stated in the treaty's
preamble, parties to the treaty declared their intention to

> achieve at the earliest possible date the cessation of the nuclear
> arms race and to undertake effective measures in the direction of
> nuclear disarmament.

The preamble also recalled the commitment in the 1963 Partial Test Ban
Treaty to continue negotiations to end all nuclear tests for all time.

Although the First Review Conference in 1975 concluded successfully from the perspective of Canada and other supporters of the
treaty, it proved to be a highly political exercise, particularly in the
areas of nuclear disarmament and security issues. The neutral and
non-aligned (NNA) countries, insisting that they had lived up to
their obligations under the treaty, accused the nuclear powers (particularly the superpowers) of not fulfilling their commitments under
Article IV (calling for the sharing of nuclear equipment, materials
and technology for peaceful uses).

The debate in the closing days and hours of the conference was
marked by acrimony and accusations. It was only at the last moment,
after great efforts by Sweden's Inga Thorsson and Canada's William
Barton, that the conference succeeded in adopting by consensus a
final document. Nevertheless, this Final Declaration of the conference reflected the frustration felt by many states, particularly the
NNA countries, over the lack of implementation of the basic bar-
gains of the treaty during the previous five years.

The demands of the NNA remained outstanding at the time of the
Second Review Conference in 1980. However, the atmosphere and

disarmament climate were relatively hopeful. The SALT II treaty had been recently signed, and promising trilateral (United Kingdom, United States, Soviet Union) negotiations for a Comprehensive Test Ban (CTB) treaty were still officially taking place.

Despite marathon sessions of informal negotiations, the conference ended without a consensus final document because of lack of agreement on issues relating to nuclear disarmament, particularly on a Comprehensive Test Ban. While consensus was reached on texts dealing with international safeguards, the sharing of the benefits of peaceful uses of nuclear energy, and the posing of full-scope safeguards as a condition for nuclear co-operation (a goal that had been strongly pursued by Canada and other like-minded countries), there was no agreement on a final document. This was a major setback and has been interpreted by some as meaning that the Second Review Conference was a failure.

During the final approach to the Third Review Conference, which opened 27 August 1985 in Geneva, the outlook was uncertain. It was certain that once again there would be vigorous debate on the perceived failure of the nuclear powers to implement their obligations under Article VI. As in 1980, there was a very real danger that a lack of tangible progress relating to Article VI would hold hostage any agreement on other matters relating to safeguards and international nuclear co-operation.

A major focus of debate during the Third Review Conference was Article VI. In the past five years since the last review, there has been no substantial progress on any nuclear arms control and disarmament issue. In fact, the nuclear arms race is proceeding at an ever-increasing pace in both its qualitative and quantitative aspects. In addition, the trilateral CTB talks have been abandoned.

Although the resumption of bilateral negotiations between the United States and the Soviet Union in Geneva has been a welcome development, the road ahead is likely to be a long and arduous one. The United States and the Soviet Union have set themselves high goals for the Geneva negotiations: the prevention of an arms race in space and its termination on earth; the limitation and reduction of nuclear arms; and the strengthening of strategic stability, leading ultimately to the complete elimination of nuclear weapons. Although the objectives have been agreed on, the views of the two sides on how to arrive at their shared goals differ dramatically.

In the multilateral arms control fora, forward movement is halting and prospects for real progress or agreement seem remote. The

Conference on Disarmament (CD) offers some opportunities for progress on arms control, but not, unfortunately, in areas related to nuclear matters. The Conference on Confidence- and Security-Building Measures and Disarmament in Europe began its second year with East and West still far apart in their approach to confidence-building measures. And at the Mutual and Balanced Force Reduction (MBFR) talks in Vienna, which resumed in January 1985, East and West are still unable to resolve troop data questions after more than eleven years of negotiations.

Progress towards a CTB treaty has been traditionally associated with compliance on Article VI. For Canada, the achievement of a CTB treaty remains a fundamental and abiding Canadian objective. The Canadian government policy is that a CTB is a concrete, realistic measure which would constitute a major step in curbing the development of new and more sophisticated nuclear weapons. It is regarded as an extremely important step towards halting both the vertical and horizontal proliferation of nuclear weapons. As the United Nations Secretary-General stated in early 1985: 'It is of direct importance to the future of humanity to end all nuclear explosions. No other means would be as effective in limiting the further development of nuclear weapons.'

The world community is now asking why it has been necessary for the nuclear-weapon states to have conducted a total of 1,522 nuclear explosions between 1945 and 1984. The question intensifies as one recognises that 53 nuclear explosions were carried out in 1984. How does continued testing demonstrate a commitment to Article VI of the NPT? Growing numbers of governments and expert bodies have recently been calling attention to this dilemma.

It is Canada's firm view that, with a willingness to accept sensible accommodations of interests, it should be possible for the Conference on Disarmament, which is grappling with this problem, to agree to the establishment of an *ad hoc* committee on a nuclear test ban with a realistic and practical mandate. The Government of Canada is, in fact, greatly disappointed that the sensible and sustained efforts of many in the CD, who have been working towards this modest goal, have led to so little. The CD should examine the issue of scope as well as that of verification and compliance, with a view to negotiation of a treaty.

With respect to the many complex policy decisions that must be made in the field of disarmament and arms control, the Canadian government, in its Green Paper on Foreign Policy published in the spring of 1985, has stated clearly:

the imperative of ensuring security at lower levels of nuclear weapons requires that no proposal or line of thinking on a possible solution be dismissed without careful examination.

Keeping in mind the problems of the present international security situation, Canada strove to achieve two basic objectives at the Third Review Conference: the maintenance of the NPT as the basic element of an effective international non-proliferation regime; and the reaffirmation by the Review Conference of the purpose and provision of the NPT. Specifically, Canadian goals on the disarmament side were: to ensure that the debate on Article VI issues contributed in a positive manner to the overall objectives of the NPT and did not degenerate into an acrimonious debate between the NNA and the nuclear-weapon states; to reconfirm the need for nuclear-weapon states, particularly the United States and the Soviet Union, to negotiate in good faith towards the adoption of effective measures to achieve a cessation of the nuclear arms race at an early date and a reduction in nuclear arms; to emphasise the importance of the NPT as a major contribution to international security; to reiterate Canada's strong sympathy for the concept of regional nuclear weapon-free zones (NWFZ) as specified in the NPT where these are feasible and seem likely to contribute to stability; and to continue to explore, in close consultation with Canada's NATO allies and other like-minded countries, the possibility of other measures, both in nuclear and non-nuclear arms control fields, which would help to contribute to general progress in arms control and an amelioration of the East-West political climate.

As another practical step in maintaining and strengthening the NPT, Canada and a number of like-minded countries undertook to approach non-signatory states in an effort to have more countries sign what is already the most widely adhered-to international security treaty. In reaching out to hard-core critics and non-signatories of the NPT, we made these points: to those countries that remain critics of the NPT and argue that the treaty is discriminatory, we pointed out that the same discrimination exists in the United Nations Security Council; to those nations that call for an end to the nuclear arms race while refusing themselves to sign the NPT, we suggested that their appeal would be more credible were they a party to the treaty; to those states that retain the nuclear option for perceived regional security considerations, we asked them to consider the tragic and devastating consequences of a limited regional nuclear war; and finally, to those nuclear-weapon states that insist on remaining outside the treaty, we strongly suggested that they follow the example already set by the United States, the United Kingdom and the Soviet Union, and to note that the security and sovereignty of these nations has in no way been compromised – on the contrary, it has been enhanced.

Conclusion

The efforts of Canada and other nations in attracting new adherents to the treaty already has had some success; and there are now 130 signatories with every indication of other nations signing in the near future. Whatever the numerical success of this exercise, it has the additional benefit of demonstrating to non-signatories that parties to the NPT believe in the intrinsic merit and value of the non-proliferation regime offered by the treaty.

Some criticisms of the NPT are not unfounded. Any agreement that brings together so many diverse nations will be subject to certain strains and problems of compliance. In the international community it is difficult to legislate security, yet that is what certain articles of the NPT are attempting to do. The NPT, for all its strengths, is still a fragile international instrument whose credibility and applicability constantly must be monitored and nurtured. The NPT cannot be taken for granted.

To those who continue to criticise the treaty, either from within or without, I would simply reiterate Canada's view. The NPT has weaknesses and flaws, certainly. However, it remains of fundamental importance to the international community and has, in general, served its members well.

What would happen if the non-proliferation regime, implemented and protected by the NPT, were to collapse? Would the world be better off? I think not. I believe strongly that the world would be much worse off without the NPT – more uncertain, more unstable, more dangerous; it would also be less equitable in the sharing of technological resources and expertise.

The NPT is a rare, international instrument, having at once both practical and moral dimensions. The fact that countries are continuing to sign the NPT, and continuing to feel that they should sign the NPT, is a tribute to both the moral force and practical utility of the treaty. It reflects a basic belief within the international community that proliferation is a bad thing.

The treaty has survived its first 15 years – not untarnished and not without criticism. An honest review at the Third Review Conference which assessed how the treaty has worked so far, where it has succeeded and where it may have failed, has only served to strengthen it.

It is the responsibility of Canada, and all nations of the world, to work to strengthen the NPT. Adherence to the letter and spirit of the NPT would result in a powerful non-proliferation regime guaranteeing the reduction, and eventual elimination, of nuclear weapons. That is a goal that commands our highest priority.

THE TREATY OF TLATELOLCO AND THE NPT

Miguel Marín Bosch

The dangers posed by the potential spread of nuclear weapons to more and more nations and the possible misuse of peaceful nuclear technology for military purposes have been a major concern of the international community since the late 1940s. During the following decade, that concern was translated into a number of specific proposals aimed at limiting the number of states possessing nuclear weapons and the areas where they could be stationed. For reasons of geography, the Soviet Union was moved to submit proposals to ban the deployment of nuclear weapons in Central Europe and other areas, whereas the United States favoured a policy of prohibiting the transfer of the control of those weapons to other countries with the exception of military allies.[1]

Those two different approaches to the prevention of the spread of nuclear weapons have been developed over the past three decades. The idea of a treaty prohibiting the dissemination of nuclear weapons and their acquisition by states not possessing them found concrete expression in the proposal by Ireland in 1958. Ten years later the United Nations would produce the Treaty on the Non-Proliferation of Nuclear Weapons (NPT).[2]

The establishment of nuclear-weapon-free zones has been advocated by many countries. Proposals were submitted for such zones in the Balkans, the Adriatic, the Mediterranean, Scandinavia, the Middle East, Asia, the South Pacific, Central Europe, Africa and Latin America.[3] Prohibitions now exist regarding the emplacement of nuclear weapons on the seabed and ocean floor and the stationing or orbiting of those weapons in space or on celestial bodies. Antarctica, as a demilitarised area, is *ipso facto* a nuclear-weapon-free zone.[4] But the Treaty for the Prohibition of Nuclear Weapons in Latin America (Treaty of Tlatelolco) is the first and, so far, only treaty establishing a nuclear-weapon-free zone in a densely populated area.[5]

The Treaty of Tlatelolco and the NPT embody different approaches to the prevention of the horizontal proliferation of nuclear weapons.

173

The purpose of this chapter is to identify those differences and to assess the future of the non-proliferation regime from a Latin American perspective.

The Treaty of Tlatelolco: A Description[6]

The Treaty of Tlatelolco was opened for signature in Mexico City on 14 February 1967.[7] It is the first treaty creating a nuclear-weapon-free zone that covers the territories of sovereign states and the first agreement to establish a system of international control and a permanent supervisory organ, the Agency for the Prohibition of Nuclear Weapons in Latin America (OPANAL).

The treaty consists of 31 articles, one transitional article and two additional protocols which, taken together, establish a system of mutual rights and obligations engaging three categories of states: the states of the region to which the treaty is open for signature (Article 25), extra-continental and continental states having *de jure* or *de facto* international responsibility for territories in the zone of application of the treaty, and the nuclear-weapon states, 'present and future'.

Parties to the treaty are required to enter into agreements with the International Atomic Energy Agency (IAEA) for the application of safeguards to their nuclear activities. This treaty also creates a system of inspection to deal with suspected cases of violation of its provisions and measures to be taken in the event of violation. There are, however, no provisions for monitoring compliance with the obligations assumed by extra-continental, continental or nuclear-weapon states under the additional protocols.

The zone came into being as a result of a five-year process. The proposal was initiated in 1962 by Bolivia, Brazil, Chile and Ecuador (Mexico was added in 1963) and elaborated by a preparatory commission of Latin American states. In 1967 the treaty was welcomed by the United Nations General Assembly which thereafter adopted numerous resolutions calling for speedy adherence to the treaty's additional protocols by all states concerned.[8]

In Article 1 of the treaty, the contracting parties undertake to use exclusively for peaceful purposes the nuclear material and facilities under their jurisdiction and to prohibit and prevent in their respective territories:

1. the testing, use, manufacture, production or acquisition by any means whatsoever of any nuclear weapons, by the parties themselves, directly or indirectly, on behalf of anyone else or in any other way; and
2. the receipt, storage, installation, deployment and any form of possession of any nuclear weapons, directly or indirectly, by the parties themselves, by anyone on their behalf or in any other way.

Further, they undertake to refrain from engaging in, encouraging or authorising, directly or indirectly, or in any way participating in the testing, use, manufacture, production, possession or control of any nuclear weapon.

Article 3 of the treaty defines the term 'territory' as including the territorial sea, air space and any other space over which the state exercises sovereignty in accordance with its own legislation. The zone of application of the treaty is that specified in Article 4, paragraph 1; that is, the sum of the territories of the countries for which the treaty is in force. It is foreseen in the treaty that once the requirements of Article 28 (ratification by all Latin American states, ratification of Additional Protocols I and II by all states concerned, and the conclusion of safeguards agreements with IAEA in accordance with Article 13 of the treaty) have been met, the zone will be an area larger than the current sum of the territories of the contracting parties, as specified in Article 4, paragraph 2. It is also foreseen in the treaty that upon the accession of all states concerned to the treaty and additional protocols, as appropriate, its zone of application shall extend to include the territories and the maritime area precisely defined in Article 4, paragraph 2 of the treaty.

For the purposes of this treaty, a nuclear weapon is defined in its Article 5 as:

Any device which is capable of releasing nuclear energy in an uncontrolled manner and which has a group of characteristics that are appropriate for use for warlike purposes. An instrument that may be used for the transport or propulsion of the device is not included in this definition if it is separable from the device and not an indivisible part thereof.

The right of the contracting parties to use nuclear energy for peaceful purposes, in particular for their economic development and social progress, is reaffirmed in Article 17 of the treaty.

Article 18 provides the right of the contracting parties to carry out nuclear explosions for peaceful purposes, including explosions which involve devices similar to those used in nuclear weapons or collaborate with third parties for a similar purpose, provided that those explosions are carried out in accordance with the treaty and in particular with Articles 1 and 5. Specific measures for the control of nuclear explosions for peaceful purposes are provided in paragraphs 2 and 3 of Article 18.

Article 27 of the treaty and Article 4 of Additional Protocol II provide that the treaty and its Additional Protocol II shall not be subject to reservations.

Additional Protocol I provides for the extension of the nuclear-weapon-free status to territories lying in the zone of application of the treaty which, *de jure* or *de facto*, are under the jurisdiction of states outside the zone, namely, France, the Netherlands, the United Kingdom and the United States. The latter three states have ratified the Protocol.[9] France has signed the protocol and declared that it would, in due course, take 'an appropriate decision on the ratification of Additional Protocol I, taking into account the state of ratification of the Treaty itself'.[10]

This protocol was the result of extensive negotiations among the Latin American states and between a negotiating committee of the preparatory commission of the treaty and the four states mentioned above. In 1965 the United States declared that neither the United States Virgin Islands nor Puerto Rico could be included in the nuclear-weapon-free zone because the Virgin Islands were part of the territory of the United States, and Puerto Rico had a special relationship with the United States. The Canal Zone, the United States added, could be included, provided that the rights of transit through the Panama Canal were not affected, as well as the Guantanamo base, if Cuba joined the treaty. The general conference and the council of OPANAL have examined the question of the Panama Canal Zone in view of the fact that the Panamanian government declared that the treaty applies to the totality of the territory of Panama, including the so-called Canal Zone.

During the drafting of the treaty, a clear commitment by the nuclear-weapon states to respect the nuclear-weapon-free status of the zone was considered an important condition for the effectiveness of the zone. The search for a formula to embody this commitment led to contacts between the preparatory commission of the treaty and the nuclear-weapon states, which resulted in Additional Protocol II.

By 1979 all five nuclear-weapon states had adhered to Additional Protocol II.[11] It has been said that the effectiveness of the treaty has been adversely affected by interpretative declarations to the protocols, which impose conditions contrary to the letter and spirit of the treaty and which amount to reservation, since they modify the terms of the Treaty of Tlatelolco. Others have held that the declarations made on ratifying the additional protocols to the treaty are entirely consistent with the provisions of those protocols and the treaty.

The Treaty of Tlatelolco applies to the territories of the 33 independent states of Latin America and the Caribbean, as well as the territories for which, *de jure* or *de facto*, France, the Netherlands, the United Kingdom and the United States are internationally responsible. The treaty enters into force for those states which have ratified it, subject to the requirements set out in Article 28, paragraph 1: namely, that all the states included in the zone have acceded to the treaty, that all the states concerned have acceded to the additional protocols, and that safeguards agreements have been concluded with IAEA.[12] However, since these requirements might considerably delay the zone from coming into being, paragraph 2 of the same article allows signatory states to waive these requirements, wholly or in part. As of 1 May 1985, the treaty was in force for 23 Latin American states that have ratified it and that have waived the said requirements: Antigua and Barbuda, Bahamas, Barbados, Bolivia, Colombia, Costa Rica, Dominican Republic, Ecuador, El Salvador, Grenada, Guatemala, Haiti, Honduras, Jamaica, Mexico, Nicaragua, Panama, Paraguay, Peru, Surinam, Trinidad and Tobago, Uruguay and Venezuela. Also covered are the territories of the Netherlands, the United Kingdom and the United States.

Of the remaining states in the region, Brazil and Chile have ratified the treaty but have not waived the requirements. Argentina has signed the treaty and has stated that it shares its aims and objectives.[13] Belize and Guyana have not yet been invited by the General Conference of OPANAL to accede to the treaty, since parts of their territories are subjects of a dispute or claim by other Latin American states (Article 25, paragraph 2). Five states have not signed the treaty: Cuba,[14] Dominica, Saint Lucia, Saint Christopher and Nevis, and Saint Vincent and the Grenadines. The four latter states have gained independence only recently and are expected to complete soon the constitutional actions needed to accede to the treaty. At the latest meeting of the General Conference of OPANAL no new accessions to the treaty were recorded.[15] Also excluded from the zone are the territories of France.

The Treaty of Tlatelolco: Divergent Views

Some provisions of the Treaty of Tlatelolco have given rise to different interpretations. This is especially true with regard to peaceful nuclear explosions (PNEs), the geographical extent of the zone and transit of nuclear weapons through the zone.

The treaty specifically permits PNEs, including explosions that involve devices similar to those used in nuclear weapons, provided this is done in accordance with Articles 1 and 5. And yet, upon signing the treaty, three states – Argentina, Brazil and Nicaragua – reserved their right to carry out PNEs, 'including explosions which involve devices similar to those used in nuclear weapons'. Only Nicaragua is a party to the treaty, and it has stated that it reserves

> its sovereign right to use nuclear energy, as it deems fit, for such peaceful purposes as the removal of large amounts of earth for the construction of interoceanic or any other type of canal, irrigation works, electric power stations, etc., and to allow the transit of atomic materials through its territory.[16]

On the other hand, some countries interpret the treaty as prohibiting the manufacture of nuclear explosive devices for peaceful purposes unless and until nuclear devices are developed which can be distinguished from nuclear weapons.[17] In this respect, three nuclear-weapon states have referred to nuclear explosive devices for peaceful purposes in their declarations to Additional Protocol II. The Soviet Union has stated that 'the carrying out by any party to the treaty of explosions of nuclear devices for peaceful purposes would constitute a violation of its obligations as defined in Article 1, and would be incompatible with its non-nuclear status'. The United Kingdom has stated that

> Article 18 of the Treaty, when read in conjunction with Articles 1, and 5 thereof, would not permit the Contracting Parties to the Treaty to carry out explosions of nuclear devices for peaceful purposes unless and until advances in technology have made possible

the development of devices for such explosions which are not capable of being used for weapons purposes.

The United States stated that it wished to point out

the fact that the technology of making nuclear explosive devices for peaceful purposes is indistinguishable from the technology of making nuclear weapons and the fact that nuclear weapons and nuclear explosive devices for peaceful purposes are both capable of releasing nuclear energy in an uncontrolled manner and have the common group of characteristics of large amounts of energy generated instantaneously from a compact source. Therefore, we understand the definition contained in Article 5 of the Treaty as necessarily encompassing all nuclear explosive devices.[18]

Some have viewed these interpretative declarations as *de facto* reservations which run counter to the clear-cut provisions of Article 18 of the treaty. Other countries consider that the treaty has sanctioned any nuclear explosion as long as its purpose is peaceful, and in that connection refer to the verification procedures of the treaty (Article 16).

The Soviet Union, the United Kingdom and the United States view the matter of PNEs in terms of Article V of the NPT. But the promised negotiations on agreements to make available to non-nuclear-weapon states party to the NPT the 'potential benefits' from PNEs have yet to begin, although the NPT specifies that they would 'commence as soon as possible after the treaty enters into force' (that is, 1970).

Another source of controversy with regard to the Treaty of Tlatelolco is that of unsettled territorial disputes, such as those between Venezuela and Guyana, Guatemala and Belize, as well as between Panama and the United States regarding the Canal Zone. But these do not represent insurmountable obstacles.

Differences exist also concerning the geographical extent of the zone. According to the treaty, its zonal application will embrace the territory, territorial sea, air space and any other space over which each of the zonal states exercises sovereignty in accordance with 'its own legislation'. Such legislation, however, varies from state to state. For example, a number of Latin American countries have declared a 200-mile limit for their territorial sea. In signing Additional Protocol II of the treaty, France, the Soviet Union, the United

Kingdom and the United States made declarations to the effect that they would not recognise any legislation which did not, in their view, comply with the relevant rules of international law, such as the Law of the Sea.[19]

An additional difference exists on the question of transit. As the treaty has not explicitly prohibited either transit or transport of nuclear weapons, this issue is highly relevant in the context of this chapter. The Preparatory Commission for the Denuclearisation of Latin America (COPREDAL) did not consider it necessary to include the term 'transport' in the article dealing with the obligations of the parties, on the grounds that if the carrier state were one of the zonal states, transport prohibition would be covered by Article 1(b) of the treaty which prohibits any form of possession of any nuclear weapon, 'directly or indirectly, by the parties themselves, by anyone on their behalf or in any other way'. If the carrier were a state not party to the treaty, transport would be identical with 'transit'. In that case, the principles and rules of international law would have to apply, according to which it is the prerogative of the territorial state, in the exercise of its sovereignty, to grant or deny permission for transit. In adhering to Additional Protocol II of the treaty, France, the United Kingdom and the United States made declarations of understanding to that effect, while the Soviet Union reaffirmed its position that authorising the transit of nuclear weapons in any form would be contrary to the objectives of the treaty. China, on the other hand, considers that nuclear-weapon states must implement a prohibition of the passage of any means of transportation or delivery carrying nuclear weapons through Latin American territory, territorial sea or air space. Two states, Mexico and Panama, have taken the general decision not to grant permission for transit of nuclear weapons through their territories. In this regard, these states have noted that the statute of military denuclearisation of Latin America 'in all its express aims and provisions' is to keep the whole region 'forever free from nuclear weapons', and thus any exception to a total ban on transit contradicts the treaty's purpose.

The issue of assurances not to use nuclear weapons against parties to the treaty continues to be subject to differing interpretations concerning the effect of Article 27 of the treaty, which states that it 'shall not be subject to reservations'. China, on signing Additional Protocol II on 21 August 1973, reiterated its undertaking that 'China will never use or threaten to use nuclear weapons against non-nuclear Latin American countries and the Latin America nuclear-weapon-free zone'. The other assurances given of non-use of nuclear weapons have not been unconditional. The United Kingdom and the United States have reserved the right to reconsider their obligations with regard to a state in the nuclear-weapon-free zone in the event of any act of aggression or armed attack by that state which is carried out with the support or assistance of a nuclear-weapon state. The Soviet Union has made a similar reservation with regard to a party to the treaty committing an act of aggression with the support of, or together with, a nuclear-weapon state. France, on signing Additional Protocol II, declared: 'The French Government interprets the undertaking made in Article 3 of the Protocol as being without prejudice to the full exercise of the right of self-defence confirmed by Article 51 of the Charter of the United Nations.'

The fact that Additional Protocol II has been signed and ratified by all five nuclear-weapon states has been regarded as a significant achievement contributing to the effectiveness of the treaty and fulfilling one of the conditions for its full implementation. Disappointment has been expressed by some of the governments concerned because of interpretative declarations and statements issued which, in some cases, have been regarded as *de facto* reservations, substantially limiting the scope of the obligations. Some have expressed the view that, in addition to the self-conferred exemptions arising from unilateral declarations, the nuclear-weapon states are not subject to any form of verification of compliance with the obligations they undertake as parties to Protocol II of the Treaty of Tlatelolco. These concerns were raised at the Eighth General Conference of OPANAL held in Kingston, Jamaica, from 16 to 19 May 1983.

In this view, the establishment of machinery for verification of compliance with the Treaty of Tlatelolco is necessary to create an acceptable balance of rights and obligations between zonal states and nuclear-weapon states under the treaty. It also has been said that Article 51 of the United Nations Charter cannot be invoked to justify the use of threat of use of nuclear weapons in the exercise of the right of self-defence in the case of armed attack not involving the use of nuclear weapons, since nuclear war would threaten the very survival of mankind. The Secretary General of OPANAL, at the 1983 General Conference, touched on another question:

Although Article 5 of the treaty clearly establishes that nuclear-powered vehicles cannot be considered as nuclear devices, it is certain that the nuclear-powered submarines that took part in the

South Atlantic conflict were not on a peace mission, they participated in warlike actions, which lead to the conclusion that one
of the nuclear Powers used this energy militarily to defend its
interests, which would be contrary to the political philosophy that
inspired Tlatelolco.[20]

On the other hand, the view has been expressed that nuclear-powered
warships are not prohibited by the Treaty of Tlatelolco, with the title
of the treaty and its Article 5 cited as evidence for this position.

Furthermore, attention has been drawn to the allegation by Argentina and other Latin American states that warships which participated in the South Atlantic conflict in 1982 could have been
carrying nuclear weapons, which caused concern and uneasiness
among the states of the region. However, the Government of the
United Kingdom has stated that it has scrupulously observed its
obligations under Additional Protocols I and II of the treaty and has
not deployed nuclear weapons in areas for which the treaty is in
force.

According to the preamble of the treaty, 'the establishment of
militarily denuclearised zones is closely linked with the maintenance of peace and security in the respective regions'. In this
regard, there has been growing concern over the deterioration of the
security situation in the region, but there are different perceptions of
the reasons for this. One view is that the root causes are the interven-
tions and interference in the internal affairs of states, the increasing
frequency of intimidating military manoeuvres within the region by
some nuclear-weapon states, the repeated acts of hostility and aggression – including direct military actions and mining of ports of states
parties to the treaty – and the maintenance and strengthening of
foreign military bases to, *inter alia*, preserve anachronistic colonial
situations. Furthermore, according to this view, these acts aggravate
the poverty, inequality and misery which have been imposed on
some countries of the region since the end of the last century through
domination and imperialist exploitation, and against which the countries of the region have been struggling since that time – a struggle
which the international community has recognised as not being the
consequence of an ideological East-West confrontation.

Another view is that the root causes are to be found elsewhere, in
so far as in one part of the region there have been continued activities
supported by a distant extra-continental nuclear-weapon state aimed
at fomenting and exploiting the internal difficulties of some states.

Such activities have included, *inter alia*, the surreptitious supply of arms, ammunition, military equipment and other support to elements seeking to subvert and overthrow by force legitimate, freely elected governments. According to this view, in their efforts to protect themselves against such activities and to establish conditions of peace and stability that are essential for the economic and social development of their peoples, a number of countries in the area have sought and received assistance from a major power.

The Treaty of Tlatelolco and the NPT

Twenty-one Latin American countries are party to both the Treaty of Tlatelolco and the NPT. The only parties to the Treaty of Tlatelolco that have yet to ratify the NPT are Colombia and Trinidad and Tobago. For most there seems to be no conflict between their adherence to the Treaty of Tlatelolco and the NPT. The latter contains an unequivocal provision (Article VII) that the NPT in no way 'affects the right of any group of states to conclude regional treaties in order to assure the total absence of nuclear weapons in their respective territories'. Nevertheless, one party to the Treaty of Tlatelolco felt compelled to clarify further its position. Upon signing the NPT, the Government of Mexico noted that nothing in that treaty could be interpreted as affecting in any way whatsoever its rights and obligations under the Treaty of Tlatelolco.[21]

Differences between the Tlatelolco approach and the NPT become apparent among those states of the region that hold the NPT to be discriminatory. These include Argentina, Brazil, Chile, Cuba and Guyana. But differences also exist among states outside the region with regard to those two treaties. These were brought out most clearly during the discussions among the experts that carried out the 1975 study on nuclear-weapon-free zones, and the follow-up study requested by the United Nations General Assembly in 1984. Unfortunately, the group of experts was unable to complete its task in 1984 and requested an extension. But the meeting at the beginning of 1985 ended in failure since the group 'was unable to reach agreement on the study as a whole and in particular on the conclusions resulting from the study'.[22]

The group of experts was divided on such questions as the concept of nuclear-weapon-free zones, the peaceful uses of nuclear energy, and on specific proposals regarding Africa, Asia, Europe, the

Mediterranean, the Middle East and the South Pacific. From the debates it became apparent that for many experts, particularly those belonging to military alliances, a nuclear-weapon-free zone was nothing more than a regional version of the NPT. For others, principally the experts from Latin America, this approach was unacceptable.

The experts also were divided as to the value of the definitions regarding nuclear-weapon-free zones adopted by the General Assembly in its Resolution 3472 B (XXX) of 11 December 1975. In that resolution the General Assembly set the following criteria regarding nuclear-weapon-free zones: they should be spontaneously arrived at by states of a given region and they should be recognised by the General Assembly; the treaty or convention establishing them should ensure the total absence of nuclear weapons, the procedure for the delimitation of the zone, and an international system of verification and control. The General Assembly also defined the principal obligations of the nuclear-weapon states towards nuclear-weapon-free zones and towards the states included therein: total respect for the statute of total absence of nuclear weapons; refraining from contributing to any act in violation of the treaty or convention; and refraining from using or threatening to use nuclear weapons against the states included in the zone.

Although supported by an overwhelming majority, the resolution drew strong criticism from a handful of delegations. The NATO countries took the position that, regardless of the importance of the question of nuclear-weapon-free zones, it was 'wrong and dangerous' that the General Assembly attempt to impose obligations on states against their will.[23]

The Soviet Union, the United Kingdom and the United States continue to insist that the NPT 'is a cornerstone of international efforts to erect and to sustain effective barriers to the further spread of nuclear weapons'.[24] Those states and their allies have made it clear that adherence to the NPT is a necessary first step, if not a *sine qua non* condition, for the establishment of a nuclear-weapon-free zone.

Conclusion

Since the 1950s writings on the non-proliferation of nuclear weapons have been characterised by a fascination with the horizontal aspect of the dissemination of those weapons. At that time, the 'nuclear club' was limited to three nations: the United States (1945), the Soviet Union (1949) and the United Kingdom (1952). France would join them in 1960 and China in 1964. A decade later India would carry out a peaceful nuclear explosion but forgo the production of nuclear weapons.

Recently, attention has been drawn to the potential danger posed by the growing number of countries now capable of producing nuclear weapons without the need of conducting a test. That danger has been described as a 'silent spread' of such a capability to countries which, it is said, today include Israel, South Africa and Pakistan, and which will soon include Argentina, Brazil and Iraq.[25]

What is often overlooked, however, is the fact that the potential acquisition of nuclear weapons by other countries poses much less of a danger than the constant spread, and a not so 'silent' one at that, of nuclear warheads throughout the world. Indeed, 40 years ago, the earth was a nuclear-weapon-free zone. Today there are some 50,000 nuclear weapons deployed around the globe, on land and on sea. The establishment of nuclear-weapon-free zones is aimed at reducing the areas into which such weapons can spread. And that is precisely what is *not* prohibited by the NPT, which permits the stationing of nuclear weapons on the territories of non-nuclear-weapon states that have adhered to it.

The term 'nuclear-weapon state', as defined in Article IX of the NPT, has in fact acquired a different meaning since 1 January 1967. The NPT defined a 'nuclear-weapon state' as one having manufactured and exploded a nuclear weapon or other nuclear explosive devices prior to that date. One could argue that members of military alliances which include one or more nuclear-weapon states having access to the possibility of deciding, permanently or provisionally, on the use of nuclear weapons could be considered as nuclear-weapon states. Were that acceptable, there would certainly be more than five nuclear-weapon states. On the other hand, this problem does not occur with regard to the Treaty of Tlatelolco since it does not define the term 'nuclear-weapon state'.

The Treaty of Tlatelolco is of 'a permanent nature and shall remain in force indefinitely' (Article 30, paragraph 1). In contrast, the NPT calls for a conference to be held 25 years after its entry into force to decide by a majority of parties 'whether the Treaty shall continue in force indefinitely, or [its duration] shall be extended for an additional fixed period or periods' (Article X, paragraph 2). Thus in 1995 the continuing viability of the NPT regime will undergo its most severe test. It had already received close scrutiny at the First and Second Review Conferences (in 1975 and 1980 respectively) and it came under still sharper criticism at the Third Review Conference held in Geneva in September 1985. But the depositary governments once again managed to placate the growing discontent among the non-nuclear-weapon parties and put off until 1990 any serious move that could undermine the status of the treaty.

The Treaty of Tlatelolco, on the other hand, will in all likelihood continue to move towards complete adherence by the states of the region. Its viability can only be threatened by the nuclear-weapon states. And precisely three of them, in particular the two superpowers, also hold the key to the future of the NPT. Unless they begin to comply with the spirit of Article VI and proceed to reduce their nuclear arsenals and to halt nuclear weapon tests, there is the danger that the NPT regime will crumble and, as a result, produce an effect exactly opposite to its original purpose.

The day after the NPT regime falls apart, the world will be left with Latin America as the only densely populated region free of nuclear weapons. But even there, the situation is potentially dangerous, as demonstrated by the South Atlantic conflict of 1982 and the continuing escalation of the Central American crisis, including naval manoeuvres and increased foreign military presence.

End Notes

1. See United Nations, *The United Nations and Disarmament, 1945-1970* (New York, 1970), pp. 257-346 and United Nations, *The United Nations and Disarmament, 1970-1975* (New York, 1976), pp. 75-113.
2. For the text of the NPT, see United Nations, *Status of Multilateral Arms Regulation and Disarmament Agreements*, 2nd edn (New York, 1983), pp. 71-101.
3. United Nations, *Comprehensive Study of the Question of Nuclear-Weapon-Free Zones in all its Aspects: Special Report of the Conference of the Committee on Disarmament* (New York, 1976), pp. 10-28.
4. For the texts of the Treaty on the Prohibition of the Emplacement of Nuclear Weapons and Other Weapons of Mass Destruction on the Seabed and the Ocean Floor and in the Subsoil Thereof (Seabed Treaty in force since 1972), the Treaty on Principles Governing the Activities of States in the Exploration and Use of Outer Space, including the Moon and Other Celestial Bodies (Outer Space Treaty, in force since 1967), and the Antarctic Treaty of 1959, see *Status of Agreements*, pp. 12-19, 32-45 and 102-19.
5. For the text of the Treaty of Tlatelolco, see *Status of Agreements*, pp. 46-70.
6. This section and the next include material presented by the author to, and the discussion within, the Ad Hoc Group of Qualified Governmental Experts appointed by the Secretary-General of the United Nations in order to assist him in the

preparation of a study to review and supplement the 1975 *Comprehensive Study*. The new study was requested by the General Assembly in its resolution 37/99 F of 13 December 1982. The Ad Hoc Group included experts from Algeria, Argentina, Australia, Bulgaria, China, Cuba, Egypt, Federal Republic of Germany, Finland, France, India, Japan, Mexico, Nigeria, Pakistan, Poland, Romania, Tanzania, Soviet Union, United Kingdom, United States and Yugoslavia. The study was not completed because of differences among the experts.

7. For a description of the Treaty of Tlatelolco and its negotiating history, see the following books and articles: Alfonso Garcaía Robles: *La desnuclearizatión de la América Latina*, 2nd edn (El Colegio de México, México, 1966); *The Denuclearization of Latin America* (Carnegie Endowment for Peace, New York, 1967); *El Tratado de Tlatelolco, Génesis, alcance y propósitos de la proscripción de las armas nucleares en la América Latina* (El Colegio de México, México, 1967); 'The Treaty for the Prohibition of Nuclear Weapons in Latin America (Treaty of Tlatelolco), *World Armament and Disarmament SIPRI Yearbook, 1969-70* (SIPRI, Stockholm, 1970), pp. 218-58; and *La proscripción de las armas nucleares en la América Latina* (El Colegio Nacional, México, 1975).

8. For Additional Protocol I, see resolutions 2286 (XXII) of 5 December 1967, 3262 (XXIX) of 9 December 1974, 3473 (XXX) of 11 December 1975, 32/76 of 12 December 1977, 33/58 of 14 December 1978, 34/71 of 11 December 1979, 35/143 of 12 December 1980, 36/83 of 9 December 1981, 37/71 of 9 December 1982, 38/61 of 15 December 1983 and 39/51 of 12 December 1984. For Additional Protocol II, see resolutions 2286 (XXII) of 5 December 1967, 2456 B (XXIII) of 20 December 1968, 2666 (XXV) of 7 December 1970, 2830 (XXVI) of 16 December 1971, 2935 (XXVII) of 29 November 1972, 3079 (XXVIII) of 6 December 1973, 3258 (XXIX) of 9 December 1974, 3467 (XXX) of 11 December 1975, 31/67 of 10 December 1976, 32/79 of 12 December 1977, and 33/61 of 14 December 1978.

9. For the full text of reservations and declarations made by governments at the time of signature and ratification of Additional Protocol I, see *Status of Agreements*, pp. 64-70.

10. United National General Assembly, *Official Records of the General Assembly, Thirty-eighth Session, First Committee*, 38th meeting, p. 23, and ibid.

11. For the declarations made by the nuclear-weapon states upon signing Additional Protocol II or upon depositing their instruments of ratification, see *Status of Agreements*, pp. 64-70.

12. The following states concerned have concluded safeguards agreements with the IAEA: Colombia, Costa Rica, Dominican Republic, Ecuador, El Salvador, Guatemala, Honduras, Jamaica, Mexico, Nicaragua, Panama, Paraguay, Peru, Surinam, Uruguay and Venezuela.

13. United Nations document A/38/496, Annex VII.

14. For Cuba's position, see United National General Assembly, *Official Records of the General Assembly, Tenth Special Session, Plenary Meetings*, 8th meeting, p. 72.

15. The IX General Conference of OPANAL was held in Mexico City at the beginning of May 1985.

16. The text of those declarations are reproduced in *Status of Agreements*, pp. 63-4.

17. For its part, upon signing the NPT in 1968, Mexico stated that, at that time, there was no indication that it was possible to distinguish between a nuclear weapon and a peaceful nuclear explosive device, ibid, p. 97.

18. Ibid., pp. 64-70.

19. Ibid. The recent United Nations Convention on the Law of the Sea, signed at Montego Bay, Jamaica, on 10 December 1982, which is not yet in force, in its

Article 3 stipulates: 'Every State has the right to establish the breadth of its territorial sea up to a limit not exceeding twelve nautical miles, measured from baselines determined in accordance with the Convention.' See United Nations, *The Law of the Sea*, sales no. E.83.V.5.

20. United Nations document A/38/496, Annex III.
21. For the text of the Mexican declaration, see *Status of Agreements*, p. 97.
22. See footnote 6 above.
23. United Nations General Assembly, *Official Records of the General Assembly, Thirty-ninth Session, First Committee*, 2108th meeting, 5 December 1975.
24. Lewis Dunn, 'The Non-Proliferation Treaty and Future Global Security: An American Perspective', unpublished paper prepared for the York University, Toronto, Conference on the 1985 NPT Review Conference, held 16-17 May 1984, p. 14.
25. Leonard S. Spector, 'Silent Spread', *Foreign Policy*, no. 58 (Spring 1985), pp. 53-78. In this regard, it would be interesting to compare what the reaction was in the United States to the acquisition of a nuclear weapon capability by the United Kingdom and France, on the one hand, and by the Soviet Union, China and India, on the other.

THE NPT AND THE MIDDLE EAST

S. Freier

Introduction

This chapter is written by an Israeli and probably expresses perceptions and views held by most of those compatriots who take an actual
interest in nuclear developments in this area. The absence of public
discussion in a country where defence concerns loom so large is due
to the ever-present conventional threat posed by the Arab countries
– some populous, some wealthy – stretching from the Persian Gulf to
Libya. The Stockholm International Peace Research Institute reports
that Saudi Arabia is the biggest arms importer in the Third World,
followed by Libya, the first equipped by the United States, the latter
by the Soviet Union, but both committed enemies of Israel. Peace
with Egypt, once heralded as ushering in a new prospect, is cold.
Sinai was surrendered in return for an exchange of ambassadors and
some 40 agreements designed to infuse life into cultural, commercial
and scientific exchanges as well as to bolster tourism. The Egyptian
ambassador has long since been withdrawn and, except for some
joint work in agriculture, the agreements have remained dead letters,
and anti-Israeli and anti-Jewish propaganda abounds.

Constant Aspects of the Middle Eastern Situation

Apart from the different ways of asserting revulsion from Israel,
there are other constant features of the Middle Eastern situation
which merit mention in a discussion of the Treaty on the Non-
Proliferation of Nuclear Weapons (NPT) and this area. First among
these is the fact that agreements in the region have a short life span.
Indeed, it is sufficient to recall the fusion of Egypt and Syria some 25
years ago into one country – the United Arab Republic – soon
thereafter dissolved; or the proposed union of Iraq and Syria, much
publicised in presidential meetings and embraces, soon to be

followed by a hostility which persists to this day. These examples suffice to illustrate that in this region even the most solemn pledges are of a more brittle nature than elsewhere, and no government in Israel can fail to take account of this fact.

Second is the proposition that the presence or absence of Israel makes little difference to peace in the Middle East. Israel has been made out to be the obstacle to peace in the Middle East, at different times for different reasons, but throughout, just for being there. Even a cursory look at the relations between the states of the region reveals a changing pattern of alliances and hostilities which exists apart from any issue pertaining to Israel or the Palestinian problem. Iran and Iraq are at war; Syria and Iraq are enemies; Jordan officially seeks arms in order to defend itself against a possible Syrian attack; Libya is poised against Egypt and until recently against Sudan. Jordan and the PLO are friends; Iraq and Egypt are friends. Going back a few years, and a few years again, the ensuing constellations just could not be foreseen. It is only at times of war with Israel that the countries of the region coalesce. Also, the Middle East reflects the colliding policies of the United States and the Soviet Union, in the context of their global confrontation, which tend to acerbate rather than assuage local conflicts.

The third feature is that, contrary to appearances, Israel has a very small margin of error, the stakes are its very survival; no other country's survival is at stake. In the 1973 war, Israel refrained from anticipating the Egyptian and Syrian attack, even when it was recognised as imminent, in order not to be branded aggressor. It paid dearly for this delay. Israel erred in believing that it could prevail on Lebanon to make peace with it. It could not, a heavy price in lives was exacted all round, and the definite denial of bases for hostile incursions into Israel – the principal motivation for that war – was not achieved.

The above three propositions have a bearing on the nuclear proliferation risks in the Middle Eastern area and on the value of international undertakings, such as the NPT or a nuclear-weapon-free zone (NWFZ), as measures of credible restraint. Before engaging in this discussion, it is helpful to list some general notions about the NPT, as they are perceived in Israel.

Aspects of the NPT Relevant to the Middle East

The NPT is good in four respects. Its adherents commit themselves formally not to acquire or develop nuclear weapons, they accept

International Atomic Energy Agency (IAEA) inspection, they do not export nuclear materials to non-nuclear states unless these supplies are safeguarded, and the NPT generates a general feeling of reassurance with respect to the nuclear policies of its adherents. These are the virtues of the NPT and they often are considered its only attributes.

However, the NPT cannot serve as a reassurance in areas in which wars are endemic or warlike threats exist. The acceptance of recurring wars to settle conflicts is bound to fuel an arms race, which creates a penchant for more sophisticated and powerful weaponry. Such a situation eventually could encourage attempts to procure nuclear weapons. There are some 20 to 30 countries technically able to mount a nuclear weapons programme. The most advanced among them shelter under alliances, such as NATO or the Warsaw Treaty Organisation (WTO). None of these countries is solely responsible for its defence but trusts its alliance to offer a common, protective shield. It is the stability of these alliances which guarantees the restraint of these states, rather than a commitment on principle to forswear nuclear weapons. Even so, France has equipped itself with indigenous nuclear arms, ostensibly in order not to confine its protection to the comportment of the United States alone if Western Europe were invaded.

One has to admit that it is the reliability of the defensive provisions of a country which acts as the principal curb on the indigenous procurement of nuclear arms. In the absence of such contingencies, faithful abidance by the provisions of the NPT becomes questionable and the following quotations assume special importance. On the workings of the safeguards system, Dr Hans Blix, the present Director General of the IAEA, made the following cautious comments:

> The safeguards do not, of course, reveal what future intention the State may have. It might change its mind on the question of nuclear weapons and wish to produce them despite possible adherence to the NPT. Neither such adherence nor full-scope safeguards are full guarantees that the State will not one day make nuclear weapons.[1]

Also, the NPT permits a state to withdraw from the treaty upon three months' notice. On this provision, Dr Rudolf Rometsch, former Deputy Director General of the IAEA, remarked in 1977:

the 'abrogation risk' has to be understood and accepted. This is a new notion in the non-proliferation discussion. It designates the risk that a sovereign State might at any time – according to the rules or by breaking them – abrogate a safeguards agreement or a treaty partnership. We have to live with such risks.[2]

Both these quotations tell us that the NPT can be subverted. Libya and Iraq, for instance, are parties to the NPT. It is accepted that Libya opted for the acquisition of nuclear technology, plants and materials under the NPT after vainly trying to buy bombs, and that adherence to the NPT was mainly a more arduous alternative towards the same end. With respect to Iraq, also party to the NPT, the Israeli bombing of the reactor invited near universal condemnation on the manner that Israel chose to forestall a perceived threat. However, a perusal of moderate assessments attributes proliferation risks to Iraq, Iran and Libya, despite their adherence to the NPT,[3] all while rating their present capabilities as low.

Channels are provided whereby the Security Council and the General Assembly of the United Nations can intervene if a country is suspect of failing to live up to its commitment to the NPT or chooses to publicly withdraw from the treaty. However, the discretion of the United Nations and its organs are largely at the sport of political convenience. India's explosion of a nuclear device in 1974 incurred only passing censure, while a year after the bombing of the Iraqi reactor in 1982, the IAEA General Conference rejected the credentials of the Israeli delegation to the conference. Had it not been for the insistence of the United States on the charter and rules of the IAEA, irrespective of United States criticism of the Israeli action, the IAEA would have acted in defiance of its charter and rules in the case of Israel.

There are aspects of the NPT debate which do not engage emotions in the Middle East. The failure of the nuclear powers to live up to their obligations under Articles IV (to assist in realising the benefits of nuclear energy for peaceful purposes) and VI (to curb vertical proliferation), or the objection to an arbitrary division between states which have licence under the NPT to go on making nuclear weapons, and other states which are denied such licence, and the curious stance of moral indignation displayed by the 'haves' *vis-à-vis* aspiring 'have-nots', are issues which do not receive the attention accorded them in most other regions of the world.

Nuclear Capabilities and Intentions

A proliferation threat is generally assessed on the basis of incentives, disincentives and capabilities. Earlier in this chapter the point was made that in areas of ongoing military conflict, the incentive exists of eventually creating nuclear capabilities. The capabilities in the Middle East may be summarised as follows. For obvious reasons, I do not quote Israeli sources.

Indicative of Israeli intent and capabilities, the following quotes from 'Nuclear Arms Control – Background and Issues' by the National Academy of Science of the United States (page 267) are offered:

> The declared policy of Israel has long been that it would not be the first to introduce nuclear weapons into the Middle East. Nevertheless, Israel is generally believed to have the capability to manufacture a nuclear weapon on very short notice if it has not already done so.

> Israel has a strong base of highly trained nuclear scientists, engineers and technicians. It has an unsafeguarded research reactor capable of producing enough plutonium for at least one bomb a year and an unsafeguarded reprocessing facility.

> Israel has been careful to maintain a studied ambiguity between its declared nuclear policy and its nuclear capabilities. Apparently, it wishes to maintain an implicit nuclear deterrent while avoiding an open confrontation on the nuclear issue with its neighbours.

Israel has not signed the NPT for reasons spelled out above (liability of undertakings in the Middle East and the anti-Israel bias in all international organs), but has insisted on negotiating a nuclear-weapon-free zone patterned on the Tlatelolco Treaty as a more credible alternative to the NPT. It submitted a formal proposal to the United Nations (A/C. 1/35/L.8 of 30 October 1980) which was never taken up by its neighbours, and its earnest in the matter was never put to a test.

The substantial difference between the NPT and an NWFZ in Israeli eyes is threefold:

1. inspection under the NPT is negotiated by a member country with the IAEA while an NWFZ is negotiated among the states of the 'zone';
2. inspection by the IAEA is conducted by an international team of inspectors and agreement must be obtained beforehand from the inspected country regarding the identity of the inspector, the dates of the visits and the particular installation to be inspected. An NWFZ includes provisions for mutual inspections by the contracting parties of a character designed to reassure rather than to stress the limitations of access; and
3. adherence to the NPT can be abrogated on three-months' notice. An NWFZ presumably would place more obstacles on the withdrawal of a member of such a zone.

The importance of reliable agreements negotiated by the parties to a NWFZ in the Middle Eastern region will be dwelt upon later in the chapter.

Egypt is party to the NPT, has an ambitious programme for the installation of several power reactors, and is acquiring a sound technological base. Its present capability is modest, but its potential capability within a few years high. It is not known whether Egypt intends to endow itself with a military nuclear capability.

Iraq's present capability is low, its potential capability high. On Iraqi intentions I quote:[4]

Most telling is a 1975 statement by Saddam Hussein, then a member of the Revolutionary Command Council. In an interview with a Beirut magazine, he declared his nation's expanding nuclear program was 'the first Arab attempt at nuclear arming'.

In 1977, after the conclusion of the nuclear contracts with France and Italy, Naim Haddad, also a member of Iraq's Revolutionary Command Council, reportedly stated at a meeting of the Arab League, 'The Arabs must get an atom bomb. The Arab countries should possess whatever is necessary to defend themselves.' Haddad's unqualified enthusiasm for nuclear weapons at a time when Iraq was building a large nuclear program that would provide it with virtually all of the necessary components caused considerable concern in Israel and other countries.

Three years later in July 1980, *The Times* (London) quoted Saddam Hussein, now Iraq's president, as saying, 'We have no program concerning the manufacture of the atomic bomb.' The article went on to state, however, that

> President Husain [sic] implied several times that Arab nations would be able to use atomic weapons, adding – after his denial of any intention to make a bomb – that 'whoever wants to be our enemy can expect that enemy to be totally different in the very near future.' Circumspect though this phrase may appear, it is no secret that Iraq's nuclear reactor is expected to be commissioned in five months.

While not a direct contradiction of his disavowal of nuclear weapons, Hussein's statements raised serious doubts as to its credibility.

It is, however, not on the basis of these quotations that the Israeli government decided to destroy the Iraqi reactor in 1981. Iraq negotiated with France in 1974-75 the purchase of a dual-purpose gas-graphite reactor.[5] This type of reactor had served the nuclear-weapon countries in the past as a source of plutonium – in addition to electricity – with a production capacity of 400 kg of plutonium annually in the case of France. When France declined to supply this type of reactor, Iraq settled for a research reactor of the Osiraq type with a rated output of 70 ms(th), one of the biggest research reactors in the world. Both Iraq's original request and the plants, which were eventually agreed to and supplied, provided the Israeli government and interested public with a clear indication of Iraq's military schemes in the nuclear realm; Iraq's adherence to the NPT gave them no reassurance to the contrary. The Italians supplied hot cells which would serve for reprocessing, even though Iraq was not ready either in capacity or in outfittings to reprocess an irradiated fuel load by the time the reactor was bombed. Judging by the rate of Iraqi progress in acquisitions and building, it was assumed that under ordinary circumstances (that is, without extraordinary aid from Pakistan or other countries) it could take Iraq about five years to have a bomb.

At this point the Israeli government had to answer a number of questions:

1. Did the Iraqis want a bomb and would an Iraqi bomb constitute a threat to Israel? The answer was affirmative in both cases.

2. Could the danger be averted by diplomatic means? Discussions with France and Italy elicited the response that, as far as the conscience of the supplier nations was concerned, NPT and IAEA inspections were considered satisfactory, an attitude, however, which did not reassure the Israelis. In particular, no one denied that the Iraqi programme seemed odd and that Iraq might have in mind intentions other than those declared by it.
3. Was there any more reliable way to thwart an Iraqi threat? One possibility was to wait until the Iraqi programme matured, after which uncertainty over Iraqi intent breeds concern. This entailed two risks: the international community would do nothing and France, with its oil and military supplies, had a greater stake than just the sale of a reactor in its relations with Iraq; and if the installation had to be destroyed after start-up, which was scheduled for 1981, radioactivity would be released and more than buildings would be destroyed. Another possibility to thwart an Iraqi threat was through non-diplomatic means of intervention.

On the strength of these reflections, the Israeli government decided that the installation should be destroyed before start-up and that international censure was the lesser evil. Although it is not known which of the alternative measures were discussed, the decision taken is.[6]

Although the Israeli government's explanation to the public before and after the event was handled poorly, the government acted in accordance with its understanding of its responsibilities to the safety of Israel. Many people believe that the Israeli government could have restrained its actions and acted differently, but all agree that Iraq eventually wanted to have the bomb; that Israel would have no guarantee that Iraq would not be able to carry through with its programme; that Israel should not wait for hard evidence of this before it acted against the Iraqi threat; and that Israel failed to demonstrate how its interpretation of the Iraqi endeavour was much more widely shared, with some anxiety, by Syria, Saudi Arabia, Jordan and Egypt, as well as the industrialised countries.

On Libya's thinking, the following report from Professor Spector is enlightening:[7]

As the dealings with Pakistan and India unfolded, a high-ranking Libyan official openly confirmed his country's continuing interest in obtaining nuclear arms – despite its ratification of the Non-

Proliferation Treaty. According to Jeremy Stone, Director of the Federation of American Scientists, during a late 1978 Libyan-sponsored conference in Tripoli, Ahmed el-Shahati, head of the Foreign Liaison Office of the Libyan People's Congress, stated 'unequivocally that Libya is seeking nuclear weapons'. As Stone later wrote:

> That evening I dined privately with Shahati and his group of Western-trained people-to-people entrepreneurs. I opened the discussion by saying that our scientists were often quite tolerant of anti-American statements and widely varying politics. But we did draw the line at the use of science for killing innocent people. Were they going to persist in supporting terrorists, and were they seeking an atomic bomb? They were. Shahati made no bones about it, saying they would seek all weapons with which to defend themselves. To be sure I understood, I asked again were they seeking to maintain the right to get a bomb or actually trying to get the bomb itself? It was the latter.

The Federation subsequently wrote an open letter to Soviet ambassador Anatoly Dobrynin, urging the Soviet Union to reconsider its planned power reactor sale to Libya on the ground that Tripoli could not be relied upon to honor its renunciation of nuclear weapons under the Non-Proliferation Treaty. While it is unlikely that this letter was an important factor in Soviet decision-making, the Soviets have repeatedly postponed transferring the facility to Tripoli, as noted earlier, quite possibly out of concern over Khadafi's nuclear intentions.

Also, one cannot discount the various co-operation agreements to which Libya is a party, each of which purports to enhance its nuclear potential. Such agreements exist with Argentina, which reportedly received arms from Libya during the Falklands War in return for increased nuclear aid. Co-operation with two Belgian firms (Belgatom and Belgonucleaire), resulting in the United States making representations to the Belgian government without apparent success, and Libya's shipments to Pakistan of uranium purchased in Niger were widely reported and assumed to imply nuclear technology transfer in return.

The Prospects

If policies continue to be formed in the context of the present climate
in the Middle East, it is likely that Iraq, Libya, Iran and possibly
Egypt, will each wish to develop a nuclear weapon capability, irrespective of their formal commitment to NPT. This will not be in response to the assumed potential of Israel, which has hardly been
adduced as an incentive, but as an expression of the assertiveness of
these countries on the Middle Eastern scene, both with respect to
each other and *vis-à-vis* the existence of Israel.

Israel has long resisted pressures to adhere to the NPT. It places
no reliance on such adherence on the part of its declared enemies and
would – in the prevailing international climate – find itself arraigned
before the Security Council for the most spurious reasons if it were to
accede formally to the NPT. It should be remembered that for the
past many years, Israel has occupied more time of the Security
Council than all other local conflicts combined, and has been the
whipping boy of the United Nations for longer than that on any
pretext.

Israel, therefore, proposed that the countries of the region negotiate
a nuclear-weapon-free zone. The guiding idea was derived from the
Treaty of Tlatelolco, from all such treaties proposed for the various
zones on the globe, and from the recommendation of the Independent Commission on Disarmament and Security Issues (the so-
called Palme Commission) adopted by the General Assembly of the
United Nations.[8] It said:

> The Commission believes that the establishment of nuclear-
> weapon-free zones on the basis of arrangements freely arrived at
> among the states of the region or sub-region concerned, con-
> stitutes an important step towards non-proliferation, common
> security and disarmament. They could provide mutual reassur-
> ance to states preferring not to acquire or allow deployment of
> nuclear weapons as long as neighbouring states exercise similar
> restraint. This would improve the chances for the region not to
> become enveloped in the competition of the nuclear-weapon
> states. The nuclear-weapon states would have to undertake a
> binding commitment to respect the status of the zone, and not to
> use or threaten to use nuclear weapons against the states of the
> zone.

It was obvious to Israel that negotiation between the parties concerned was considered to be the principal confidence-building measure and that the commitment to a nuclear-weapon-free zone precluded the settlement of disputes even by conventional warfare. It seemed inconceivable that states of a region would contemplate enduring military engagements and at the same time place their faith in the loyal mutual administration of a nuclear-weapon-free zone. Israel's proposal had no support. Instead, an Egyptian proposal repeatedly has been adopted at the General Assembly of the United Nations, setting the sequence of acts thus.[9] First, sign the NPT and accept full-scope safeguards that go with it; and then last, 'pending the establishment of the zone, the States declare their support for establishing such a zone and deposit this declaration with the Security Council for consideration'.

The draft resolution on a nuclear-weapon-free zone in the Middle East contains no reference to negotiation between the parties at any time. Israel voted in favour of the Egyptian draft resolution but reserved its stance on the modalities, insisting that the priority of regional initiative and negotiation be adhered to also with respect to the Middle East.

More bluntly, Israel read the Egyptian proposal to serve notice that the Arab countries would not negotiate with Israel, would retain the option of waging wars against it, would wish to ascertain that Israel's adherence to the NPT did invalidate a potential threat arising from its technical competence in the nuclear realm, that Israel eventually could be dealt with, with impunity, and that ultimately there would never be a need to arrive at the stage of negotiating a nuclear-weapon-free zone. This reaction to Israel's proposal introduced a further measure of reluctance to its adherence to the NPT.

One would wish to conclude on a hopeful note. The portents of the Middle East contain no perceptible basis for hope at the present. It would appear that pressure should be brought to bear on all parties to sit down and to begin negotiating a nuclear-weapon-free zone. Alternatively, states that are apprehensive for their security should be embraced in protective alliances of such conviction as to obviate the need for an arms race. One may doubt whether either is feasible, but for all its virtues in the Middle East, it is not on the NPT – pitted against manifest designs that pervade the region and the unreliability of undertakings – that confidence can be built.

End Notes

1. Introductory remarks by Dr Hans Blix, Director General of the IAEA, presented on 11 December 1981 at the meeting with representatives of the media.
2. R. Rometsch, 'Fuel Cycle Safeguards', remarks at the Annual Meeting of the Institute of Nuclear Materials Management, Arlington, Virginia, June 1977.
3. Congressional Research Service, The Library of Congress, *An Assessment of the Proliferation Threat of Today and Tomorrow and Replies to Questions Asked by Senator William Proximire*, CRS-12; and 'Nuclear Arms Control – Background and Issues', National Academy of Sciences, Washington, D.C., pp. 270-1.
4. Leonard S. Spector, *Nuclear Proliferation Today* (A Carnegie Endowment Book, New York, 1984), p. 173.
5. *La Recherche*, no. 54 (March 1975).
6. There are many other issues which really do not touch the core of the affair, such as the quarrel between the experts on the plutonium-producing capacity of Osiraq concerning environmental differences between France and Iraq; the amount of radioactivity that would be released if the bombing of the reactor were delayed beyond start-up; the reliability of IAEA and French inspection; what Iraq could or could not do with the highly enriched uranium supplies of reactor fuel.
7. Spector, *Nuclear Proliferation Today*, p. 154. The reason for quoting putative transactions reflects the inevitable fact that their veracity is not of academic interest in the eyes of neighbours upon whom the designs of Libya are manifestly, and not putatively, directed.
8. Resolution 37/99B adopted by the United Nations General Assembly on 13 December 1982 and distributed as Document UNGA A/CN.10/38 of 8 April 1983.
9. See, for example, United Nations General Assembly Resolution 33/75 adopted on 9 December 1982.

THE FUTURE OF THE NPT:
A VIEW FROM THE INDIAN SUBCONTINENT

Ashok Kapur

Introduction

To study vertical and horizontal proliferation as objective realities in contemporary international relations, it is necessary to note four major tendencies in world affairs:

1. the trend of rapid and controlled vertical proliferation by the five nuclear-weapon states (NWS), particularly the United States and the Soviet Union. This is based on the notion that nuclear arms help national security. Vertical proliferation requires continued nuclear testing;
2. the tendency (and hypocrisy) of vertical proliferators and the crypto-nuclear states (such as Canada) which benefit from the full protection of the Western nuclear umbrella. These states participate in the making and implementation of NATO policies to preach the importance of horizontal non-proliferation. Their insinuation that the five NWS are responsible and the rest of the world is irresponsible and unstable, and that nuclear arms are good for the five NWS but not for the rest of the world, is conceptually and politically flawed;
3. the tendency of non-nuclear-weapon states (NNWS) to oppose the one-sided Non-Proliferation Treaty regime because it extends into international nuclear relations the concept that permanent members of the United Nations Security Council and particularly the two self-appointed guardians of world order have special rights and responsibilities;
4. the consensus at present among near-nuclear states (especially India, Pakistan, Argentina, South Africa and Israel) of the utility of their nuclear option and nuclear ambiguity.

201

These are irreversible tendencies in international nuclear relations today. The argument is not that the Treaty on The Non-Proliferation of Nuclear Weapons (NPT) is an East-West regime meant only to promote atomic monopoly, but that the NPT is widely perceived in the Third World – especially in India, Argentina and Brazil – to be a device to promote atomic colonialism. This perception is not without foundation. The record of multilateral and Western national diplomacy after the Atoms for Peace programme of the mid-1950s has been to strengthen supplier controls which restrict peaceful nuclear technology transfers. With respect to its peaceful technology transfer obligations which are laid down in the 1956 statute of the International Atomic Energy Agency (IAEA), it is significant that these statutory obligations have been compromised by the increasingly stringent (and, one might add, increasingly ineffective) requirements of the NPT system after 1968. With the ascendancy of the IAEA safeguards constituency over the one dealing with peaceful technology transfers, prospects of increased peaceful transfers as required in Article IV of the NPT are remote. Complaints about the IAEA's weak record of peaceful technology transfers are made by Third World states which are party to the NPT, as well as those states not party to the NPT but entitled to IAEA facilities by virtue of their membership in the IAEA.

The argument is not that the superpowers' claim of the NPT promoting 'international security' is without any meaning, rather in asserting that it is not self-evident that the NPT serves the interests of the global collectivity. The NPT does not serve the security interests of any middle or regional power located in areas of secondary international conflict outside the NATO and Warsaw Treaty Organisation (WTO) spheres: the Middle East, South Asia, Southern Africa and South America. The NPT is a political-cultural document which serves the interests of the superpowers and their military allies. It is 'international' in the sense that the NPT enjoys a consensus between Washington and Moscow as well as a consensus within the two military alliances. But even this East-West consensus has begun to erode in the wake of Soviet criticism that the Western world promotes selective proliferation in Israel, South Africa and Pakistan.

The NPT has near-universal membership. However, this fact is not significant, since a majority of NPT parties (with the exception of the five NWS and their allies) does not shape international nuclear-military relations, and all the near-nuclear states of significance are formally outside the NPT system. Adherence of non-nuclear countries to the NPT is a symbolic but an empty gesture. Furthermore, adherence of states such as Libya which have actively sought the bomb is an act of deception. Thus, in one sense, the NPT system continues to live and grow, and is not compromised until another state acquires usable nuclear arms. But in another and probably more significant sense, the practice of nuclear ambiguity by Israel, India, Pakistan, South Africa and Argentina (although the circumstances vary in each case) severely erodes the NPT regime. Nuclearisation of regional conflict zones in contemporary world politics already has compromised the NPT system. This pattern of development in four different continents has undermined the legal, psychological, technical, political-military and conceptual bases of anti-proliferation as the strategy was understood by the fathers of the NPT in the 1960s.

The Third NPT Review Conference

Background to Third Review Conference

The First Review Conference in 1975 produced a final statement, a last-minute compromise which 'saved' the conference. The Second Review Conference in 1980 was a failure: there was no final report and Yugoslavia's threat to withdraw from the NPT left a shadow on this conference. The Third Review Conference was a repeat of the second, but a formula to report 'progress' saved it.

The Third Review Conference took place in a background of continuing erosion of the political, psychological and technical underpinnings of the so-called NPT/IAEA regime, often mistaken to be 'the' non-proliferation regime. The IAEA's role as a barrier against further nuclear proliferation is now a limited one. The credibility of IAEA safeguards as the central instrument of anti-proliferation has been undermined by several events: Israel's attack on the safeguarded Baghdad reactor in 1981; the suspected failures of safeguards on Pakistan's KANUPP reactor in the mid-1970s and early 1980s (the IAEA subsequently reported that no diversion had occurred, but the matter is not yet resolved); testimony of an IAEA inspector (subsequently fired) casting doubt on the credibility of safeguards even as an accounting mechanism. A recent work by two former international officials[1] also casts doubt on the effectiveness of IAEA safeguards.

The NPT supposedly was a bargain between Article III (non-proliferation) and Article VI (nuclear disarmament). This bargain has been dead for almost a decade. As a policy objective and a line of pressure against both superpowers Article VI is without force. It cannot be used as a lever to pressure either the United States or the Soviet Union to disarm. The resulting undermining of the credibility of the peace and disarmament proponents that are left in the Third World has brought the new constituencies to seek regional order through controlled militarisation and nuclearisation in all major centres of regional conflicts; none seeks its own disarmament. Rhetorical poses and speeches are used by these constituencies to propose disarmament or neutralisation of their external enemies; the resulting rejections are then used to legitimise their own militarisation and nuclearisation.

The NPT was, and remains, a cultural document, extending into international nuclear relations the 1945 pattern of allocating special rights and responsibilities to wartime allies, particularly the United States and the Soviet Union. It is not, therefore, surprising that the NPT aroused counter-cultural and diplomatic opposition by secondary emerging powers wanting to exempt regional power-politics from interventionist pressures of the superpowers.

Since the mid-1960s operative objectives and purposes of the NPT in Western thinking have changed. The motivation initially was to settle the West German nuclear debate, and secondly the Swedish debate. The NPT succeeded in fulfilling these European aspects of treaty deliberations. Then the Soviet Union, which traditionally takes a hard line stance against proliferation, gave the NPT a universal meaning. The United States was slow to understand the Soviet motivation, but later recognised the merit of the Soviet Union's attitude on the subject. At this time in the mid-1960s, the IAEA was an agency in search of a mission. Safeguards gave the IAEA a lease on life, and from Vienna the safeguards/nuclear controls constituency emerged. After India's nuclear test the NPT became the umbrella under which supplier controls were strengthened, a process which began in the NPT context in the early 1970s. (In the pre-NPT context this process began in the 1950s when uranium suppliers were practising a strategy of supplier controls.) By the mid-1970s the orientation of the NPT had shifted decisively towards a strategy of controls and denial, and away from nuclear disarmament and curbing of vertical proliferation. Moreover, since the mid-1970s, various European and North American governments as well as the private nuclear industry have revealed a high tolerance for the flow of sensitive nuclear technology and supplies to Pakistan, a strategic ally of the United States. This trend exemplified the Western practice of selective proliferation, despite its public stance continually stressing the need to strengthen the NPT regime.

Thus the purposes of the NPT during the 1968-85 period have changed: from managing the Germans, to using the NPT as a fig leaf for nuclear trade and controls on undesirable activity, to establishing the practice of selective proliferation by Western parties to the NPT, especially the United States, the Federal Republic of Germany, the United Kingdom, Belgium, the Netherlands, Italy, Sweden and Canada.

Present Setting

Article VI of the NPT has no force. Its implementation is not possible under present conditions in the United States and among other NWS. To have practical meaning, Article VI would require a Comprehensive Test Ban (CTB) treaty. Recently, the Soviet Union advertised its willingness to accept a CTB treaty, but exact conditions for this initiative are not known.

Article IV of the NPT has no force. The position of this article also will be tested in the 1986 International Conference on Peaceful Uses of Nuclear Energy. It is most unlikely that this conference will result in a positive movement towards greater international cooperation on this point. The stranglehold of the United States and the Soviet Union on the work of the IAEA is likely to continue, obstructing the plea for increasing the role of the IAEA in the application of nuclear energy for peaceful purposes.

The Third World is bored by the NPT: bored by the tiresome speeches by the West and the Soviet Union about the need to strengthen the NPT regime; bored by the lack of progress in the field of disarmament by the United States and the Soviet Union; bored by the one-sided attempts by the West and the Soviet Union to strengthen controls on suppliers and safeguards arrangements which do not visibly alter the picture of vertical and horizontal proliferation.

While new nuclear-weapon-free zones (NWFZ) other than in Latin America are unlikely to emerge in the areas of regional conflict (that is, South Asia, Middle East, South Africa), tentative tendencies in New Zealand, Greece and the Scandinavian countries to seek NWFZ should be noted. However, nuclearisation of India, Pakistan, Israel, South Africa, Argentina and Brazil has occurred and appears to be irreversible.

Attitudes of India and Pakistan to the NPT Review Conference

While the incorporation of the Eighteen-Nation Disarmament Committee into the Committee on Disarmament (CD) was at the initiative of the non-aligned states, they have failed to use the CD in a creative manner. The CD in Geneva, the G-21, is in disarray. Although India's strong disarmament position is expressed repeatedly, most recently in the New Delhi Declaration, the disarmament constituency in India has been dead since the late 1960s. Where are the modern equivalents of Nehru, Krishna Menon and Arthur Lall in the Indian disarmament scene? Who and where are the disarmers in the major Third World capitals? Do they carry weight in national decision-making? It is significant that disarmament briefs in Third World capitals, including India's, are vetted by defence officials. This is as it should be because Third World military elites are repeatedly used to check hostile neighbours in order to contain dangers of super-power interventionist pressures and to manage local social and military conflicts. Foreign ministry officials who are tainted by foreign influences cannot be trusted with disarmament issues. In this setting it is appropriate that India had no interest in the Third NPT Review Conference. It did not attend even as an observer. Its well-known position on the NPT maintains that the treaty is conceptually and politically flawed, and now deserves no mention.

India's position on the NPT is independent of its China policy, its Pakistan policy and its nuclear policy. It is independent of the NPT policies of parties and non-parties of the NPT. The philosophical and legal bases of India's argument against the treaty maintains that reciprocal obligations should be the basis of international relations, and contracts must be respected, not changed unilaterally. Pakistan, on the other hand, has spoken the language of the NPT since November 1972, when Bhutto raised the possibility of a South Asian NWFZ (a few months after he decided in January 1972 to make the bomb). But Pakistan's posture of 'we will join the NPT if certain conditions are met' is not meant to facilitate its entry into the NPT. It is calculated to embarrass India, to make impossible demands and to legitimise its own nuclear activities. Significantly, Pakistan did not accept the Partial Test Ban Treaty even though India did. To imply that Pakistan follows India in regional arms control issues is therefore factually wrong.

Since 1972 Pakistan's NPT position has changed. In the 1960s Pakistan stressed the discriminatory effect of the NPT and geopolitical realities. In recent years it has focused on the need for negative security assurances. Pakistan cannot get India to agree on bilateral, reciprocal inspection; nor will Pakistan's nuclear activity help its security position *vis-à-vis* India and the Soviet Union. Still, it is likely to continue to play the NPT-game in the context of its decision to jump into the lap of the United States in 1981; and it will keep its nuclear option open. But Pakistan is not likely to succeed either as an NPT actor or as a proliferator against India unless direct nuclear assistance is given from China and/or the United States. The latter possibility cannot be excluded during the coming decade. Pakistan is potentially the biggest United States base in the area, complementing bases in Diego Garcia, Sri Lanka and access rights in select Indian Ocean littoral areas.

Nuclear Proliferation in the Indian Subcontinent

Indian and Pakistani elites have shown great deliberation in their decisions to use force. Military encounters in the past have been followed by quick return to normalcy. Indians and Pakistanis are rational, occasionally bloody, always calculating and usually difficult with each other. These attitudes underscore a process of slow, conscious and controlled nuclearisation of the Indian subcontinent.[2] The motivations influencing nuclear activities and behaviour on the subcontinent can be distinguished among those concerning attitudes and policies regarding the NPT/IAEA regime; those concerning attitudes and policies regarding respective nuclear options; and finally, those which may account for the quest for nuclear arms.

Scholars should not assume that the positions of India and Pakistan on the NPT reveal motivations in their nuclear options; or that motivations in the utility of a nuclear option reveal a motivation in nuclear arms. The motivations in each category are different. The literature on this subject reveals a tendency to assume that a combination of technical capacity and refusal to join a multilateral non-proliferation scheme automatically means that the country in question is going nuclear or intends to do so as soon as it can.[3] This worst-case assumption is wrong and dangerously counter-productive.

On the contrary, in assessing the international nuclear proliferation situation, we must consider that India and Pakistan at present find it in their security interests not to proceed to a nuclear weapons decision, yet avoid publicity for a non-nuclear-weapon status. That is, a country can be restrained without publicly adopting institutional means reflecting restraint. Both India and Pakistan have refused to sign the NPT, citing various reasons.[4] The nuclear posture and the nuclear activities of both countries are calculated to keep nuclear options open, and yet not to develop and deploy nuclear arms. This adds up to the practice of nuclear ambiguity, an important concept just beginning to penetrate Western consciousness. The position of a state that is seeking to keep the nuclear option open without actually going nuclear, and that deliberately does not declare its non-nuclear status, obviously is very different from the position of a state that restrains itself by joining the NPT regime. Both states may be potential proliferators, but the signals each conveys to its neighbours and the world are different.

In addition to categorising state-centric motivations, analysts should study nuclear proliferation by distinguishing between three types of proliferation: imminent proliferation; active proliferation; and latent proliferation. 'Imminent proliferation' refers to proliferation expected to happen quickly, but which actually does not occur; for example, Israel and India which were supposed to go nuclear in the mid-1960s.[5] Imminent proliferation reflects a state of the Western mind rather than actual realities in India, Pakistan, South Africa, Israel or Argentina. 'Active proliferation' is synonymous with vertical proliferation. Since 1945 active proliferation, coupled with images of imminent proliferation by irresponsible and unstable leaders outside NATO/WTO who want a quick bomb, has been the most common.[6]

In other words, what is known as imminent proliferation – what was seen as imminent proliferation by many Western analysts – is actually 'latent proliferation'. Latent proliferation is a profound tendency in contemporary world affairs found in all the major centres of regional conflict where select states see themselves as upwardly mobile in the international system. Latent proliferation is a dynamic activity. It means that in the cases of India and Pakistan, the proliferation curves have risen slowly since the 1940s for India and since the mid-1960s for Pakistan, controlled by decision-makers who avoid high risks and are not careless.

In this context it must be recognised that nuclearisation of India and Pakistan has occurred; the capability to make one or more nuclear bombs exists, and has existed for some time. However, such weapons-capable nuclearisation is neither equivalent to nor inevitably leads to deployed nuclear forces. At present there are strong incentives in both India and Pakistan against accepting NPT and full-scope safeguards, in favour of an extended nuclear option stance, and against adopting a nuclear weapons posture.[7]

In summary, both India and Pakistan have strong incentives to practise calculated nuclear ambiguity; that is, neither to adopt a nuclear weapons stance nor to adopt a purely non-nuclear posture. This, of course, is a type of behaviour distinguishing these two countries and other near-nuclear states from the five NWS. The novelty lies in attitudes and policies seeking to stretch out the nuclear option, actively seeking to preserve the position of nuclear ambiguity, and using near-nuclear status as a basis for active diplomacy. Many objectives are served by such diplomacy, principally: building support and coalition among external partners; mobilising domestic nationalism; encouraging restraint among external enemies through implied threat of imminent punishment; maintaining an active and current nuclear development programme; helping regional powers negotiate with more technologically advanced states and the superpowers.[8]

These objectives occur in pre-bomb diplomacy, where not only the threat to go nuclear under select conditions is useful in peacetime, but the option for conversion to nuclear-weapon state remains open should a military crisis occur, or should the strategic environment change and adversely affect the national interest. A study of nuclear ambiguity, therefore, requires careful assessment of external and domestic settings of a pre-bomb diplomatic practitioner.

The major elements of India's nuclear behaviour are straightforward and well understood. First, India possesses a nuclear weapon capability, demonstrated by its 1974 nuclear test and since enhanced by progress in its space programme. Its ballistics laboratories, space programme and research reactors are unsafeguarded. It has a reprocessing capability, and discussion continues regarding India's preparations for a second nuclear test and possible fusion device.[9] Second, the Chinese threat did not motivate India to go for nuclear arms, but it did motivate India to develop its option. At present, China can be contained by conventional military means.[10] Third, India's rejection of the NPT, couched in legal and philosophical terms, used the argument of discrimination. This argument was real and hard to dismiss, but the primary motivation for rejecting the NPT was to keep the nuclear weapons option open against China since the 1960s and now against Pakistan, as well as making sure that neither superpower took India for granted. An anti-NPT stance also finds support in Indian public opinion, and today no Indian government could possibly agree to the NPT. Fourth, there is no decisive motivation at present for Indian nuclear arms. They are not needed against either China or Pakistan because conventional arms and diplomatic alignments are sufficient for India's current security needs. However, were Pakistan to explode a bomb, the pressure would be there from the Indian bureaucracy and public opinion for another peaceful nuclear explosion (PNE) test.[11]

The main elements in Pakistan's nuclear behaviour are fewer but no less complex than those of India. First, Pakistan claims that the major motivation behind its nuclear programme is fear of India, yet India is not a realistic target for Pakistan's military capability. If Pakistan goes nuclear, India also goes nuclear. A Pakistani bomb is likely to legitimise an Indian nuclear stance, provoking an arms race which Pakistan cannot win. However, Pakistani fear of Hindus cannot easily be dismissed. It is one factor behind Pakistan's nuclear development, but it is not the factor which is likely to result in a Pakistani nuclear weapons stance. Second, Pakistan's nuclear path was neither always of a military nature nor always anti-Indian. In the latter 1960s Bhutto sold his nuclear programme to the Pakistani public on an anti-Indian appeal, but those were the days when the Ayub government was falling and Pakistanis wanted war. During the 1950s and 1960s Pakistan's nuclear programme was neither anti-Indian nor military in orientation. Today under Zia, its nuclear programme helps Pakistan obtain modern conventional arms from the United States. Pakistan is not solely or even necessarily anti-Indian because it is not evident that Pakistan's military leadership or the public wants war with India.[12]

What can Pakistan do with its bomb? Today the South Asian strategic agenda, to the extent a coherent one exists, is in the hands of intelligence officers, military men and their political masters; not in the hands of the nuclear planners, and definitely not in the hands of the disarmers. In South Asia there are no disarmers left. The nuclear planner can deliver the goods in the form of the odd test, but others in government control the decision-making. This means that Indian and Pakistani nuclear programmes do not suffer from the problem of technological drift or scientific determinism. But just because India and Pakistan can explode a bomb does not mean that they will; as yet, there is no imperative.

Conditions for Nuclear Weapons Development and Deployment

One consideration which favours a posture and a policy of nuclear ambiguity could include the acquisition of a nuclear weapon capability; that is, in the form of components of a small nuclear force which may be assembled and deployed at short notice upon a national decision. According to available literature, both India and Pakistan already possess a nuclear weapon capability. This is certainly true of India, given the variety of its atomic and space activities. Pakistan at least possesses the capability to explode a bomb for purposes of a political demonstration, but its present capacity to mount a small national force of a dozen or so weapons is questionable.

Judging from current evidence, India has developed, but not deployed, nuclear arms. The India-China competition has not been a determining factor in India's nuclear weapons consideration, even though Chinese nuclear deployments provide the opportunity to justify Indian nuclear weapons development. India has declined to adopt a nuclear weapons stance despite the Chinese presence. Nor has consideration of political prestige motivated the Indian government to deploy nuclear arms. Further, the Indian government's official stance still favours nuclear disarmament, a ban on nuclear weapons testing (not to be confused with a ban on nuclear testing which India does not support), and non-proliferation through nuclear disarmament of all countries, rather than the NPT to which it remains opposed.

Only two kinds of conditions are likely to govern an Indian decision to deploy nuclear arms in the contemporary regional security environment. First, if Pakistan were to explode a nuclear device – whatever the reason – no Indian government (irrespective of its ideology) could resist the political and bureaucratic pressure to develop a nuclear weapons posture. Second, if it became clear that the Soviet Union were no longer interested in Pakistan's status as a buffer state, then it could make sense for India to acquire some sort of minimum deterrent and to revise its alignments with China and the United States. The centre of gravity of Indian diplomatic and strategic actions has shifted to the northwestern sector of South Asia because this centre of Soviet actions is where geostrategic change is possible or likely.

To the extent that these speculations assume a change in the regional power structure and related international alignments, Western reactions to nuclear weapons development and deployment by India need not repeat reactions to India's 1974 nuclear test. If India's nuclear policy has been built on a foundation combining concerns over defence with an effort to accommodate Soviet interests, then foreign policy and East-West strategic considerations, rather than single-issue non-proliferation considerations, are likely to shape Western reactions to Indian nuclear weapons development. On the other hand, if India went nuclear because Pakistan did, and Pakistan went nuclear because India did, then standard anti-proliferation concerns and irrational fears of 'irresponsible' Third World leaders are likely to shape Western reactions.

The Long-Term 'Solution'

This chapter argues the need to distinguish between the NPT and the issues of both non-proliferation and nuclear proliferation. Having served its intended purposes in part (that is, *vis-à-vis* the Federal Republic of Germany), the NPT has no enduring utility. The NPT/ IAEA regime is full of loop-holes, and nothing of lasting value can be done to fill them. Only dead-ends await attempts to strengthen the regime. Ironically, the NPT has had important negative side-effects. It has destroyed the credibility of disarmers in the Third World who believed that Article VI of the NPT was sincerely intended and hence lobbied for the treaty for that reason. It legitimised nuclear options of the near-nuclear states. Hidden options became public as a consequence of the NPT's interventionist pressures, its attack on national sovereignty and, above all, its neglect of the national security needs of objectors of the NPT. Selective proliferation has taken place under the NPT/IAEA regime. The effectiveness of Article I is suspect when NPT parties have transferred sensitive and hard-to-obtain technology, equipment and material to a nuclearising country while speaking at the very same time of strengthening the regime. What should the West do?

Attempts to apply different rules to different states must be abandoned. In this case, invidious distinctions between the rights and duties of NWS and NNWS must be avoided. Such distinctions are likely to be labelled culturally, and possibly racially, discriminatory. Attempts at regime-making must be conceptually, legally and morally defensible. Specifically, why is nuclearisation of NATO/ WTO alliances acceptable, while that of the near-nuclear states is not? This hypocrisy must be amended.

The West needs to study the motivations of near-nuclear states by distinguishing between motivations which shape policies opposing the NPT/IAEA, the utility of nuclear ambiguity and nuclear option, and the disutility at present of nuclear arms. Academic study of nuclear ambiguity which is diplomatically sound, militarily useful and economically cost-effective is required. Unfortunately, many Western academics are a part of the problem because they have not critically evaluated the framework of governmental thinking. Rethinking is needed by academic and governmental practitioners. There must be a pause in the mindless drive towards the elusive goal of anti-proliferation, and thorough study must precede further policy action.

End Notes

This paper was written while the author was a Senior Associate Member, St. Antony's College, Oxford. It draws in part on research supported by the Social Sciences and Humanities Research Council of Canada. The author wishes to thank K.J. Holsti for his comments on an earlier draft and to Robert Reford for his help.

1. D. Fischer and P. Szasz, *Safeguarding the Atom: A Critical Appraisal* (Taylor & Francis, London, 1985; for SIPRI).
2. Because of the limitations of time and space, this section does not discuss details of each country's nuclear activities. Existing public sources are adequate. In any case, unclassified information is unavailable about some vital points; for example, whether Pakistan has enriched uranium beyond 3 per cent, whether Kahuta has experienced technical difficulties, or the reliability of Indian heavy water supplies.
3. This tendency is inherent in the Treaty on the Non-Proliferation of Nuclear Weapons (1968), the United States Nuclear Non-Proliferation Act (1978), United Nations resolutions on the subject, most writings issued under the auspices of the Stockholm International Peace Research Institute and, in most instances, of Western scholarly advocacy, which favours the NPT and opposes nuclear proliferation. Nevertheless, in the judgement of this author, it is peculiar that Western academic practitioners have gone along with the fallacious assumption since it was legitimised by the NPT in 1968.
4. The main, formal and public reasons for India's rejection of the NPT are: it is discriminatory; it divides the world into two types of nations, viz. the nuclear-weapon states and the non-nuclear-weapon states; it legalises possession of nuclear arms and indeed legitimises such possession by allotting special rights to the nuclear-weapon states; it is one-sided because there is no acceptable balance of obligations between the NWS and the NNWS; priority should be given to control of vertical proliferation, which is a danger to world peace; and so on.

   The main, formal and public reasons for Pakistan's rejection of the NPT are: it is discriminatory; Pakistan cannot sign the NPT because of (unspecified) 'geo-political realities'; Pakistan will sign the NPT if India, Israel and South Africa sign it.

   These reasons are frequently cited in official international conference statements by the two countries. Whether there are other centrally relevant motivations which underline the public postures of the two countries against the NPT is another question, and it is beyond the scope of this chapter.

5. 'Imminent proliferation' in the Middle East and South Asia was the central thrust of speeches from 1963 onwards by President John F. Kennedy and his brother Robert F. Kennedy. For examples of their statements, see quotations in A. Hodes, 'Implications of Israel's Nuclear Capability', *The Wiener Library Bulletin*, no. xxii (Autumn 1968), p. 2. Robert Kennedy was quite categorical in his expectation that about a dozen countries would go nuclear by 1968, the year the NPT was signed. This indicates an interesting relationship between a fallacious prediction which was made by prestigious and authoritative sources and their quest for international agreement for an anti-proliferation regime. Here I suggest that the fear of the unknown was unleashed to mobilise international support for the status quo, which favoured the nuclear 'haves'.

   In 1966 British writing reflected a debate on this point. A. Buchan, in his introduction to *A World of Nuclear Powers?* (The American Assembly, 1966), spoke of a chain reaction of nuclear proliferation from the 6th to the 16th nuclear power. This reflected establishment thinking. In contrast, L. Beaton, in his *Must the Bomb Spread?* (Pelican Books, 1966), made no such sweeping generalisation about a dangerous chain reaction. Beaton saw Japan, India and Israel as the 'most likely candidates' to acquire nuclear arms during 1965-75, but he predicted that they 'will engage in serious national debate on the question for years to come' (p. 69). In retrospect, it seems that Buchan was wrong but policy relevant. Beaton was right, but his analysis did not quite fit the official orthodoxy.

6. I cannot resist noting that the proliferating list of horizontal proliferators and proliferating images of irresponsible proliferators are proliferated by the active proliferators themselves, and here we have the basis for a proliferating academic industry!

7. For a fuller discussion, see my 'Pakistan' in J. Goldblat (ed.), *Non-Proliferation: The Why and the Wherefore* (Taylor and Francis, London, 1985; for SIPRI), pp. 141-9; and my *India's Nuclear Option* (Praeger, New York, 1976).

8. This paper does not address in detail the uses of calculated nuclear ambiguity by India and Pakistan. It should suffice to note that key practitioners in South Asia (as well as in Israel and South Africa), such as Bhutto (1972-77) and Zia ul-Haq (1977 to present) in Pakistan; and Bhabha (1948-66), Indira Gandhi (1967-68 and 1974-84) and Rajiv Gandhi (1984 to present), have used their nuclear activities to pursue some of the listed objectives of nuclear ambiguity. Empirical analysis is needed to develop case histories of the patterns, objectives and consequences of the uses of nuclear ambiguity in the foreign and military policies of secondary powers; and the objectives, strategies and consequences of the role of key bureaucratic players within the near-nuclear states also deserve study.

9. 'Shadow of an Indian H-Bomb', *Foreign Report*, 13 December 1984, pp. 1-2.

10. There are two Chinese divisions in Tibet; ten Indian divisions in the Himalayas, according to information relayed in confidence to the author by a South Asian specialist.

11. But it should be remembered that a decision to have another nuclear test is not necessarily a decision to deploy a nuclear force. Another PNE would mean another blow to the NPT regime, a signal to Pakistan to avoid a nuclear race, a signal to Washington and Beijing to rein in Pakistan and, last but not least, another test would temporarily disarm the Indian nuclear arms lobby, as did the first test.

12. Moreover, Pakistani domestic politics reveal a troublesome agenda. Tariq Ali has raised the question: Can Pakistan survive? This is a valid question. It is possible – and I hope I am wrong – that by the late 1980s or 1990s there will be either no Pakistan or a fragmented Pakistan. In this case, my topic may refer only to India, which seeks a status of middle power in the international system. I rather

suspect that India's quest for nuclear power has less to do with meeting the nuclear challenges of China and Pakistan, and more to do with its self-image, its search for a regional position, and international recognition of its middle power status. Thus Indian nuclearisation today may be studied in the context of India's development of economic and military strength – policies which are a far cry from Nehru's pleas for development and disarmament.

THE THIRD NPT REVIEW CONFERENCE, GENEVA, 27 AUGUST TO 21 SEPTEMBER 1985: A RETROSPECTIVE*

David A.V. Fischer

Overview

Object

Under Article VIII (3) of the Treaty on the Non-Proliferation of Nuclear Weapons (NPT), a conference is held every five years 'to review the operation of this Treaty with a view to assuring that the purposes of the Preamble and the provisions of the Treaty are being realised'. The Fourth Review Conference will take place in 1990. In 1995 'a conference shall be convened to decide whether the Treaty shall continue in force indefinitely, or shall be extended for an additional fixed period or periods'.

Summary

For the year preceding the conference, the media had been full of gloomy forecasts. To the surprise of many, the conference was a considerable success, in sharp contrast to the Second Review Conference in 1980, and a good deal better than the First Review Conference in 1975. Unlike 1980, the conference was able to reach consensus on a final report that strongly reaffirmed support of the NPT, contained many useful recommendations, and succeeded (at the last moment) in finding acceptable formulas on the three most difficult and divisive issues.

By far, the most profound was the lack of progress in nuclear arms control called for by Article VI of the treaty; in particular, the resistance of the United States (and the more muted resistance of the United Kingdom) to negotiating a Comprehensive Test Ban (CTB) treaty which, in the words of the NPT preamble, would ban 'all test explosions of nuclear weapons for all time'. In the Partial Test Ban Treaty of 1963, as well as in the NPT preamble, the three nuclear-weapon nations state and restate their determination to achieve such a ban and 'to continue negotiations to this end'.

One of the hidden issues here is 'Star Wars' (the Strategic Defense Initiative (SDI)). The Soviet Union's conditional moratorium on nuclear testing (6 August 1985 until 31 December 1985, unless the United States follows suit) and pressure for a CTB treaty appear partly aimed at preventing any test of nuclear explosives in research and development on anti-missile defences, while United States resistance to a CTB treaty is partly inspired by the need for such testing (and for Midgetman, MX and Trident II D-5 warheads). But it also reflects a broad change in United States policy since 1980.

The United Nations and the United Kingdom found themselves virtually isolated in this matter. Fortunately, on the night before the conference was due to end, it proved possible to reach agreement on a compromise text: the conference called for a resumption of CTB treaty negotiations in 1985, the United States stated that it set more store by deep, verifiable nuclear arms cuts, and the Soviet Union recalled its willingness to proceed with CTB treaty negotiations forthwith.

The second divisive issue was what the conference should do about the 7 June 1981 Israeli attack on the Iraqi Tammuz reactor and the related issue of the abilities of Israel and South Africa to make and use nuclear weapons. Here, too, the United States took exception to the majority conference position. In the end, the United States accepted a formula expressing the conference's 'profound concern' about the attack and recalling the terms of resolutions of other bodies – the United Nations General Assembly, the United Nations Security Council and the International Atomic Energy Agency (IAEA).

The third issue centred on the proposal of Australia (supported by Canada and several Western European countries but opposed by the Federal Republic of Germany, Switzerland and Belgium) that a non-proliferation commitment and full-scope safeguards should be a condition of supply of nuclear plants and materials. The agreed compromise came close to the Australian proposal: it urged all states 'to take effective steps towards achieving a commitment to non-proliferation' and full-scope safeguards as a basis for supplies. Canada, together with Australia, took the lead on the full-scope safeguards issue and Canada was the only country that went to some length to point out that safeguards on isolated plants were not only politically unsatisfactory but also that they were more complex, costly and gave less assurance that there was no diversion at the plant than if it were a part of a fully safeguarded fuel cycle.

At the eleventh hour, the Final Declaration consensus was nearly wrecked by Iran-Iraq hostility. In the early hours of Saturday morning, after an all-night session, the Australian disarmament ambassador prevailed upon the Iranians to withdraw a statement referring to Iraqi attacks on its nuclear facilities. The conference ended just before 6:00 a.m. on Saturday, 21 September 1985.

Thus in sharp contrast to 1980, the conference was, in the end, able to agree on what it wished to say to the world. Many factors have caused the change:

1. the unexpected spurt in membership of the NPT, rising by 17 from 113 in 1980 to 130 on the eve of the conference, showing that the treaty is alive and growing;
2. a greater awareness in the Third World of the mortal danger that nuclear war would present to every country and the importance of every measure to avert it;
3. increasing recognition by the Third World that the NPT is one of the few successes in this regard;
4. deeper fear of proliferation in all its forms (shown, for instance, in the relatively new concern about the stationing of nuclear weapons on the territories of NPT non-nuclear-weapon states (NNWS) – a form of creeping proliferation in the eyes of some and seen as new mobile nuclear-armed emergency forces of the superpowers);
5. recognition that the NPT has done much to stem proliferation, but growing fear of the nuclear potential of the threshold nations;
6. greater appreciation of the value of IAEA safeguards and growing support of full-scope safeguards as a condition of supply;
7. more optimism about the prospects for nuclear-weapon-free zones (NWFZ) with the success of the South Pacific Nuclear-Free Zone and some progress, at least on paper, towards an NWFZ as part of a 'Zone of Peace, Friendship and Neutrality' in South East Asia;
8. a growing desire for both negative and positive security assurances (negative: an undertaking not to engage in or threaten nuclear attack; positive: a promise to come to the aid of a state attacked or threatened by nuclear attack); and
9. a more realistic appreciation of the limited role nuclear energy can play in the development of Third World economies (no Third World country has launched a nuclear power programme since 1975, and many programmes are in serious difficulties).

Partly because of this, the rancour caused by suppliers' controls (the

Nuclear Suppliers Group's Guidelines of 1977 and the United States Nuclear Non-Proliferation Act of 1978) on nuclear exports has largely dissipated.

In 1980 the animosity generated by these controls dominated the work of one of the two committees; this time, the controls were hardly mentioned. Among the OECD countries, only Switzerland pursued the problem of export controls (because of the difficulties Switzerland is having with the United States in securing agreement to the reprocessing and recycling of Swiss spent fuel imported from the United States).

The conference managed to avoid several pitfalls: no defections or serious threats of defection; no proposals for amendment or revision of the NPT; and no polemics between the United States and the Soviet Union. On the contrary, the conference proceedings were generally business-like and low-keyed, thanks in part to very effective direction by the president, the chairmen of the committees, and the chairmen of the working groups.

Outcome

The positive results of the conference are summed up in its short, unanimous declaration, the strongest endorsement yet of the immense value of the NPT as 'essential to international peace and security', and in its lengthy and detailed report which records consensus on every major issue before the conference; the need for universal acceptance of the treaty; strengthening IAEA safeguards; international plutonium storage; NWFZ; security assurances; South Africa and Israel (as well as other unnamed threshold states); full-scope safeguards; the IAEA's role and programme in promoting technology transfer; and, finally, except for the United States and United Kingdom, the need to stop all nuclear tests.

With so many favourable portents, it seemed as though the conference would end in harmony and on time. However, two days before it was due to close, Ambassador Garcia Robles of Mexico, veteran of all NPT negotiations and reviews, with the somewhat reluctant support of the neutral and non-aligned groups (NNA), introduced three contentious resolutions. These bluntly called upon the NWS to begin negotiating a CTB treaty within the year, to accept an immediate moratorium on all tests, and to place a 'freeze' on new nuclear weapons development. Since there was no prospect of reaching a consensus on any of the resolutions, Western delegations generally interpreted them as a means of bringing pressure on the

United States to accede to an acceptable formula on the CTB treaty. At the same time, Iraq, frustrated by the United States unwillingness to accept any condemnation of the Israeli attack on Tammuz, tabled a lengthy and strongly worded resolution on this subject. Eventually, through the work largely of Ambassador Dhanapala of Sri Lanka, the conference agreed to the compromise noted above and Ambassador Robles agreed not to press his resolutions. The conference also found a way around the issue of the Israeli attack, and Iraq withdrew its draft resolution. The Iran-Iraq issue, which arose at the last moment, was settled by including statements by the two delegations in the report of the conference.

The Main Issues

Arms Control

The central focus at the Third Review Conference was the nuclear arms race and how this affected further movement towards an enhanced non-proliferation regime. In this context the main issues debated were vertical proliferation, nuclear arms control and disarmament (Article VI), a Comprehensive Test Ban treaty and the preambular paragraph to the NPT.

The Comprehensive Test Ban Treaty. With the exception of the United States and the United Kingdom, virtually all the participants in the conference (including NATO and ANZUS countries and Japan, as well as the Soviet bloc and the Third World) called upon the NWS to resume negotiations and conclude a CTB treaty as soon as possible. The Soviet Union made much of its conditional moratorium and of its readiness to accept a CTB treaty. Others saw the moratorium as an unverifiable ploy in the arms control manoeuvres between the superpowers and it received a rather lukewarm reception. Soviet Union readiness to negotiate a CTB treaty was more warmly welcomed and gave the Soviet Union a distinct tactical advantage. There were doubtless some who suspected that the Soviet Union did not seriously desire a permanent cessation of all tests, but was merely profiting from apparent United States intransigence and the fact that the Soviet Union had just completed tests on a new range of missiles. On the other hand, stopping SDI is proclaimed to be the first aim of Soviet Union foreign policy, and if a CTB treaty were to help do this (by inhibiting the use of nuclear explosives to produce the energy needed for X-ray laser beams to intercept and destroy missiles), the Soviet Union may well believe that a CTB treaty is worth the candle.

The United States argued that a CTB treaty would not eliminate a single nuclear weapon, and that the first aim of arms control agreements must be to make deep cuts in nuclear armaments. Although the United States accepted a CTB treaty as a long-term goal, too much focusing on it might be counter-productive, diverting attention to a secondary issue.

In the context of the NPT, these arguments cut little ice. Other delegates pointed out that a CTB treaty is the only arms control measure explicitly mentioned in the NPT, that the nuclear-weapon states' commitment to it in the Partial Test Ban Treaty as well as in the NPT is quite clear. They saw the CTB treaty as the only arms control measure that would simultaneously inhibit proliferation, put some brakes on the arms race, commit the NWS by treaty to significant restraint, and eliminate some of the irksome discrimination that the NPT makes between an NWS and NNWS.

Pressure on the United States mounted during the conference, but in the end the United States gave away nothing in substance, merely accepting the wording referred to above, specifically:

> The conference except for certain states . . . deeply regretted that a comprehensive multilateral Nuclear Test Ban Treaty banning all nuclear tests by all states in all environments for all time had not been concluded so far and, therefore, called on the nuclear-weapon states party to the treaty to resume trilateral negotiations in 1985 and on all nuclear-weapon states to participate in the urgent negotiation and conclusion of such a treaty as a matter of the highest priority in the Conference on Disarmament.

> At the same time, the conference noted that certain states party to the treaty, while committed to the goal of an effectively verifiable comprehensive Nuclear Test Ban Treaty, considered deep and verifiable reductions in existing arsenals of nuclear weapons as the highest priority in the process of pursuing the objectives of Article VI.

> The conference also noted the statement of the Soviet Union, as one of the nuclear-weapon states party to the treaty, recalling its repeatedly expressed readiness to proceed forthwith to negoti-

ations, trilateral and multilateral, with the aim of concluding a comprehensive Nuclear Test Ban Treaty and the submission by it of a draft treaty proposal to this end. (NPT/CONF.III/61)

The turn of events illustrated (if any illustration were necessary) that all the NNWS put together, with full support of the other superpower, are unable directly to budge by one millimetre a superpower unwilling to comply with an NPT commitment if it believes that such compliance conflicts with its defence priorities. Indirectly, however, the isolation of the United States may have some effect. Senator Carl Levin, of the Senate Armed Services Committee, publicly deplored both the unwillingness of the United States to sit down with the Soviet Union and the isolation of the United States from its allies. His strong views on this subject were lucidly expressed in an article in the *Washington Post* on 19 September. The day before, Senator Kennedy and 18 of his fellow senators sent a letter to all parties to the treaty urging the three NWS to resume negotiations on a verifiable CTB treaty.

Paradoxically, the current Republican Administration in the United States might be more able to secure a CTB treaty – if it so wished – than any possible Democratic successor. Unless the latter came in with a truly sweeping majority, it might face insuperable difficulties in persuading two-thirds of the United States Senate to ratify a treaty strongly opposed by the Pentagon, the Joint Chiefs of Staff and the Republican members of the Armed Services Committees of both houses. The record of Senate approval of arms control agreements is not encouraging.

Unless there is a major change in the political mood of the United States, the prospects of having a Comprehensive Test Ban treaty before the Fourth Review Conference in 1990 seem rather slim. At best, serious negotiations might be under way.

Other Recommendations on Arms Control. In other arms control areas, the conference (*inter alia*):

1. reaffirmed that nuclear proliferation 'would seriously increase the danger of a nuclear war';
2. expressed deep concern about the programme of the threshold states and proclaimed that 'any further detonation of a nuclear explosive device by any NNWS would constitute a most serious breach of the non-proliferation objective';

3. noted specific concerns about the nuclear weapon capability of South Africa and Israel, the calls for total prohibition of nuclear exchanges with either country, and a prohibition of the exploitation of Namibian uranium;

4. concluded that, since there had been no new arms control agreements, the objectives of Article VI (and related preambular paragraphs) had not been achieved and reaffirmed the commitment of all parties to these objectives. It called upon all states, particularly the NWS, to intensify their efforts and demonstrate their commitment. The United States delegate maintained in private that this was, in fact, an admission by the NWS that they had not done what they promised to do and an undertaking to do better. This, he maintained, was quite a step for the United States to take, and should be recognised as such;

5. welcomed ongoing United States-Soviet Union negotiations and hoped that they would lead to early and effective agreements aimed at preventing an arms race in space and terminating it on earth;

6. took note of General Assembly resolutions appealing for a quantitative and qualitative 'freeze', first by the superpowers, and then by all NWS;

7. reaffirmed the 'particular importance' of security assurances to NPT NNWS, took note of the 'continued determination' of the three NPT NWS to honour the 'positive' assurances they gave in 1968 (see Security Council Resolution 255 (1968)) to help any NPT NNWS attacked or threatened by nuclear attack;

8. regretted that 'no legally binding' instrument embodying such assurances had been achieved, and called upon the Conference on Disarmament to seek an acceptable common approach to this matter;

9. recommended further study of the possibility of applying IAEA safeguards to more plants in the NWS, when IAEA resources permit, and 'consideration of the separation of the civil and military facilities in the nuclear weapon states'. This stemmed from a Swedish proposal, with some support from other NNWS, and aimed at preparing the ground for an eventual 'cut-off' of the production of fissile material for military purposes; and

10. noted the steps being taken to create a nuclear-free zone in the South Pacific and encouraged the 'process of establishing such zones in different parts of the world'. The conference also endorsed Egypt's efforts to get matters moving on a Middle East

nuclear-weapon-free zone and noted that South Africa's nuclear weapon capability was the chief hurdle in the way of an African zone.

Safeguards and the Nuclear Fuel Cycle

With Australia, Canada and the 'White Angels' (a mocking reference to the Scandinavian countries) in the lead, some progress was made towards accepting full-scope (comprehensive) safeguards as the norm for nuclear exports. The conference eventually adopted a formula (see summary) which came much closer to the Australian draft than to the FRG/Belgian/Swiss counter-proposal that full-scope safeguards should be a long-term goal. But Bonn, defending the absent French as well as its own position, had difficulty until near the end in getting national agreement to the compromise. It remains to be seen what practical effect the conference's consensus on this point will have, but at least it obliges NPT exporters to be seen to be 'taking effective steps'.

The Australian draft and the conference's consensus goes beyond previous proposals for full-scope safeguards. They also call for 'a commitment to non-proliferation'. The simplest way of making such a commitment is obviously to accept the NPT, but presumably a formal declaration would suffice.

The proposed commitment may explain why the United States (and the United Kingdom) were unusually reticent on this issue. Taken literally, the required commitment would prohibit exports to non-NPT Spain, which depends partly on United States fuel for its quite large power programme and which has in practice accepted full-scope safeguards but has not made any formal non-proliferation commitment. Brazil, Chile, Cuba and North Korea are in much the same position: in practice, all their significant nuclear plants are believed to be under safeguards, but they have not made any non-proliferation commitments.

Canada made the point that full-scope safeguards are not only desirable as a matter of broad non-proliferation policy but also are needed to ensure effective safeguards. The IAEA's experience in Pakistan (with the CANDU KANUPP reactor) and India (with the TARAPUR reprocessing plant) shows that safeguards at such plants become more costly, less confident and probably more intrusive if key phases in the country's fuel cycle are not under safeguards or are under safeguards only when handling safeguarded fuel.

The conference recognised that safeguards in NPT NNWS are effective and do not hamper the nuclear industry or international nuclear co-operation. It addressed several recommendations to the IAEA and to states designed to increase the coverage of safeguards and make them more effective. The German Democratic Republic took the main initiatives in this matter.

There was some discussion of how to improve or complement safeguards at sensitive steps in the fuel cycle. The conference made the, by now, ritual endorsement of the concept of multinational or regional fuel cycle centres, but no optimism was visible. Australia, Canada and the 'White Angels' also proposed that the conference press for the creation of an International System for Plutonium Storage (to keep stocks of separated plutonium under international custody) and expressed some concern about growing stocks of separated plutonium. Belgium, the Federal Republic of Germany and others would not agree to any expression of concern but reluctantly went along with a formula recommending the IAEA to establish an 'internationally agreed effective' International System for Plutonium Storage.

A Point for Canada

The conference observed that spent fuel and nuclear waste storage are chiefly national concerns but saw 'advantage in international cooperation' in these matters.

Exports of nuclear plants to non-NPT (and to NPT) NNWS have dwindled almost to vanishing point except in the Far East, while the volume of nuclear waste continually grows. If the first trend continues, the issue of full-scope safeguards may become largely academic while the second arouses growing safety and proliferation concerns.

Canada could set a helpful example to other Western exporters in this regard. At the General Conference of the IAEA, which took place immediately after the NPT conference, Turkey reported that it was likely to buy a large CANDU reactor under a novel financing arrangement. CANDUs have excellent safety and operating records, and the head of the Pakistani Atomic Energy Commission once described them as ideal for developing countries. But CANDUs and their research counterparts, the NRX reactors, can easily produce weapons-grade plutonium (with a high proportion of Pu_{239}) and they have figured prominently in imports by countries whose nuclear activities have at times aroused concern (India, Pakistan, Taiwan, South Korea, Argentina). Canada has adopted the 'once through' fuel cycle: spent fuel from the many CANDUs and NRXs in Canada is not reprocessed but is stored underground for an indefinite period or permanently disposed of.

Lord Marshall, now head of the United Kingdom Central Electricity Generating Board, once vividly described spent fuel stores as 'Plutonium Mines' in which, after a decade or two of radiation decay, the plutonium becomes more easily accessible. The description is particularly apt if the spent fuel still contains a high proportion of Pu_{239}.

Turkey is an NPT party and an ally of Canada, but CANDUs go on operating for a long time, and Turkey is located in a troubled region where one would not wish to see 'plutonium mines'. Canada's negotiations with Turkey might thus provide it with a unique opportunity to arrange that spent fuel from the CANDU be returned to Canada and handled there in accordance with standard practice for Canada's own reactors. Turkey might welcome such an arrangement which would spare it the safety problems and cost of permanent spent fuel storage.

Peaceful Uses of Nuclear Explosions (PNEs)

The conference reaffirmed Article V of the NPT which obliges the NWS to make available to NPT NNWS 'the potential benefits from any peaceful applications of nuclear explosions'. It confirmed that the IAEA would be the appropriate channel for this purpose.

But the conference also noted that the potential benefits of PNEs 'have not been demonstrated' and that the IAEA has had no requests for PNE services since 1980. Might one hope that this brief reference is the funeral service for this technology?

Peaceful Nuclear Co-operation

Besides reaffirming at length the provisions of Article IV of the NPT, the conference showered compliments on the IAEA and (chiefly at the United Kingdom's initiative) made several proposals for making the IAEA's and states' nuclear aid programmes more effective. The non-aligned countries made a half-hearted attempt to revive a paper they had submitted to the 1980 conference but did not press it. The conference also commended the (limited) progress made in the IAEA's Committee on Supply Assurances and in preparations for the United Nations Conference on International Co-operation in the Peaceful Uses of Nuclear Energy (UNCICPUNE) which was to be held in 1982 (in retaliation against the Carter Administration's nuclear export policies) and might now take place in 1987. The conference relegated for further study an Egyptian proposal to revive the idea of an International Fund to help finance nuclear power plants in developing countries.

Israel, South Africa, Iraq, Iran

As noted in the summary, Israel's bombing of the Tammuz reactor in Iraq and Iraqi bombing of Iranian plants – rather than the more central and ecumenical issues of the nuclear arms race and nuclear testing – nearly wrecked the conference. At the last moment the conference was able to find formulas to paper over the wide differences of view. The United States would not accept any direct censure of Israel or any call for sanctions against it. In the end the conference resolved the matter by expressing its 'profound concern' about the Israeli attack, noting various General Assembly and IAEA resolutions and decisions and recalling and quoting a Security Council resolution to which the United States had subscribed and in which the Council considered that the attack 'constituted a serious threat to the entire IAEA safeguards regime which is the foundation of the Non-Proliferation Treaty'.

The conference also noted the 'great and serious concerns' expressed about the nuclear capability of South Africa and Israel, and noted the calls made to stop all nuclear contacts with both countries and all exploitation of Namibian uranium until Namibia becomes independent.

The solution found to the flare-up between Iran and Iraq at 5:00 a.m. on Saturday, 21 September was to attach a statement by each delegation to the final report of the conference. Physical exhaustion and Australian persuasiveness played their part.

Conclusions

On balance, the Third Review Conference was a considerable success and has helped to fortify the Nuclear Non-Proliferation Treaty by demonstrating that it commands wide-spread and strong support from all groups – non-aligned, neutral, Western and Socialist. There is general agreement that Articles I, II and III (horizontal proliferation) have been complied with, Article IV (peaceful cooperation) partly fulfilled and that Article V ('peaceful nuclear explosions') is a dead letter, and that the NPT and its regime have been an effective brake on further 'horizontal' proliferation. Far from unravelling, the treaty is more viable than in 1980.

The basic reason for this is a subtle but highly significant change in the attitude of the non-aligned countries. In 1980 they still saw the NPT chiefly as a proffered nuclear cornucopia. Today, judging by their statements and their obvious wish to make a success of the conference, they increasingly seem to see it as a means of enhancing their own security in their own regions as well as world-wide. It provides them with a verified non-nuclear regime and serves as the means to obtain or strengthen security assurances and to encourage NWFZ. The NPT is also a legal instrument, perhaps the only visible lever, for putting pressure on the nuclear-weapon powers.

Despite this generally positive development, the future of the NPT remains uncertain. It will largely depend on:

1. continuation of the United States/Soviet Union partnership in non-proliferation matters, as witnessed by the November 1985 Reagan-Gorbachov communiqué;
2. progress by the superpowers in nuclear arms control and disarmament, especially a CTB treaty;
3. whether the growing support of the Third World continues to take root during the next ten years or, at least, is maintained, which will depend upon the NPT continuing to prove its effectiveness as a barrier against proliferation, to contribute to regional and global security, and to evince progress in arms control;
4. whether the main threshold countries (Israel, India, Pakistan and South Africa) continue to refrain from openly demonstrating their nuclear explosive capability, where a South African or Israeli test or a nuclear explosive race between India and Pakistan could disrupt the regime or lead to withdrawals from the treaty;
5. what progress is made by Argentina and Brazil in mutual confidence-building arrangements (or full application of the Treaty of Tlatelolco) and in establishing additional NWFZ;
6. stronger and more consistent support from Western Europe; and
7. whether China and France move more closely into the regime.

Many of the recommendations of the conference will, no doubt, remain no more than pious wishes, at least for several years to come: a CTB treaty; a nuclear 'freeze'; a moratorium on testing; NWFZ in Africa, the Middle East and Europe; meaningful positive or negative security assurances to NPT NNWS (except in the framework of

NWFZ); full-scope safeguards as a universal condition of supply. Nevertheless, they do have a declaratory value as specific statements of the wishes of most of the 86 countries that attended the conference.

With so many imponderables, it would be rash to make any predictions about the long-term future of the treaty or the mood of 1995 when the parties must decide on its extension. By the time of the Fourth Review Conference in 1990, we should see whether the developing countries have indeed lowered their hopes about nuclear energy and about the treaty as a source of aid. Unless there is a vast revival in Third World prospects for nuclear power so that the atom is again seen as the best hope for transforming Third World economies, one would expect the present trend in Third World perceptions to continue. And the prospects for such an early revival of nuclear power in the North as well as the South seem today remote.

The question then will be whether the non-proliferation regime, of which the treaty is the cornerstone, effectively serves our security interests, first by keeping nuclear weapons out of our regions and second by reducing the danger of superpower nuclear conflict. If the answer is, on balance, yes, then one might hope that most parties will go into the 1995 conference in a positive mood attuned to a consensus, which already should be apparent at the preparatory meetings for the conference as it was in 1984 and 1985.

In this perspective, three groups of countries have most of the strands of fate in their hands: the United States/Soviet Union/United Kingdom; the non-party NWS (China and France, whose adhesion would be an enormous boost); and the threshold countries. The remaining parties – the vast majority – can chiefly help by seeking to influence the main actors and by refraining from actions – for instance, exports – that would damage the regime. One implication of this is that the non-nuclear parties, especially of the West which were certainly the least co-ordinated group at Geneva, must get their own act together if they wish to influence events.

September 1985 again showed that there is the constant risk from the seemingly extraneous wrecking factors: Israeli-Arab tensions, the Gulf war, apartheid. By 1995, although the Arab/Israeli problem probably still will be with the world, the latter two may be settled in some fashion; it is hard to imagine the Gulf war lasting another nine years without some manner of resolution. We cannot tell what other risks the future may hold, but we might be able to do more to reduce those that are now so obvious.

ANNEX

Organisation of the Conference

The conference elected as President Ambassador Mohamed Ibrahim Shaker, Deputy Permanent Representative of Egypt to the United Nations (and formerly representative of the IAEA to the United Nations), and it appointed 26 vice-presidents. The Secretary-General was Mr Benjamin Sanders, Director in the United Nations Department of Disarmament Affairs, from the Netherlands.

The conference allocated its work to three main committees (two in 1980):

Main Committee I: Non-proliferation in general – especially vertical, disarmament, international peace and security
(Chairman: Ambassador Jayantha Dhanapala of Sri Lanka)

Main Committee II: Non-proliferation – chiefly horizontal, safeguards, nuclear-weapon-free zones (NWFZ)
(Chairman: Ambassador Milos Vejvoda of Czechoslovakia)

Main Committee III: Peaceful applications of nuclear energy
(Chairman: Ambassador Ryukichi Imai of Japan).

Because of the divisive political issues with which Main Committee I had to deal, three working groups were delegated the task of formulating recommendations:

Group I: Articles I and II dealing with obligations of the NWS and NNWS
(Chairman: Ambassador Richard Butler of Australia)

Group II: Security assurances and aspects of Article VII on NWFZ
(Chairman: Dr Hubert Thielicke of the German Democratic Republic)

Group III: Article VI and Preambular Paragraphs 8-12 on disarmament, arms control, and the CTB treaty
(Chairman: Ambassador Jayantha Dhanapala of Sri Lanka, also Chairman of Main Committee I).

Delegates from 86 parties registered for attendance at the conference. The geopolitical breakdown was approximately: Western Europe, North America, Japan, Australasia – 25 countries, including 6 neutrals; the Soviet bloc – 10 countries, including Afghanistan; the Group of 77 non-aligned – 51 countries composed of 17 from Africa, 12 from Latin America, 13 from Asia, 8 from the Middle East, and Yugoslavia.

Ten states applied for, and were granted, observer status: Algeria, Cuba, Argentina, Israel, Bahrain, Pakistan, Brazil, Spain, Chile and Tanzania. Colombia and the Yemen Arab Republic, not having ratified the treaty, took part as signatories of the NPT without having a vote. Non-voting inter-governmental organisations present as observers were: the Agency for the Prohibition of Nuclear Weapons in Latin America (OPANAL); the League of Arab States; the Organisation of African Unity; the Organisation of American States. In addition, the Palestine Liberation Organisation was granted observer list were: France, China, India and the European Economic Community.

The neutral and non-aligned countries formed a group for the purpose of proposing measures relating particularly to arms control and the CTB treaty (but generally not on other matters dealt with by the conference), effectively splitting Western countries on these two issues.

The committees completed their work and reported to the conference on Tuesday, 17 September. This accomplishment sharply contrasted with both previous review conferences where one or both of the committees was unable to reach agreement on a report.

End Notes

* Much of the material in this paper is taken from a more detailed report that Dr. Harald Mueller and the author have prepared for the Centre for European Policy Studies.

APPENDICES

APPENDIX A

TREATY ON THE NON-PROLIFERATION
OF NUCLEAR WEAPONS

OPENED FOR SIGNATURE AT LONDON, MOSCOW AND WASHINGTON:
1 July 1968

ENTERED INTO FORCE: 5 March 1970

THE DEPOSITORY GOVERNMENTS: The Union of Soviet Socialist Republics,
the United Kingdom of Great Britain and Northern Ireland and the United States
of America

— —

The States concluding this Treaty, hereinafter referred to as the 'Parties to the
Treaty',
Considering the devastation that would be visited upon all mankind by a nuclear
war and the consequent need to make every effort to avert the danger of such a war and
to take measures to safeguard the security of peoples,
Believing that the proliferation of nuclear weapons would seriously enhance the
danger of nuclear war,
In conformity with resolutions of the United Nations General Assembly calling for
the conclusion of an agreement on the prevention of wider dissemination of nuclear
weapons,
Undertaking to co-operate in facilitating the application of International Atomic
Energy Agency safeguards on peaceful nuclear activities,
Expressing their support for research, development and other efforts to further the
application, within the framework of the International Atomic Energy Agency safeguards system, of the principle of safeguarding effectively the flow of source and special fissionable materials by use of instruments and other techniques at certain
strategic points,
Affirming the principle that the benefits of peaceful applications of nuclear technology, including any technological by-products which may be derived by nuclear-
weapon States from the development of nuclear explosive devices, should be
available for peaceful purposes to all Parties to the Treaty, whether nuclear-weapon
or non-nuclear-weapon States,
Convinced that, in furtherance of this principle, all Parties to the Treaty are entitled
to participate in the fullest possible exchange of scientific information for, and to contribute alone or in co-operation with other States to, the further development of the
applications of atomic energy for peaceful purposes,
Declaring their intention to achieve at the earliest possible date the cessation of the
nuclear arms race and to undertake effective measures in the direction of nuclear
disarmament,
Urging the co-operation of all States in the attainment of this objective,
Recalling the determination expressed by the Parties to the 1963 Treaty banning
nuclear weapons tests in the atmosphere, in outer space and under water in its Preamble

to seek to achieve the discontinuance of all test explosions of nuclear weapons for all time and to continue negotiations to this end,

Desiring to further the easing of international tension and the strengthening of trust between States in order to facilitate the cessation of the manufacture of nuclear weapons, the liquidation of all their existing stockpiles, and the elimination from national arsenals of nuclear weapons and the means of their delivery pursuant to a Treaty on general and complete disarmament under strict and effective international control,

Recalling that, in accordance with the Charter of the United Nations, States must refrain in their international relations from the threat or use of force against the territorial integrity or political independence of any State, or in any other manner inconsistent with the Purposes of the United Nations, and that the establishment and maintenance of international peace and security are to be promoted with the least diversion for armaments of the world's human and economic resources,

Have agreed as follows:

Article I

Each nuclear-weapon State Party to the Treaty undertakes not to transfer to any recipient whatsoever nuclear weapons or other nuclear explosive devices or control over such weapons or explosive devices directly, or indirectly; and not in any way to assist, encourage, or induce any non-nuclear-weapon State to manufacture or otherwise acquire nuclear weapons or other nuclear explosive devices, or control over such weapons or explosive devices.

Article II

Each non-nuclear-weapon State Party to the Treaty undertakes not to receive the transfer from any transferor whatsoever of nuclear weapons or other nuclear explosive devices or of control over such weapons or explosive devices directly, or indirectly; not to manufacture or otherwise acquire nuclear weapons or other nuclear explosive devices; and not to seek or receive any assistance in the manufacture of nuclear weapons or other nuclear explosive devices.

Article III

1. Each non-nuclear-weapon State Party to the Treaty undertakes to accept safeguards, as set forth in an agreement to be negotiated and concluded with the International Atomic Energy Agency in accordance with the Statute of the International Atomic Energy Agency and the Agency's safeguards system, for the exclusive purpose of verification of the fulfilment of its obligations assumed under this Treaty with a view to preventing diversion of nuclear energy from peaceful uses to nuclear weapons or other nuclear explosive devices. Procedures for the safeguards required by this Article shall be followed with respect to source or special fissionable material whether it is being produced, processed or used in any principal nuclear facility or is outside any such facility. The safeguards required by this Article shall be applied on all source or special fissionable material in all peaceful nuclear activities within the territory of such State, under its jurisdiction, or carried out under its control anywhere.

2. Each State Party to the Treaty undertakes not to provide: (a) source or special fissionable material, or (b) equipment or material especially designed or prepared for the processing, use or production of special fissionable material, to any non-nuclear-weapon State for peaceful purposes, unless the source or special fissionable material shall be subject to the safeguards required by this Article.

3. The safeguards required by this Article shall be implemented in a manner designed to comply with Article IV of this Treaty, and to avoid hampering the economic or technological development of the Parties or international co-operation in the field

of peaceful nuclear activities, including the international exchange of nuclear material and equipment for the processing, use or production of nuclear material for peaceful purposes in accordance with the provisions of this Article and the principle of safeguarding set forth in the Preamble of the Treaty.

4. Non-nuclear-weapon States Party to the Treaty shall conclude agreements with the International Atomic Energy Agency to meet the requirements of this Article either individually or together with other States in accordance with the Statute of the International Atomic Energy Agency. Negotiation of such agreements shall commence within 180 days from the original entry into force of this Treaty. For States depositing their instruments of ratification or accession after the 180-day period, negotiation of such agreements shall commence not later than the date of such deposit. Such agreements shall enter into force not later than eighteen months after the date of initiation of negotiations.

Article IV

1. Nothing in this Treaty shall be interpreted as affecting the inalienable right of all the Parties to the Treaty to develop research, production and use of nuclear energy for peaceful purposes without discrimination and in conformity with Articles I and II of this Treaty.

2. All the Parties to the Treaty undertake to facilitate, and have the right to participate in, the fullest possible exchange of equipment, materials and scientific and technological information for the peaceful uses of nuclear energy. Parties to the Treaty in a position to do so shall also co-operate in contributing alone or together with other States or international organizations to the further development of the applications of nuclear energy for peaceful purposes, especially in the territories of non-nuclear-weapon States Party to the Treaty, with due consideration for the needs of the developing areas of the world.

Article V

Each Party to the Treaty undertakes to take appropriate measures to ensure that, in accordance with this Treaty, under appropriate international observation and through appropriate international procedures, potential benefits from any peaceful applications of nuclear explosions will be made available to non-nuclear-weapon States Party to the Treaty on a non-discriminatory basis and that the charge to such Parties for the explosive devices used will be as low as possible and exclude any charge for research and development. Non-nuclear-weapon States Party to the Treaty shall be able to obtain such benefits, pursuant to a special international agreement or agreements, through an appropriate international body with adequate representation of non-nuclear-weapon States. Negotiations on this subject shall commence as soon as possible after the Treaty enters into force. Non-nuclear-weapon States Party to the Treaty so desiring may also obtain such benefits pursuant to bilateral agreements.

Article VI

Each of the Parties to the Treaty undertakes to pursue negotiations in good faith on effective measures relating to cessation of the nuclear arms race at an early date and to nuclear disarmament, and on a treaty on general and complete disarmament under strict and effective international control.

Article VII

Nothing in this Treaty affects the right of any group of States to conclude regional treaties in order to assure the total absence of nuclear weapons in their respective territories.

Article VIII

1. Any Party to the Treaty may propose amendments to this Treaty. The text of any proposed amendment shall be submitted to the Depositary Governments which shall circulate it to all Parties to the Treaty. Thereupon, if requested to do so by one-third or more of the Parties to the Treaty, the Depositary Governments shall convene a conference, to which they shall invite all the Parties to the Treaty, to consider such an amendment.

2. Any amendment to this Treaty must be approved by a majority of the votes of all the Parties to the Treaty, including the votes of all nuclear-weapon States Party to the Treaty and all other Parties which, on the date the amendment is circulated, are members of the Board of Governors of the International Atomic Energy Agency. The amendment shall enter into force for each Party that deposits its instrument of ratification of the amendment upon the deposit of such instruments of ratification by a majority of all the Parties, including the instruments of ratification of all nuclear-weapon States Party to the Treaty and all other Parties which, on the date the amendment is circulated, are members of the Board of Governors of the International Atomic Energy Agency. Thereafter, it shall enter into force for any other Party upon the deposit of its instrument of ratification of the amendment.

3. Five years after the entry into force of this Treaty, a conference of Parties to the Treaty shall be held in Geneva, Switzerland, in order to review the operation of this Treaty with a view to assuring that the purposes of the Preamble and the provisions of the Treaty are being realised. At intervals of five years thereafter, a majority of the Parties to the Treaty may obtain, by submitting a proposal to this effect to the Depositary Governments, the convening of further conferences with the same objective of reviewing the operation of the Treaty.

Article IX

1. This Treaty shall be open to all States for signature. Any State which does not sign the Treaty before its entry into force in accordance with paragraph 3 of this Article may accede to it at any time.

2. This Treaty shall be subject to ratification by signatory States. Instruments of ratification and instruments of accession shall be deposited with the Governments of the United Kingdom of Great Britain and Northern Ireland, the Union of Soviet Socialist Republics and the United States of America, which are hereby designated the Depositary Governments.

3. This Treaty shall enter into force after its ratification by the States, the Governments of which are designated Depositaries of the Treaty, and forty other States signatory to this Treaty and the deposit of their instruments of ratification. For the purposes of this Treaty, a nuclear-weapon State is one which has manufactured and exploded a nuclear weapon or other nuclear explosive device prior to 1 January 1967.

4. For States whose instruments of ratification or accession are deposited subsequent to the entry into force of this Treaty, it shall enter into force on the date of the deposit of their instruments of ratification or accession.

5. The Depositary Governments shall promptly inform all signatory and acceding States of the date of each signature, the date of deposit of each instrument of ratification or of accession, the date of the entry into force of this Treaty, and the date of receipt of any requests for convening a conference or other notices.

6. This Treaty shall be registered by the Depositary Governments pursuant to Article 102 of the Charter of the United Nations.

Article X

1. Each Party shall in exercising its national sovereignty have the right to withdraw from the Treaty if it decides that extraordinary events, related to the subject matter

of this Treaty, have jeopardized the supreme interests of its country. It shall give notice of such withdrawal to all other Parties to the Treaty and to the United Nations Security Council three months in advance. Such notice shall include a statement of the extraordinary events it regards as having jeopardized its supreme interests.

2. Twenty-five years after the entry into force of the Treaty, a conference shall be convened to decide whether the Treaty shall continue in force indefinitely, or shall be extended for an additional fixed period or periods. This decision shall be taken by a majority of the Parties to the Treaty.

Article XI

This Treaty, the English, Russian, French, Spanish and Chinese texts of which are equally authentic, shall be deposited in the archives of the Depositary Governments. Duly certified copies of this Treaty shall be transmitted by the Depositary Governments to the Governments of the signatory and acceding States.

IN WITNESS WHEREOF the undersigned, duly authorized, have signed this Treaty.

DONE in triplicate, at the cities of London, Moscow and Washington, the first day of July, one thousand nine hundred and sixty-eight.

APPENDIX B

STATUS OF STATES (INCLUDING STATES NOT MEMBERS OF THE UNITED NATIONS) IN RELATION TO THE TREATY ON THE NON-PROLIFERATION OF NUCLEAR WEAPONS

A. Parties to the Non-Proliferation Treaty

Afghanistan	1970	Greece	1970
Antigua and Barbuda	1981	Grenada	1975
Australia	1973	Guatemala	1970
Austria	1969	Guinea	1985
Bahamas, The	1976	Guinea-Bissau	1976
Bangladesh	1979	Haiti	1970
Barbados	1980	Holy See	1971
Belgium	1975	Honduras	1973
Benin	1972	Hungary	1969
Bhutan	1985	Iceland	1969
Bolivia	1970	Indonesia	1979
Botswana	1969	Iran	1970
Brunei	1985	Iraq	1969
Bulgaria	1969	Ireland	1968
Burkina Faso	1970	Italy	1975
Burundi	1971	Ivory Coast	1973
Cameroon	1969	Jamaica	1970
Canada	1969	Japan	1976
Cape Verde	1979	Jordan	1970
Central African Republic	1970	Kenya	1970
Chad	1971	Kiribati	1985
Congo	1978	Lao People's Democratic	
Costa Rica	1970	Republic	1970
Cyprus	1970	Lebanon	1970
Czechoslovakia	1969	Lesotho	1970
Democratic Kampuchea	1972	Liberia	1970
Denmark	1969	Libyan Arab Jamahiriya	1975
Dominica	1968	Liechtenstein	1978
Dominican Republic	1981	Luxembourg	1975
Ecuador	1969	Madagascar	1970
Egypt	1981	Malaysia	1970
El Salvador	1972	Maldives	1970
Equatorial Guinea	1984	Mali	1970
Ethiopia	1970	Malta	1970
Fiji	1972	Mauritius	1969
Finland	1969	Mexico	1969
Gabon	1974	Mongolia	1969
Gambia	1975	Morocco	1970
German Democratic Republic	1969	Nauru	1982
Germany, Federal Republic of	1975	Nepal	1970
Ghana	1970	Netherlands	1975

New Zealand	1969	Sudan	1973
Nicaragua	1973	Suriname	1976
Nigeria	1968	Swaziland	1969
Norway	1969	Sweden	1970
Panama	1977	Switzerland	1977
Papua New Guinea	1982	Syrian Arab Republic	1969
Paraguay	1970	Thailand	1972
Peru	1970	Togo	1970
Philippines	1972	Tonga	1971
Poland	1969	Tunisia	1970
Portugal	1977	Turkey	1980
Republic of Korea	1975	Tuvalu	1979
Romania	1970	Uganda	1982
Rwanda	1975	Union of Soviet Socialist	
Sao Tome & Principe	1983	Republics	1970
St Kitts and Nevis	1983	United Kingdom of Great Britain	
St Lucia	1979	and Northern Ireland	1968
St Vincent and The Grenadines	1984	United States of America	1970
Senegal	1970	Uruguay	1970
Seychelles	1985	Venezuela	1975
Sierra Leone	1975	Vietnam	1982
Singapore	1976	Yemen (Aden)	1979
Solomon Islands	1981	Yugoslavia	1970
Somalia	1970	Zaire	1970
Sri Lanka	1979		

B. Countries that have signed but not ratified the Treaty

Colombia
Kuwait
Trinidad & Tobago

C. Countries that have neither signed nor ratified the Treaty

Albania	Malawi
Algeria	Mauritania
Angola	Monaco
Argentina	Mozambique
Bahrain	Niger
Brazil	Oman
Burma	Pakistan
Chile	Qatar
China*	Saudi Arabia
Comoros	South Africa
Cuba	Spain
Djibouti	Tanzania, United Republic of
France*	United Arab Emirates
Guyana	Vanuatu
India**	Zambia
Israel	Zimbabwe
Korea, Democratic People's Republic of	

  *   Nuclear-weapon state
 **   India has detonated a 'peaceful nuclear device'.

APPENDIX C

NPT/CONF.III/64/I
ANNEX I
FINAL DECLARATION*

THE STATES PARTY TO THE TREATY ON THE NON-PROLIFERATION OF NUCLEAR WEAPONS WHICH MET IN GENEVA FROM 27 AUGUST TO 21 SEPTEMBER 1985 TO REVIEW THE OPERATION OF THE TREATY SOLEMNLY DECLARE:

– their conviction that the Treaty is essential to international peace and security,
– their continued support for the objectives of the Treaty which are:

  – the prevention of proliferation of nuclear weapons or other nuclear explosive devices;
  – the cessation of nuclear arms race, nuclear disarmament and a Treaty on general and complete disarmament;
  – the promotion of co-operation between States Parties in the field of peaceful uses of nuclear energy,

– the reaffirmation of their firm commitment to the purposes of the Preamble and the provisions of the treaty,
– their determination to enhance the implementation of the Treaty and to further strengthen its authority.

Review of the Operation of the Treaty and Recommendations

Articles I and II and preambular paragraphs 1-3

The Conference noted the concerns and convictions expressed in preambular paragraphs 1 to 3 and agreed that they remain valid. The States Party to the Treaty remain resolved in their belief in the need to avoid the devastation that a nuclear war would bring. The Conference remains convinced that any proliferation of nuclear weapons would seriously increase the danger of a nuclear war.

The Conference agreed that the strict observance of the terms of Articles I and II remains central to achieving the shared objectives of preventing under any circumstances the further proliferation of nuclear weapons and preserving the Treaty's vital contribution to peace and security, including to the peace and security of non-Parties.

The Conference acknowledged the declarations by nuclear-weapons States Party to the Treaty that they had fulfilled their obligations under Article I. The Conference further acknowledged the declarations that non-nuclear-weapons States Party to the Treaty had fulfilled their obligations under Article II. The Conference was of the view therefore that one of the primary objectives of the Treaty had been achieved in the period under review.

The Conference also expressed deep concern that the national nuclear programmes of some States non-Party to the Treaty may lead them to obtain a nuclear weapon

* Editor's Note: This appendix is reproduced directly from the Final Document of the Third Review Conference of the Parties to the Treaty on the Non-Proliferation of Nuclear Weapons, drafted in Geneva on 25 September 1985. No editorial changes either in style or substance have been made.

capability. States Party to the Treaty stated that any further detonation of a nuclear explosive device by any non-nuclear-weapon State would constitute a most serious breach of the non-proliferation objective.

The Conference noted the great and serious concerns expressed about the nuclear capability of South Africa and Israel. The Conference further noted the calls on all States for the total and complete prohibition of the transfer of all nuclear facilities, resources or devices to South Africa and Israel and to stop all exploitation of Namibian uranium, natural or enriched, until the attainment of Namibian independence.

Article III and preambular paragraphs 4 and 5

1. The Conference affirms its determination to strengthen further the barriers against the proliferation of nuclear weapons and other nuclear explosive devices to additional States. The spread of nuclear explosive capabilities would add immeasurably to regional and international tensions and suspicions. It would increase the risk of nuclear war and lessen the security of all States. The Parties remain convinced that universal adherence to the Non-Proliferation Treaty is the best way to strengthen the barriers against proliferation and they urge all States not party to the Treaty to accede to it. The Treaty and the regime of non-proliferation it supports play a central role in promoting regional and international peace and security, *inter alia*, by helping to prevent the spread of nuclear explosives. The non-proliferation and safeguards commitments in the Treaty are essential also for peaceful nuclear commerce and co-operation.

2. The Conference expresses the conviction that IAEA safeguards provide assurance that States are complying with their undertakings and assist States in demonstrating this compliance. They thereby promote further confidence among States and, being a fundamental element of the Treaty, help to strengthen their collective security. IAEA safeguards play a key role in preventing the proliferation of nuclear weapons and other nuclear explosive devices. Unsafeguarded nuclear activities in non-nuclear-weapon States pose serious proliferation dangers.

3. The Conference declares that the commitment to non-proliferation by nuclear-weapon States Party to the Treaty pursuant to Article I, by non-nuclear-weapon States Party to the Treaty pursuant to Article II, and by the acceptance of IAEA safeguards on all peaceful nuclear activities within non-nuclear-weapon States Party to the Treaty pursuant to Article III is a major contribution by those States to regional and international security. The Conference notes with satisfaction that the commitments in Articles I-III have been met and have greatly helped prevent the spread of nuclear explosives.

4. The Conference therefore specifically urges all non-nuclear-weapon States not party to the Treaty to make an international legally-binding commitment not to acquire nuclear weapons or other nuclear explosive devices and to accept IAEA safeguards on all their peaceful nuclear activities, both current and future, to verify that commitment. The Conference further urges all States in their international nuclear co-operation and in their nuclear export policies and, specifically as a necessary basis for the transfer of relevant nuclear supplies to non-nuclear-weapon States, to take effective steps towards achieving such a commitment to non-proliferation and acceptance of such safeguards by those States. The Conference expresses its view that accession to the Non-Proliferation Treaty is the best way to achieve that objective.

5. The Conference expresses its satisfaction that four of the five nuclear-weapon States have voluntarily concluded safeguards agreements with the IAEA, covering all or part of their peaceful nuclear activities. The Conference regards those agreements as further strengthening the non-proliferation regime and increasing the authority of IAEA and the effectiveness of its safeguards system. The Conference calls on the nuclear-weapon States to continue to co-operate fully with the

IAEA in the implementation of these agreements and calls on the IAEA to take full advantage of this co-operation. The Conference urges the People's Republic of China similarly to conclude a safeguards agreement with the IAEA. The Conference recommends the continued pursuit of the principle of universal application of IAEA safeguards to all peaceful nuclear activities in all States. To this end, the Conference recognizes the value of voluntary offers and recommends further evaluation of the economic and practical possibility of extending application of safeguards to additional civil facilities in the nuclear-weapon States as and when IAEA resources permit and consideration of separation of the civil and military facilities in the nuclear-weapon States. Such an extending of safeguards will enable the further development and application of an effective regime in both nuclear-weapon States and non-nuclear-weapon States.

6. The Conference also affirms the great value to the non-proliferation regime of commitments by the nuclear-weapon States that nuclear supplies provided for peaceful use will not be used for nuclear weapons or other nuclear explosive purposes. Safeguards in nuclear-weapon States pursuant to their safeguards agreements with IAEA can verify observance of those commitments.

7. The Conference notes with satisfaction the adherence of further Parties to the Treaty and the conclusion of further safeguards agreements in compliance with the undertaking of the Treaty and recommends that:

   (a) The non-nuclear-weapon States Party to the Treaty that have not concluded the agreements required under Article III (4) conclude such agreements with IAEA as soon as possible;

   (b) The Director-General of IAEA intensify his initiative of submitting to States concerned draft agreements to facilitate the conclusion of corresponding safeguards agreements, and that Parties to the Treaty, in particular Depositary Parties, should actively support these initiatives;

   (c) All States Party to the Treaty make strenuous individual and collective efforts to make the Treaty truly universal.

8. The Conference notes with satisfaction that IAEA in carrying out its safeguards activities has not detected any diversion of a significant amount of safeguarded material to the production of nuclear weapons, other nuclear explosive devices or to purposes unknown.

9. The Conference notes that IAEA safeguards activities have not hampered the economic, scientific or technological development of the Parties to the Treaty, or international co-operation in peaceful nuclear activities and it urges that this situation be maintained.

10. The Conference commends IAEA on its implementation of safeguards pursuant to this Treaty and urges it to continue to ensure the maximum technical and cost effectiveness and efficiency of its operations, while maintaining consistency with the economic and safe conduct of nuclear activities.

11. The Conference notes with satisfaction the improvement of IAEA safeguards which has enabled it to continue to apply safeguards effectively during a period of rapid growth in the number of safeguarded facilities. It also notes that IAEA safeguards approaches are capable of adequately dealing with facilities under safeguards. In this regard, the recent conclusion of the project to design a safeguards regime for centrifuge enrichment plants and its implementation is welcomed. This project allows the application of an effective regime to all plants of this type in the territories both of nuclear-weapon States and non-nuclear-weapon States Parties to the Treaty.

12. The Conference emphasizes the importance of continued improvement in the effectiveness and efficiency of IAEA safeguards, for example, but not limited to:

(a) Uniform and non-discriminatory implementation of safeguards;
(b) The expeditious implementation of new instruments and techniques;
(c) The further development of methods for evaluation of safeguards effectiveness in combination with safeguards information;
(d) Continued increases in the efficiency of the use of human and financial resources and of equipment.

13. The Conference believes that further improvement of the list of materials and equipment which, in accordance with Article III (2) of the Treaty, calls for the application of IAEA safeguards should take account of advances in technology.
14. The Conference recommends that IAEA establish an internationally agreed effective system of international plutonium storage in accordance with Article XII (A) 5 of its statute.
15. The Conference welcomes the significant contributions made by States Parties in facilitating the application of IAEA safeguards and in supporting research, development and other supports to further the application of effective and efficient safeguards. The Conference urges that such co-operation and support be continued and that other States Parties provide similar support.
16. The Conference calls upon all States to take IAEA safeguards requirements fully into account while planning, designing and constructing new nuclear fuel cycle facilities and while modifying existing nuclear fuel cycle facilities.
17. The Conference also calls on States Parties to the Treaty to assist IAEA in applying its safeguards, *inter alia*, through the efficient operation of State systems of accounting for and control of nuclear material, and including compliance with all notification requirements in accordance with safeguards agreements.
18. The Conference welcomes the Agency's endeavours to recruit and train staff of the highest professional standards for safeguards implementation with due regard to the widest possible geographical distribution, in accordance with Article VII D of the IAEA Statute. It calls upon States to exercise their right regarding proposals of designation of IAEA inspectors in such a way as to facilitate the most effective use of safeguards manpower.
19. The Conference also commends to all States Parties the merits of establishment of international fuel cycle facilities, including multination participation, as a positive contribution to reassurance of the peaceful use and non-diversion of nuclear materials. While primarily a national responsibility, the Conference sees advantages in international co-operation concerning spent fuel storage and nuclear waste storage.
20. The Conference calls upon States Parties to continue their political, technical and financial support of the IAEA safeguards system.
21. The Conference underlines the need for IAEA to be provided with the necessary financial and human resources to ensure that the Agency is able to continue to meet effectively its safeguards responsibilities.
22. The Conference urges all States that have not done so to adhere to the Convention on the physical protection of nuclear material at the earliest possible date.

Article IV and preambular paragraphs 6 and 7

1. The Conference affirms that the NPT fosters the world-wide peaceful use of nuclear energy and reaffirms that nothing in the Treaty shall be interpreted as affecting the inalienable right of any Party to the Treaty to develop research, production and use of nuclear energy for peaceful purposes without discrimination and in conformity with Articles I and II.
2. The Conference reaffirms the undertaking by all Parties to the Treaty, in accordance with Article IV and preambular paragraphs 6 and 7, to facilitate the fullest possible exchange of equipment, materials and scientific and technological

information for the peaceful uses of nuclear energy and the right of all Parties to the Treaty to participate in such exchange. In this context, the Conference recognizes the importance of services. This can contribute to progress in general and to the elimination of technological and economic gaps between the developed and developing countries.

3. The Conference reaffirms the undertaking of the Parties to the Treaty in a position to do so to co-operate in contributing, alone or together with other States or international organizations, to the further development of the applications of nuclear energy for peaceful purposes, especially in the territories of the non-nuclear-weapon States Party to the Treaty, with due consideration for the needs of the developing areas of the world. In this context the Conference recognizes the particular needs of the least developed countries.

4. The Conference requests that States Parties consider possible bilateral co-operation measures to further improve the implementation of Article IV. To this end, States Parties are requested to give in written form their experiences in this area in the form of national contributions to be presented in a report to the next Review Conference.

5. The Conference recognizes the need for more predictable long-term supply assurances with effective assurances of non-proliferation.

6. The Conference commends the recent progress which the IAEA's Committee on Assurances of Supply (CAS) has made towards agreeing a set of principles related to this matter, and expresses the hope that the Committee will complete this work soon. The Conference further notes with satisfaction the measures which CAS has recommended to the IAEA Board of Governors for alleviating technical and administrative problems in international shipments of nuclear items, emergency and back-up mechanisms, and mechanisms for the revision of international nuclear co-operation agreements and calls for the early completion of the work of CAS and the implementation of its recommendations.

7. The Conference reaffirms that in accordance with international law and applicable treaty obligations, States should fulfil their obligations under agreements in the nuclear field, and any modification of such agreements, if required, should be made only by mutual consent of the parties concerned.

8. The Conference confirms that each country's choices and decisions in the field of peaceful uses of nuclear energy should be respected without jeopardizing their respective fuel cycle policies. International co-operation in this area, including international transfer and subsequent operations should be governed by effective assurances of non-proliferation and predictable long-term supply assurances. The issuance of related licences and authorization involved should take place in a timely fashion.

9. While recognizing that the operation and management of the back-end of the fuel cycle including nuclear waste storage are primarily a national responsibility, the Conference acknowledges the importance for the peaceful uses of nuclear energy of international and multilateral collaboration for arrangements in this area.

10. The Conference expresses its profound concern about the Israeli military attack on Iraq's safeguarded nuclear reactor on 7 June 1981. The Conference recalls Security Council Resolution 487 of 1981, strongly condemning the military attack by Israel which was unanimously adopted by the Council and which considered that the said attack constituted a serious threat to the entire IAEA safeguards regime which is the foundation of the Non-Proliferation Treaty. The Conference also takes note of the decisions and resolutions adopted by the United Nations General Assembly and the International Atomic Energy Agency on this attack, including Resolution 425 of 1984 adopted by the General Conference of the IAEA.

11. The Conference recognizes that an armed attack on a safeguarded nuclear facility, or threat of attack, would create a situation in which the Security Council would

have to act immediately in accordance with provisions of the United Nations Charter. The Conference further emphasizes the responsibilities of the Depositaries of NPT in their capacity as permanent members of the Security Council to endeavour, in consultation with the other members of the Security Council, to give full consideration to all appropriate measures to be undertaken by the Security Council to deal with the situation, including measures under Chapter VII of the United Nations Charter.

12. The Conference encourages Parties to be ready to provide immediate peaceful assistance in accordance with international law to any Party to the NPT, if it so requests, whose safeguarded nuclear facilities have been subject to an armed attack, and calls upon all States to abide by any decisions taken by the Security Council in accordance with the United Nations Charter in relation to the attacking State.

13. The Conference considers that such attacks could involve grave dangers due to the release of radioactivity and that such attacks or threats of attack jeopardize the development of the peaceful uses of nuclear energy. The Conference also acknowledges that the matter is under consideration by the Conference on Disarmament and urges co-operation of all States for its speedy conclusion.

14. The Conference acknowledges the importance of the work of the International Atomic Energy Agency (IAEA) as the principal agent for technology transfer amongst the international organizations referred to in Article IV (2) and welcomes the successful operation of the Agency's technical assistance and co-operation programmes. The Conference records with appreciation that projects supported from these programmes covered a wide spectrum of applications, related both to power and non-power uses of nuclear energy notably in agriculture, medicine, industry and hydrology. The Conference notes that the Agency's assistance to the developing States Party to the Treaty has been chiefly in the non-power uses of nuclear energy.

15. The Conference welcomes the establishment by the IAEA, following a recommendation of the First Review Conference of the Parties to the Treaty, of a mechanism to permit the channelling of extra-budgetary funds to projects additional to those financed from the IAEA Technical Assistance and Co-operation Fund. The Conference notes that this channel has been used to make additional resources available for a wide variety of projects in developing States Party to the Treaty.

16. In this context, the Conference proposes the following measures for consideration by the IAEA:

  (i) IAEA assistance to developing countries in siting, construction, operation and safety of nuclear power projects and the associated trained manpower provision to be strengthened.

 (ii) To provide, upon request, assistance in securing financing from outside sources for nuclear power projects in developing countries, and in particular the least developed countries.

(iii) IAEA assistance in nuclear planning systems for developing countries to be strengthened in order to help such countries draw up their own nuclear development plans.

(iv) IAEA assistance on country-specific nuclear development strategies to be further developed, with a view to identifying the application of nuclear technology that can be expected to contribute most to the development both of individual sectors and developing economies as a whole.

 (v) Greater support for regional co-operative agreements, promoting regional projects based on regionally agreed priorities and using inputs from regional countries.

(vi) Exploration of the scope for multi-year, multi-donor projects financed from the extra-budgetary resources of the IAEA.

(vii) The IAEA's technical co-operation evaluation activity to be further developed, so as to enhance the Agency's effectiveness in providing technical assistance.

17. The Conference underlines the need for the provision to the IAEA of the necessary financial and human resources to ensure that the Agency is able to continue to meet effectively its responsibilities.

18. The Conference notes the appreciable level of bilateral co-operation in the peaceful uses of nuclear energy, and urges that States in a position to do so should continue and where possible increase the level of their co-operation in these fields.

19. The Conference urges that preferential treatment should be given to the non-nuclear-weapon States Party to the Treaty in access to or transfer of equipment, materials, services and scientific and technological information for the peaceful uses of nuclear energy, taking particularly into account needs of developing countries.

20. Great and serious concerns were expressed at the Conference about the nuclear capability of South Africa and Israel and that the development of such a capability by South Africa and Israel would undermine the credibility and stability of the non-proliferation Treaty regime. The Conference noted the demands made on all States to suspend any co-operation which would contribute to the nuclear programme of South Africa and Israel. The Conference further noted the demands made on South Africa and Israel to accede to the NPT, to accept IAEA safeguards on all their nuclear facilities and to pledge themselves not to manufacture or acquire nuclear weapons or other nuclear explosive devices.

21. The Conference recognizes the growing nuclear energy needs of the developing countries as well as the difficulties which the developing countries face in this regard, particularly with respect to financing their nuclear power programmes. The Conference calls upon States Party to the Treaty to promote the establishment of favourable conditions in national, regional and international financial institutions for financing of nuclear energy projects including nuclear power programmes in developing countries. Furthermore, the Conference calls upon the IAEA to initiate and the Parties to the Treaty to support the work of an expert group study on mechanisms to assist developing countries in the promotion of their nuclear power programmes, including the establishment of a Financial Assistance Fund.

22. The Conference recognizes that further IAEA assistance in the preparation of feasibility studies and infrastructure development might enhance the prospects for developing countries for obtaining finance, and recommends such countries as are members of the Agency to apply for such help under the Agency's technical assistance and co-operation programmes. The Conference also acknowledges that further support for the IAEA's Small and Medium Power Reactor (SMPR) Study could help the development of nuclear reactors more suited to the needs of some of the developing countries.

23. The Conference expresses its satisfaction at the progress in the preparations for the United Nations Conference for the Promotion of International Co-operation in the Peaceful Uses of Nuclear Energy (UNCPICPUNE) and its conviction that UNCPICPUNE will fully realize its goals in accordance with the objectives of resolution 32/50 and relevant subsequent resolutions of the General Assembly for the development of national programmes of peaceful uses of nuclear energy for economic and social development, especially in the developing countries.

24. The Conference considers that all proposals related to the promotion and strengthening of international co-operation in the peaceful uses of nuclear energy

which have been produced by the Third Review Conference of the NPT, be transmitted to the Preparatory Committee of the UNCPICPUNE.

Article V

1. The Conference reaffirms the obligation of Parties to the Treaty to take appropriate measures to ensure that potential benefits from any peaceful applications of nuclear explosions are made available to non-nuclear weapon States Party to the Treaty in full accordance with the provisions of article V and other applicable international obligations, that such services should be provided to non-nuclear weapon States Party to the Treaty on a non-discriminatory basis and that the charge to such Parties for the explosive devices used should be as low as possible and exclude any charge for research and development.
2. The Conference confirms that the IAEA would be the appropriate international body through which any potential benefits of the peaceful applications of nuclear explosions could be made available to non-nuclear weapon States under the terms of article V of the Treaty.
3. The Conference notes that the potential benefits of the peaceful applications of nuclear explosions have not been demonstrated and that no requests for services related to the peaceful applications of nuclear explosions have been received by the IAEA since the Second NPT Review Conference.

Article VI and preambular paragraphs 8-12

A.

1. The Conference recalled that under the provisions of article VI all parties have undertaken to pursue negotiations in good faith:

   – on effective measures relating to cessation of the nuclear arms race at an early date;
   – on effective measures relating to nuclear disarmament;
   – on a Treaty on general and complete disarmament under strict and effective international control.

2. The Conference undertook an evaluation of the achievements in respect of each aspect of the article in the period under review, and paragraphs 8 to 12 of the preamble, and in particular with regard to the goals set out in preambular paragraph 10 which recalls the determination expressed by the parties to the Partial Test Ban Treaty to:

   – continue negotiations to achieve the discontinuance of all test explosions of nuclear weapons for all time.

3. The Conference recalled the declared intention of the parties to the Treaty to achieve at the earliest possible date the cessation of the nuclear arms race and to undertake effective measures in the direction of nuclear disarmament and their urging made to all States parties to co-operate in the attainment of this objective. The Conference also recalled the determination expressed by the parties to the 1963 Treaty banning nuclear weapons tests in the atmosphere, in outer space and under water in its preamble to seek to achieve the discontinuance of all test explosions on nuclear weapons for all time and the desire to further the easing of international tension and the strengthening of trust between States in order to facilitate the cessation of the manufacture of nuclear weapons, the liquidation of all existing stockpiles, and the elimination from national arsenals of nuclear weapons and the means of their delivery.
4. The Conference notes that the Tenth Special Session of the General Assembly of

the United Nations concluded, in paragraph 50 of its Final Document, that the achievement of nuclear disarmament will require urgent negotiations of agreements at appropriate stages and with adequate measures of verification satisfactory to the States concerned for:

(a) Cessation of the qualitative improvement and development of nuclear-weapon systems;
(b) Cessation of the production of all types of nuclear weapons and their means of delivery, and of the production of fissionable material for weapons purposes;
(c) A comprehensive, phased programme with agreed time-tables whenever feasible, for progressive and balanced reduction of stockpiles of nuclear weapons and their means of delivery, leading to their ultimate and complete elimination at the earliest possible time.

5. The Conference also recalled that in the Final Declaration of the First Review Conference, the parties expressed the view that the conclusion of a treaty banning all nuclear-weapon tests was one of the most important measures to halt the nuclear arms race and expressed the hope that the nuclear-weapon States party to the Treaty would take the lead in reaching an early solution of the technical and political difficulties of this issue.
6. The Conference examined developments relating to the cessation of the nuclear arms race, in the period under review and noted in particular that the destructive potentials of the nuclear arsenals of nuclear-weapon States parties, were undergoing continuing development, including a growing research and development component in military spending, continued nuclear testing, development of new delivery systems and their deployment.
7. The Conference noted the concerns expressed regarding developments with far reaching implications and the potential of a new environment, space, being drawn into the arms race. In that regard the Conference also noted the fact that the United States of America and the Union of Soviet Socialist Republics are pursuing bilateral negotiations on a broad complex of questions concerning space and nuclear arms, with a view to achieving effective agreements aimed at preventing an arms race in space and terminating it on Earth.
8. The Conference noted with regret that the development and deployment of nuclear weapon systems had continued during the period of review.
9. The Conference also took note of numerous proposals and actions, multilateral and unilateral, advanced during the period under review by many States with the aim of making progress towards the cessation of the nuclear arms race and nuclear disarmament.
10. The Conference examined the existing situation in the light of the undertaking assumed by the parties in Article VI to pursue negotiations in good faith on effective measures relating to cessation of the nuclear arms race at an early date and to nuclear disarmament. The Conference recalled that a stage of negotiations on the Strategic Arms Limitations Talks (SALT II) had been concluded in 1979, by the signing of the Treaty which had remained unratified. The Conference noted that both the Union of Soviet Socialist Republics and the United States of America have declared that they are abiding by the provisions of SALT II.
11. The Conference recalled that the bilateral negotiations between the Union of Soviet Socialist Republics and the United States of America which were held between 1982 and 1983 were discontinued without any concrete results.
12. The Conference noted that bilateral negotiations between the Union of Soviet Socialist Republics and the United States of America had been held in 1985 to consider questions concerning space and nuclear arms, both strategic and intermediate-range, with all the questions considered and resolved in their

interrelationship. No agreement has emerged so far. These negotiations are continuing.

13. The Conference evaluated the progress made in multilateral nuclear disarmament negotiations in the period of the Review.

14. The Conference recalled that the trilateral negotiations on a comprehensive test ban treaty, begun in 1977 between the Union of Soviet Socialist Republics, the United Kingdom of Great Britain and Northern Ireland and the United States of America, had not continued after 1980, that the Committee on Disarmament and later the Conference on Disarmament had been called upon by the General Assembly of the United Nations in successive years to begin negotiations on such a Treaty, and noted that such negotiations had not been initiated, despite the submission of draft treaties and different proposals to the Conference on Disarmament in this regard.

15. The Conference noted the lack of progress on relevant items of the agenda of the Conference on Disarmament, in particular those relating to the cessation of the nuclear arms race and nuclear disarmament, the prevention of nuclear war including all related matters and effective international arrangements to assure non-nuclear-weapon States against the use or threat of use of nuclear weapons.

16. The Conference noted that two Review Conferences had taken place since 1980, one on the Sea-bed Treaty and one on the Environmental Modification Treaty and three General Conferences of the Agency for the Prohibition of Nuclear Weapons in Latin America. In 1982, a Special United Nations General Assembly Session on Disarmament took place without any results in matters directly linked to nuclear disarmament.

17. The Conference also noted the last five years had thus not given any results concerning negotiations on effective measures relating to cessation of the nuclear arms race and to nuclear disarmament.

B.

1. The Conference concluded that, since no agreements had been reached in the period under review on effective measures relating to the cessation of an arms race at an early date, on nuclear disarmament and on a Treaty on general and complete disarmament under strict and effective international control, the aspirations contained in preambular paragraphs 8 to 12 had still not been met, and the objectives under Article VI had not yet been achieved.

2. The Conference reiterated that the implementation of Article VI is essential to the maintenance and strengthening of the Treaty, reaffirmed the commitment of all States Parties to the implementation of this Article and called upon the States Parties to intensify their efforts to achieve fully the objectives of the Article. The Conference addressed a call to the nuclear-weapon States Parties in particular to demonstrate this commitment.

3. The Conference welcomes the fact that the United States of America and the Union of Soviet Socialist Republics are conducting bilateral negotiations on a complex of questions concerning space and nuclear arms – both strategic and intermediate-range – with all these questions considered and resolved in their interrelationship. It hopes that these negotiations will lead to early and effective agreements aimed at preventing an arms race in space and terminating it on Earth, at limiting and reducing nuclear arms, and at strengthening strategic stability. Such agreements will complement and ensure the positive outcome of multilateral negotiations on disarmament, and would lead to the reduction of international tensions and the promotion of international peace and security. The Conference recalls that the two sides believe that ultimately the bilateral negotiations, just as efforts in general to limit and reduce arms, should lead to the complete elimination of nuclear arms everywhere.

4. The Conference urges the Conference on Disarmament, as appropriate, to proceed to early multilateral negotiations on nuclear disarmament in pursuance of paragraph 50 of the Final Document of the First Special Session of the General Assembly of the United Nations devoted to disarmament.
5. The Conference reaffirms the determination expressed in the preamble of the 1963 Partial Test Ban Treaty, confirmed in Article I (b) of the said Treaty and reiterated in preambular paragraph 10 of the Non-Proliferation Treaty, to achieve the discontinuance of all test explosions of nuclear weapons for all time.
6. The Conference also recalls that in the Final Document of the First Review Conference, the Parties expressed the view that the conclusion of a Treaty banning all nuclear weapons tests was one of the most important measures to halt the nuclear arms race. The Conference stresses the important contribution that such a treaty would make toward strengthening and extending the international barriers against the proliferation of nuclear weapons; it further stresses that adherence to such a treaty by all States would contribute substantially to the full achievement of the non-proliferation objective.
7. The Conference also took note of the appeals contained in five successive United Nations General Assembly resolutions since 1981 for a moratorium on nuclear weapons testing pending the conclusion of a comprehensive test ban Treaty, and of similar calls made at this Conference. It also took note of the measure announced by the Union of Soviet Socialist Republics for a unilateral moratorium on all nuclear explosions from 6 August 1985 until 1 January 1986, which would continue beyond that date if the United States of America, for its part, refrained from carrying out nuclear explosions. The Union of Soviet Socialist Republics suggested that this would provide an example for other nuclear-weapon States and would create favourable conditions for the conclusion of a Comprehensive Test Ban Treaty and the promotion of the fuller implementation of the Non-Proliferation Treaty.
8. The Conference took note of the unconditional invitation extended by the United States of America to the Union of Soviet Socialist Republics to send observers, who may bring any equipment they deem necessary, to measure a United States of America nuclear test in order to begin a process which in the view of the United States of America would help to ensure effective verification of limitations on under-ground nuclear testing.
9. The Conference also took note of the appeals contained in five United Nations General Assembly resolutions since 1982 for a freeze on all nuclear weapons in quantitative and qualitative terms, which should be taken by all nuclear-weapon States or, in the first instance and simultaneously, by the Union of Soviet Socialist Republics and the United States of America on the understanding that the other nuclear-weapon States would follow their example, and of similar calls made at this Conference.
10. The Conference took note of proposals by the Union of Soviet Socialist Republics and the United States of America for the reduction of nuclear weapons.
11. The Conference took note of proposals submitted by States Parties on a number of related issues relevant to achieving the purposes of Article VI and set out in Annex I to this document and in the statements made in the General Debate of the Conference.
12. The Conference reiterated its conviction that the objectives of Article VI remained unfulfilled and concluded that the nuclear-weapon States should make greater efforts to ensure effective measures for the cessation of the nuclear arms race at an early date, for nuclear disarmament and for a Treaty on general and complete disarmament under strict and effective international control.

The Conference expressed the hope for rapid progress in the United States-USSR bilateral negotiations.

The Conference except for certain States whose views are reflected in the following subparagraph deeply regretted that a comprehensive multilateral Nuclear Test Ban Treaty banning all nuclear tests by all States in all environments for all time had not been concluded so far and, therefore, called on the nuclear weapon States Party to the Treaty to resume trilateral negotiations in 1985 and called on all the nuclear-weapon States to participate in the urgent negotiation and conclusion of such a treaty as a matter of the highest priority in the Conference on Disarmament.

At the same time, the Conference noted that certain States Party to the Treaty, while committed to the goal of an effectively verifiable comprehensive Nuclear Test Ban Treaty, considered deep and verifiable reductions in existing arsenals of nuclear weapons as the highest priority in the process of pursuing the objectives of Article VI.

The Conference also noted the statement of the USSR, as one of the nuclear weapon States Party to the Treaty, recalling its repeatedly expressed readiness to proceed forthwith to negotiations, trilateral and multilateral, with the aim of concluding a comprehensive Nuclear Test Ban Treaty and the submission by it of a draft Treaty proposal to this end.

Article VII and the Security of Non-Nuclear-Weapon States

1. The Conference observes the growing interest in utilizing the provision of Article VII of the Non-Proliferation Treaty, which recognizes the right of any group of States to conclude regional treaties in order to assure the absence of nuclear weapons in their respective territories.
2. The Conference considers that the establishment of nuclear-weapon-free zones on the basis of arrangements freely arrived at among the States of the region concerned constitutes an important disarmament measure and therefore the process of establishing such zones in different parts of the world should be encouraged with the ultimate objective of achieving a world entirely free of nuclear weapons. In the process of establishing such zones, the characteristics of each region should be taken into account.
3. The Conference emphasizes the importance of concluding nuclear-weapon-free zone arrangements in harmony with internationally recognized principles, as stated in the Final Document of the First Special Session of the United Nations devoted to disarmament.
4. The Conference holds the view that, under appropriate conditions, progress towards the establishment of nuclear-weapon-free zones will create conditions more conducive to the establishment of zones of peace in certain regions of the world.
5. The Conference expresses its belief that concrete measures of nuclear disarmament would significantly contribute to creating favourable conditions for the establishment of nuclear-weapon-free zones.
6. The Conference expresses its satisfaction at the continued successful operation of the Treaty for the Prohibition of Nuclear Weapons in Latin America (Treaty of Tlatelolco). It reaffirms the repeated exhortations of the General Assembly to France, which is already a signatory of Additional Protocol I, to ratify it, and calls upon the Latin American States that are eligible to become parties to the treaty to do so. The Conference welcomes the signature and ratification of Additional Protocol II to this Treaty by all nuclear-weapon States.
7. The Conference also notes the continued existence of the Antarctic Treaty.
8. The Conference notes the endorsement of the South Pacific Nuclear Free Zone Treaty by the South-Pacific Forum on 6 August 1985 at Rarotonga and welcomes this achievement as consistent with Article VII of the Non-Proliferation Treaty. The Conference also takes note of the draft Protocols to the South Pacific Nuclear Free Zone Treaty and further notes the agreement at the South Pacific

Forum that consultations on the Protocols should be held between members of the Forum and the nuclear-weapon States eligible to sign them.

9. The Conference takes note of the existing proposals and the ongoing regional efforts to achieve nuclear-weapon-free zones in different areas of the world.

10. The Conference recognizes that for the maximum effectiveness of any treaty arrangements for establishing a nuclear-weapon-free zone the co-operation of the nuclear-weapon States is necessary. In this connection, the nuclear-weapon States are invited to assist the efforts of States to create nuclear-weapon-free zones, and to enter into binding undertakings to respect strictly the status of such a zone and to refrain from the use or threat of use of nuclear weapons against the States of the zone.

11. The Conference welcomes the consensus reached by the United Nations General Assembly at its thirty-fifth session that the establishment of a nuclear-weapon-free zone in the region of the Middle East would greatly enhance international peace and security, and urges all parties directly concerned to consider seriously taking the practical and urgent steps required for the implementation of the proposal to establish a nuclear-weapon-free zone in the region of the Middle East.

12. The Conference also invites the nuclear-weapon States and all other States to render their assistance in the establishment of the zone and at the same time to refrain from any action that runs counter to the letter and spirit of the United Nations General Assembly resolution 39/54.

13. The Conference considers that acceding to the Non-Proliferation Treaty and acceptance of IAEA safeguards by all States in the region of the Middle East will greatly facilitate the creation of a nuclear-weapon-free zone in the region and will enhance the credibility of the Treaty.

14. The Conference considers that the development of a nuclear weapon capability by South Africa at any time frustrates the implementation of the Declaration on the Denuclearization of Africa and that collaboration with South Africa in this area would undermine the credibility and the stability of the Non-Proliferation Treaty regime. South Africa is called upon to submit all its nuclear installations and facilities to IAEA safeguards and to accede to the Non-Proliferation Treaty. All States Parties directly concerned are urged to consider seriously taking the practical and urgent steps required for the implementation of the proposal to establish a nuclear-weapon-free zone in Africa. The nuclear weapon States are invited to assist the efforts of States to create a nuclear-weapon-free zone in Africa, and to enter into binding undertakings to respect strictly the status of such a zone and to refrain from the use or threat of use of nuclear weapons against the States of the zone.

15. The Conference considers that the most effective guarantee against the possible use of nuclear weapons and the danger of nuclear war is nuclear disarmament and the complete elimination of nuclear weapons. Pending the achievement of this goal on a universal basis and recognizing the need for all States to ensure their independence, territorial integrity and sovereignty, the Conference reaffirms the particular importance of assuring and strengthening the security of non-nuclear-weapon States Parties which have renounced the acquisition of nuclear weapons. The Conference recognizes that different approaches may be required to strengthen the security of non-nuclear-weapon States Parties to the Treaty.

16. The Conference underlines again the importance of adherence to the Treaty by non-nuclear-weapon States as the best means of reassuring one another of their renunciation of nuclear weapons and as one of the effective means of strengthening their mutual security.

17. The Conference takes note of the continued determination of the Depositary States to honour their statements, which were welcomed by the United Nations Security Council in resolution 255 (1968), that, to ensure the security of the

non-nuclear-weapon States Parties to the Treaty, they will provide or support immediate assistance, in accordance with the Charter, to any non-nuclear-weapon State Party to the Treaty which is a victim of an act or an object of a threat of aggression in which nuclear weapons are used.

18. The Conference reiterates its conviction that, in the interest of promoting the objectives of the Treaty, including the strengthening of the security of non-nuclear-weapon States Parties, all States, both nuclear-weapon and non-nuclear-weapon States, should refrain, in accordance with the Charter of the United Nations, from the threat or the use of force in relations between States, involving either nuclear or non-nuclear weapons.

19. The Conference recalls that the Tenth Special Session of the General Assembly in paragraph 59 of the Final Document took note of the declarations made by the nuclear-weapon States regarding the assurance of non-nuclear-weapon States against the use or threat of use of nuclear weapons and urged them to pursue efforts to conclude, as appropriate, effective arrangements to assure non-nuclear-weapon States against the use of threat of use of nuclear weapons.

20. Being aware of the consultations and negotiations on effective international arrangements to assure non-nuclear-weapon States against the use of threat of use of nuclear weapons, which have been under way in the Conference on Disarmament for several years, the Conference regrets that the search for a common approach which could be included in an international legally binding instrument, has been unsuccessful. The Conference takes note of the repeatedly expressed intention of the Conference on Disarmament to continue to explore ways and means to overcome the difficulties encountered in its work and to carry out negotiations on the question of effective international arrangements to assure non-nuclear-weapon States against the use or threat of use of nuclear weapons. In this connection, the Conference calls upon all States, particularly the nuclear-weapon States, to continue the negotiations in the Conference on Disarmament devoted to the search for a common approach acceptable to all, which could be included in an international instrument of a legally binding character.

Article VIII

The States Party to the Treaty participating in the Conference propose to the Depositary Governments that a fourth Conference to review the operation of the Treaty be convened in 1990.

The Conference accordingly invites States Party to the Treaty which are Members of the United Nations to request the Secretary-General of the United Nations to include the following item in the provisional agenda of the forty-third session of the General Assembly:

"Implementation of the conclusions of the third Review Conference of the Parties to the Treaty on the Non-Proliferation of Nuclear Weapons and establishment of a Preparatory Committee for the fourth Conference."

Article IX

The Conference, having expressed great satisfaction that the overwhelming majority of States have acceded to the Treaty on the Non-Proliferation of Nuclear Weapons and having recognized the urgent need for further ensuring the universality of the Treaty, appeals to all States, particularly the nuclear-weapon States and other States advanced in nuclear technology, which have not yet done so, to adhere to the Treaty at the earliest possible date.

DECLARATION BY THE GROUP OF NON-ALIGNED AND NEUTRAL STATES

The delegations of the States members of the Group of Non-aligned and Neutral States taking part in the Third Review Conference of the Parties to the Treaty on the Non-Proliferation of Nuclear Weapons submitted to the Conference the following three draft resolutions:

1. Draft resolution on a Comprehensive Nuclear Test Ban (NPT/CONF.III/L.1)
2. Draft resolution on a Nuclear Test Ban Moratorium (NPT/CONF.III/L.2)
3. Draft resolution on a Nuclear-Arms Freeze (NPT/CONF.III/L.3)

The objective pursued by the first of those three draft resolutions was achieved on the closing day of the Conference thanks to the approval by consensus, for inclusion in paragraph 12 of the Final Declaration of the Conference, of a text in which, with the exception indicated therein, it is unequivocally declared that:

> The Conference . . . deeply regretted that a comprehensive multilateral nuclear test-ban treaty banning all nuclear tests by all States in all environments for all time had not been concluded so far and, therefore, called on the nuclear weapon States party to the Treaty to resume trilateral negotiations in 1985 and called on all the nuclear-weapon States to participate in the urgent negotiation and conclusion of such a treaty as a matter of the highest priority in the Conference on Disarmament.

With regard to the other two above-mentioned draft resolutions, the sponsoring delegations wish to place on record that they have decided not to press them to a vote on this occasion for the following reasons: that there was unanimous acceptance for the reproduction of their texts together with this Declaration, immediately following the test of the Final Declaration, and that in paragraphs B-7 and B-9 of the Final Declaration, the Conference explicitly took note of the repeated appeals contained in many resolutions of the United Nations General Assembly, as well as of 'similar calls made at this Conference' in connection with a moratorium on nuclear weapons testing and a quantitative and qualitative freeze of all nuclear weapons, respectively.

GROUP OF NON-ALIGNED AND NEUTRAL STATES

Draft Resolution on a Nuclear Test Ban Moratorium
(Document NPT/CONF.III/L.2)

The Third Review Conference of the Parties to the Treaty on the Non-Proliferation of Nuclear Weapons,

Recalling that article VI of the Treaty on the Non-Proliferation of Nuclear Weapons contains an undertaking by each of the Parties 'to pursue negotiations in good faith on effective measures relating to cessation of the nuclear arms race at an early date',

Considering that the cessation of all nuclear weapon tests constitute a most important and effective measure for the qualitative cessation of the nuclear arms race,

Considering further that a moratorium on nuclear test explosions, as a provisional measure, has been called for the General Assembly of the United Nations at each of its last five sessions,

Calls upon the three Depositary States of the Treaty on the Non-Proliferation of Nuclear Weapons to institute, as a provisional measure, an immediate moratorium on all nuclear weapon tests.

GROUP OF NON-ALIGNED AND NEUTRAL STATES

Draft Resolution on a Nuclear-Arms Freeze
(Document NPT/CONF.III.L.3)

The Third Review Conference of the Parties to the Treaty on the Non-Proliferation of Nuclear Weapons,

Recalling that article VI of the Treaty on the Non-Proliferation of Nuclear Weapons contains an undertaking by each of the Parties 'to pursue negotiations in good faith on effective measures relating to cessation of the nuclear-arms race at an early date and to nuclear disarmament',

Considering that a nuclear-arms freeze, while not an end in itself, would constitute the most effective first step for a cessation of the nuclear-arms race,

Calls on three Depositary States of the Treaty on the Non-Proliferation of Nuclear Weapons:

1. To agree on a complete freeze on the testing, production and deployment of all nuclear weapons and their delivery vehicles;
2. To begin negotiations for substantial reductions of their existing stockpiles of nuclear weapons and delivery vehicles.

APPENDIX D

GLOSSARY OF TERMS AND TREATIES

I. TERMS

Agency for the Prohibition of Nuclear Weapons in Latin America (OPANAL)
The agency that is responsible for supervising compliance with the Treaty of Tlatelolco (1967). Biannual consultations are held among members in agency headquarters in Mexico City.

Atomic Colonialism
The perception by many Third World or developing countries that the current non-proliferation regime (especially the NPT) is merely a new form of colonialism designed to deprive the less-developed countries of the economic gains, technology and status that the nuclear industry (and nuclear weapons) gives to the NWS. This atomic monopoly is seen as further perpetuating North-South divisions and inequities while reinforcing East-West privileges. Third World countries in particular criticise what they see as the 'selective proliferation' tolerated by Western nuclear supplier states party to the NPT.

Atoms for Peace
Programme developed in the Eisenhower Administration (1953), which advocated the development of a 'pool' of atomic material to be used by all countries for peaceful purposes. The proposal was rejected out of hand by the Soviet Union because it did not attend to problems of the non-peaceful use of the atom. Nonetheless, this proposal resulted in many bilateral agreements with the United States for the sharing of peaceful nuclear technology. These, however, did not include safeguards against proliferation.

Baruch Plan
One of the first proposals for controlling atomic weapons; submitted by the United States to the United Nations Atomic Energy Commission in 1946. The plan advocated the setting up of an international agency to control the use of nuclear energy and safeguards against non-peaceful violations and the elimination of all atomic stockpiles after the agency had established control. The plan was rejected by the Soviet Union which feared that the United States would remain the only country with a nuclear weapon capability.

Breeder Reactor
Reactor that produces more fissile material than it consumes. Has been considered as 'sensitive technology' because these reactors can produce as much as seven times the plutonium as light water reactors.

Canadian Deuterium-Uranium Reactor (CANDU)
Canadian-designed heavy water reactor that is fueled with natural uranium or low-grade fissile material; heavy water (D_2O) acts as a coolant. Produces plutonium that might be enriched to a weapons-grade level after processing; however, this currently is not economical.

259

Committee on Disarmament (CD)

The main forum for multilateral arms control negotiations began with the 1961 establishment of the Eighteen-Nation Disarmament Committee, the body ultimately responsible for the 1964-68 negotiations leading to the NPT. Members of ENDC included the United States, Soviet Union, European countries and developing nations (formerly the Ten-Nation Disarmament Committee). In 1969 ENDC was enlarged to 26 members and was called the Conference on the Committee on Disarmament (CCD); this was expanded to the 40-member Committee on Disarmament (CD) in 1978. In addition to nuclear non-proliferation, the CD has been concerned with a Comprehensive Test Ban, chemical and radiological weapons, and cessation of the arms race in general.

Comprehensive Test Ban (CTB)

A proposal, originally arising in 1962 prior to the Partial Test Ban Treaty, that all nuclear tests (atmospheric, surface and underground) be banned. Controversy in the early years surrounded verification and, although technical advances have decreased the overall importance of this objection in more recent years, verification continues to be employed as one of the major impediments. Calls are still made for a CTB; however, to date they have been unsuccessful. A CTB is viewed by some as a way of eliminating the discrimination of the NPT towards NNWS.

Dove's Dilemma

The dilemma of whether to increase conventional arms transfers to nuclear threshold states in the hope that these states will forgo nuclear weapons development and accept conventional weapons as adequate for regional security needs. There is, of course, no guarantee that such a strategy is effective in deterring the acquisition of nuclear weapons.

Eighteen-Nation Disarmament Committee (ENDC)

See Committee on Disarmament.

Emergent Suppliers or Second- and Third-Tier Suppliers

New suppliers of nuclear materials and technology, which, since the 1980s, have included many developing countries that receive materials and technology under safeguards but then sell the same without safeguards. Emergent suppliers include countries such as Argentina, Brazil, India, China, Israel, South Korea, Spain and South Africa. By failing to achieve a consensus on export controls and safeguards, these new suppliers effectively challenge, and possibly undermine, the non-proliferation regime. Transactions (usually of components) frequently are conducted clandestinely between NPT non-signatories.

European Atomic Energy Committee (EURATOM)

The European regional organisation that co-ordinates peaceful uses of nuclear energy, research and development, and sharing of scientific and technical information among member states. Most Western European countries are members.

Full-Scope Safeguards (FSS)

Requirement that non-nuclear-weapon states accept complete safeguards on special fissionable materials and source materials in all activities utilising peaceful nuclear technology (current and future). This amounts to a commitment to non-proliferation and adherence to IAEA safeguards. In some cases suppliers may request that a consumer become a party to the NPT. The only suppliers that currently adhere to FSS are Canada, the United States, Sweden and Australia. FSS have not been formally adopted by the Nuclear Suppliers Group's Guidelines.

Gas Centrifuge Enrichment or Centrifuge Isotope Enrichment

Process by which the lighter uranium-235 is separated from the heavier uranium-238 with high speed centrifuges. Uranium-238 is the isotope of natural uranium and is not weapons-grade material; however, plutonium is produced as a product of uranium-238 in reactors, and this is considered weapons-grade material. This technology is one of the two main forms of enrichment that is on the trigger list.

Gaseous Diffusion

Enrichment of uranium-235 through a method that forces uranium in gaseous form through porous barriers to induce separation of light molecules from heavy ones, producing slight enrichment of the uranium-235.

Group of 21 (G-21)

Neutral or non-aligned nations included in the Committee on Disarmament (CD). Includes Algeria, Cuba, Indonesia, Kenya, Sri Lanka, Venezuela, Iran, Peru, Zaire, Argentina, Morocco, Pakistan, Yugoslavia, Burma, India, Ethiopia, Nigeria, United Arab Republic, Sweden, Brazil and Mexico.

Group of 77 (G-77)

Group of developing countries; often referred to as a bloc or caucusing group within the international community; especially important in voting within international organisations, particularly on North-South issues. First became active at the UNCTAD conference in 1964. Membership currently consists of at least 120 Third World countries. It has been influential at NPT review conferences; for example, at the Second Review Conference the G-77 played a significant role in pressing for reform by nuclear-weapon states with regard to Article VI of the NPT.

Horizontal Proliferation

The spread of nuclear weapons to countries not already possessing them. Article III of the NPT commits signatories to forgo the acquisition of nuclear weapons. The rate of horizontal proliferation has not been as great as had been predicted and feared, and this may be a result in part of the NPT. According to the NPT, the criterion for defining whether proliferation has occurred is the testing of a nuclear device.

Implicit Nuclear Deterrent (Nuclear Ambiguity)

Strategy of maintaining ambiguity about one's nuclear capabilities and nuclear policy in order to deter other states from aggressive action. This strategy allows the country to avoid confronting the non-proliferation regime while at the same time accomplishing certain regional security goals. This strategy is just beginning to be understood as a basis for active diplomacy by threshold states. It is seen as useful for deterring a regional competitor from conventional aggression, as well as deterring its development of a nuclear potential.

Indian Nuclear Explosion

Occurring on May 18, 1974, this 'peaceful nuclear explosion' particularly shocked the nuclear suppliers, especially Canada which provided the CIRUS reactor from which material for the explosion came. The reactor had been provided in the early 1960s on the condition that it only be used for peaceful purposes; however, safeguard procedures were not implemented (for example, external inspection). India at no time agreed that 'peaceful nuclear explosions' were to be excluded as a basis for the provision of the CIRUS reactor. The reactor also contained heavy water provided by the United States and this was subject to peaceful-uses-only provisions. In response to this event, Canada revised safeguards in 1974, and in 1976 went to full-scope safeguards (FSS). This meant that Canadian suppliers could deal only with NNWS that had ratified the NPT or those that would accept FSS on their entire nuclear programmes. Canada still maintains that the Indian CIRUS reactor can be used only for peaceful purposes, as understood in the original agreement. The United States tightened its nuclear export guidelines in 1978 with the Nuclear Non-Proliferation Act, and the Nuclear Suppliers Group (London Club) began meeting in late 1974 to outline guidelines for control of nuclear technology.

INFCIRC 66 (Rev. 2)

IAEA information circular (1965) that details the agency's safeguards system; was provisionally extended in 1966 and 1968. The 1965 safeguards covered mainly the safeguarding of reactors; this was extended in the later years to cover reprocessing, fuel conversion and fabrication plants. IAEA document Gov. 1621 clarified the duration and termination of safeguards agreements as outlined in INFCIRC 66. The document and its attempt at early safeguards have been criticised for its generality and lack of comprehensiveness (for example, failure to explicitly ban all acquisition of nuclear explosive devices and to safeguard fissile material, enrichment plants and heavy water production plants). As an early model, however, it did provide some substance for later NPT safeguards agreements.

INFCIRC 153

IAEA information circular (1971) titled 'The Structure and Content of Agreements Between the Agency and States Required in Connection with the Treaty on the Non-Proliferation of Nuclear Weapons'. This agreement was used by the IAEA to negotiate safeguards agreements between the IAEA and non-nuclear-weapon states that are parties to the NPT. It has been considered a model NPT safeguards agreement, operating at both the IAEA and the national level to control nuclear material. Still, some have criticised the model for focusing too much on nuclear material and too little on containment and surveillance.

INFCIRC 209

See Zangger Committee Trigger List.

INFCIRC 254 (London Guidelines)

IAEA information circular outlining the guidelines for nuclear transfers agreed to by the Nuclear Suppliers Group in September 1977. See Nuclear Suppliers Group.

International Atomic Energy Association (IAEA)

First proposed by United States President Eisenhower in his Atoms for Peace plan, the IAEA is an autonomous inter-governmental organisation whose goals are to promote the peaceful uses of nuclear energy, particularly for developing nations, and to discourage the application of nuclear technology to military procedures; includes design review of nuclear plants (existing and planned), recording of nuclear material received and used, receiving reports from nuclear plants and conducting inspections. One difficulty has been the fact that only 40 non-nuclear states that have signed the NPT also have entered into a safeguards agreement with the IAEA. Besides overseeing safeguards, the IAEA is involved in supporting research, conferences and training programmes: for example, the Committee on Assurances of Supply; International Nuclear Information System; Operational Safety Review Team missions (OSART); Incident Reporting System (IRS); and the International Safety Advisory Group (INSAG).

International Nuclear Fuel Cycle Evaluation (INFCE)

Committee proposed by United States President Carter in 1977. Brought together nuclear suppliers and consumers to discuss the provision of nuclear fuel and how to reduce the likelihood of diversion of nuclear material and technology. The evaluation involved 46 countries and five international organisations that participated in various working groups over a two-year period. Both the technical and institutional problems of control were studied, with the final report released in 1980. One of the conclusions reached was that many of the problems involving illicit acquisition were political and could not be addressed at the technological level alone. For example, specific stages of a fuel cycle could not be identified as more or less conducive to proliferation risk. The evaluation was an attempt to regain some degree of consensus on nuclear issues.

Irish Resolution

Introduction of the non-proliferation concept at the United Nations by Ireland in 1961. Ireland played a prominent role in the early years of the non-proliferation debate.

Latent Proliferation

The tendency of upwardly mobile states in the international system to acquire gradually a nuclear weapon capability while avoiding high-risk situations that might lead them into conflict because of the development of a nuclear potential. To be distinguished from imminent proliferation, in which it is feared that development of nuclear forces will take place quickly, and active proliferation, which is the equivalent of vertical proliferation.

Light Water Reactor

Reactor that uses normal water (H_2O) as a coolant. Heat is removed from fissioning uranium through a steam turbine. This is the most common type of power reactor. The spent fuel contains plutonium that could be processed to a weapons-grade level.

London Club

See Nuclear Suppliers Group.

Military or Weapons-Grade Fissionable Material

High quality, refined fissionable material (for example, 93 per cent fissile content for plutonium).

Mixed Fuel Cycles

Non-nuclear-weapon states having both safeguarded and unsafeguarded nuclear installations or materials. This situation may contribute to regional tensions as well as make the IAEA's work of achieving comprehensive safeguards more difficult.

Neutral and Non-Aligned (NNA)

Those nations actively refusing to align themselves militarily or politically with the Soviet bloc or the Western nations. Number is currently around 95.

Non-Proliferation Regime

The principles, norms and rules evidenced in a variety of organisations and policies that reinforce non-proliferation; for example, the NPT, the NPT-FSS system, the Zangger Committee trigger list, NSG Guidelines, national export policies, the IAEA statute and safeguards, and regional safeguards (for example, Brazil and Argentina's proposals for mutual inspections of nuclear facilities) can be viewed as part of the non-proliferation regime.

NPT Amendment Procedure

Amendment of the NPT requires approval of all the nuclear-weapon states that are parties, all states on the IAEA Board of Governors and the majority of other parties to the treaty.

Nth Countries

The unknown and potential candidates to the nuclear club.

Nuclear Chain Reaction

Fear that the nuclearisation of one state would lead to proliferation in many states. Although between eight and 15 non-nuclear-weapon states are now thought to be nuclear-capable, the chain reaction phenomenon does not appear to have occurred.

Nuclear Co-operation Networks

Civilian and inter-state networks that encourage co-operation for the purposes of providing nuclear technology and materials. May involve as many as 70 actors and the signing of hundreds of nuclear co-operation agreements. From the mid-1950s to the mid-1960s, these networks were dominated by the Soviet Union and the United States. However, in the 1960s some European states came to play a more prominent role, and more recently it seems that some Third World states (Brazil, Argentina, India) may become more involved in civilian nuclear networks.

Nuclear Fuel Cycle

The process involved in making uranium accessible for energy purposes. This proceeds through the following stages:

1. mining – extraction of uranium ore;
2. enrichment – 2 to 3 per cent for fuel, higher for weapons;
3. fuel fabrication – formation into pellets of uranium dioxide or plutonium dioxide;
4. loading and unloading of fuel into reactors;
5. reprocessing – plutonium and uranium separated from spent fuel rods; and
6. radioactive waste management – storage of wastes from reprocessing that remain radioactive for extended periods.

Attempts to prevent states from acquiring full national fuel cycles (that is, capability to carry out all procedures in the cycle) is one way of impeding proliferation.

Nuclear-Weapon States (NWS) or 'Nuclear Club'

Those states currently known to possess nuclear weapons: United States (1945), Soviet Union (1949), United Kingdom (1952), France (1960), China (1964). Threshold states, which have nuclear technology and a possible nuclear weapon capability, are not included in this designation. An NWS is defined in Article IX (3) of the NPT as a state that has 'manufactured and exploded a nuclear weapon or other nuclear explosive device prior to 1 January 1967'.

Nuclear Suppliers Group (NSG) or London Club

Fifteen of the major nuclear suppliers began meeting in late 1974 with the purpose of delineating guidelines to control the proliferation of nuclear technology having potential weapons applications. Members included the United States, Soviet Union, Canada, the United Kingdom, France, Japan and the Federal Republic of Germany. Resulted in the 1978 *NSG Guidelines* outlining safeguards and export controls on materials and technology, and an agreement to provide the latter only if the customer nations agreed to apply IAEA safeguards. Can be contrasted with the *Western Supplier Group* (United States, United Kingdom, Canada, South Africa, Belgium, France, Portugal and Australia), which was established in 1954, and the *Club of Five* (France, Canada, South Africa, Australia and the Rio Tinto Zinc Company), which was established in 1972, whose main concerns were with marketing uranium rather than with proliferation issues.

Nuclear-Weapon-Free Zone (NWFZ)

Zones prohibiting the manufacture, acquisition, use, storage, testing and usually transportation of nuclear weapons. Can be understood as an attempt to implement non-proliferation at the regional level. The Treaty of Tlatelolco (Latin America), the Outer Space Treaty, the Seabed Treaty, the Antarctic Treaty and the recently signed South Pacific Treaty specify the NWFZ currently in existence. An NWFZ has been proposed at various times for the Balkans, the Mediterranean, the Nordic countries, the Indian Ocean, the Middle East, Central Europe, Africa, the Adriatic and South East Asia. Current anti-nuclear movements also have pushed for application of the concept at the civic (municipal) level.

Osiraq Raid

The June 1981 Israeli bombing of the French-made and French-supplied Osiraq research reactor (Tammuz 1) located outside Baghdad. Although the plutonium-producing capacity of the Osiraq reactor was ambiguous and Iraq had thus far adhered to the NPT, the widely perceived intent of Iraq to acquire a nuclear weapon capability was sufficient for Israel to risk international censure in order to impede Iraqi nuclear development.

Peaceful Nuclear Explosion (PNE)

Nuclear explosions conducted for the purpose of testing nuclear capability but not assumed to have imminent military significance (that is, detonation does not have an immediate military purpose). India conducted a PNE in 1974, and Brazil and Argentina have claimed the right to conduct PNEs, although neither has done so to date.

Peaceful Uses Provision

Article IV of the NPT provides a guarantee of the provision of nuclear technology and material for peaceful purposes to all signatories in exchange for forgoing development of a nuclear weapon capability. Peaceful uses of atomic energy include application in areas of health care, nuclear medicine, biology, industry, agriculture, food processing, plant genetics, as well as provision of nuclear power. There is disagreement about PNEs under this rubric.

Proliferation Management

The concept of 'managing proliferation' has sometimes been discussed as an alternative to the current non-proliferation regime. This involves the acknowledgement that proliferation can and will occur, however undesirable, and asserts a need to develop ways to respond to it. Emphasis is on decision factors versus control of technical factors. Criticism has surrounded the fact that this is merely a change in methodology and will not effect the nature of proliferation.

Remote Continual Verification (Recover)

A new method of verification currently being explored by the IAEA; intended to supplement traditional on-site verification methods. It consists of a secure communication system that uses small computers and public telephone lines to verify status of safeguard devices.

Reprocessing

Treatment of spent reactor fuel that allows separation of plutonium, uranium and fission products.

Security Council Resolution 255

In 1968 assurance given by the NWS that they would assist any NPT NNWS should it be attacked or threatened by a nuclear attack. NNWS have since sought a legally binding assurance but have been unsuccessful.

Selective Proliferation

A term applied by many developing and Third World countries to describe the discriminatory situation whereby the nuclearisation of the Warsaw Pact and NATO countries is seen as acceptable, whereas the nuclearisation of all other NNWS is not.

Sensitive Technologies

New nuclear technologies with dual uses (that is, peaceful and weapons applications) that may threaten the non-proliferation regime in the future. These include advances in the uranium-enrichment field; development of directly-usable weapons materials; and centrifuge, chemical and laser separation methods. Some efforts have been made to control these new technologies; for example, the Hexapartite Safeguards Project dealt with international safeguards for gas centrifuge enrichment facilities.

Spent Fuel

Fuel removed from a reactor after use in generating power. Contains radioactive waste and unburned plutonium and uranium.

Threshold States

Near-nuclear states or nuclear candidates believed to be nuclear-weapon capable within certain periods if a decision were made to 'go nuclear'. These states include: India (1974 PNE); Pakistan (suspected of beginning development in 1972); Israel (assumed to have clear motivation and capability); South Africa (suspicion of a PNE); Taiwan and South Korea (currently constrained by United States pressure); Iraq, Iran, Libya (all suspected of intentions but without clear capability); Brazil and Argentina (may have technology but intentions are currently unclear); Egypt, Japan, the FRG, Italy (assumed to have technology and materials but currently do not appear to have intentions).

Unified Inventory Concept

Proposal in early 1970s that would have required the IAEA and all NPT states to establish a single record of all nuclear materials subject to safeguards in each state and to keep an updated inventory of this. Ultimately, it was hoped that universally acceptable rules would cover nuclear materials, equipment, facilities, technology and services; no agreement reached.

United Nations Conference on the Peaceful Uses of Atomic Energy

The first substantive attempt by the United States, the Soviet Union and other United Nations members to consider the advantage for all of the peaceful uses of the atom (1955).

United Nations Atomic Energy Commission (UNAEC)

The first attempt to initiate a non-proliferation regime; the impetus to form this agency was provided by Canada, the United States and the United Kingdom. Formally declared November 1945 by *The Agreed Declaration of 1945*, the UNAEC was established in 1946 and though short-lived was the precursor to the IAEA.

United States Nuclear Non-Proliferation Act (NNPA)

This 1978 act represented one of the strongest efforts in the United States to outline a uniform set of international standards for nuclear exports and the implementation of full-scope safeguards. However, it also had the converse effect of impairing United States ability to give countries incentive for complying with non-proliferation goals. The United States upgraded its guidelines in 1984 and 1985 by placing controls on the export of reprocessing technology.

Uranium Conversion or Enrichment

Process whereby a percentage of the fissionable isotope uranium-235 is increased above that of natural uranium. There are two main types of enrichment, the gaseous diffusion method and the gas centrifuge method. Uranium-235 occurs at only a 0.7 per cent level in natural uranium; it must be enriched to 3 per cent for fuel and 90 per cent for weapons-grade material.

Vertical Proliferation

Vertical or active proliferation is the development and deployment of nuclear weapons, arsenals, and corresponding systems and technology by nuclear-weapon states. Article VI of the NPT is intended to control vertical proliferation by committing the nuclear powers to make continuous efforts towards arms control and disarmament. This is seen by the NNWS as an important section of the NPT and part of the 'bargain' by which these states agreed to forgo nuclear weapons.

Zangger Committee Trigger List

In the early 1970s nuclear suppliers made a first effort to outline a multilateral agreement to control the opportunities for nuclear proliferation. This resulted in an IAEA document identifying those nuclear items likely to be of use in weapons development and outlined appropriate export controls. Members of the Zangger Committee included Australia, Austria, Belgium, Canada, Czechoslovakia, Denmark, Finland, the Federal Republic of Germany, the Democratic Republic of Germany, Ireland, Italy, Japan, Luxembourg, the Netherlands, Norway, Poland, Sweden, Switzerland, the United Kingdom, the United States, the Soviet Union and South Africa. The Zangger Committee trigger list was published in IAEA document INFCIRC 209.

II. TREATIES

Antarctic Treaty (1959)

Prohibits the militarisation of the Antarctic or its use for nuclear testing and explosions, and dumping of radioactive wastes; inspection rights are guaranteed; territorial claims are not allowed; and parties are encouraged to settle disputes peacefully and co-operate for scientific purposes. Signed by the Soviet Union, United States, New Zealand, Norway, South Africa, Japan, France, Chile, Argentina, Australia, Belgium and the United Kingdom.

Outer Space Treaty (1967)

The first treaty to apply rules of international law to outer space; had 84 signatories in 1967. Prohibits the placement of nuclear weapons or other weapons of mass destruction on celestial bodies, and bans military bases and manoeuvres on the same; encourages the peaceful and co-operative use of space by all nations and forbids claims of sovereignty.

Partial or Limited Test Ban Treaty (PTB) (1963)

Prohibits the testing of nuclear weapons in the atmosphere, as well as in outer space and underwater. Includes 100 signatories; non-signatories include France and China. The latter both occasionally still conduct atmospheric tests. The PTB was largely a 1960s response to environmental concerns about radioactive fallout. It has been successful in addressing this issue but not the issue of vertical proliferation. Underground nuclear tests have increased in frequency since the PTB.

Peaceful Nuclear Explosion Treaty (PNE) (1976)

United States/Soviet Union agreement that limits peaceful nuclear explosions to 150kt for individual explosions and 1500kt for multiple explosions. Not ratified by the United States; however, both countries have observed terms.

Seabed Treaty (1971)

Forbids the placement of nuclear weapons or other weapons of mass destruction outside each state's 12-mile territorial waters. Most nations have signed the treaty; non-signatories include France and China. Some criticism has involved the argument that placement should have been forbidden in all the oceans' seabeds, including those within 12-mile territorial waters.

South Pacific Nuclear-Free Zone Treaty (1985)

Treaty signed by eight Pacific nations (Australia, New Zealand and a number of smaller island nations) declaring the South Pacific a nuclear-free zone. The treaty prohibits the use or testing of nuclear weapons, dumping of nuclear waste, the manufacture, acquisition or receipt of nuclear explosive devices, the exportation of nuclear material without safeguards, and the stationing of nuclear weapons in the region. The signatories intend to appeal to the United States, France and the United Kingdom to abide by the terms of the treaty.

Strategic Arms Limitation Talks (SALT I) (1972)

Negotiations carried out from 1969-72 between the United States and Soviet Union to limit strategic nuclear weapons and their delivery systems as well as defensive systems. Signing of SALT I officially ushered in an era of detente, restricted ABM systems, and placed ceilings on offensive nuclear systems (missile launchers and delivery systems). These negotiations, along with progress on the signing of the Seabed Treaty (1971) and the Threshold Test Ban Agreement (1974), contributed to an optimism about nuclear-weapon states and their fulfilment of obligations to carry out 'good faith negotiations' as outlined in Article VI of the NPT. This sentiment continued to prevail at the First NPT Review Conference in 1975.

Strategic Arms Limitation Talks (SALT II) (1979)

Negotiations conducted between 1974 and 1979 between the United States and Soviet Union to reduce levels of strategic delivery vehicles and to place ceilings on MIRVed strategic missiles. The United States Congress refused to ratify the treaty which was signed by Brezhnev and Carter in 1979. This fact, along with the lack of development of arms control in other areas, led to a negative atmosphere at the Second NPT Review Conference in 1980. Non-nuclear-weapon states that were party to the NPT saw the nuclear-weapon states reneging on their obligation to conduct negotiations to reduce nuclear weapons, as outlined in Article VI of the NPT. The dissatisfaction was so great at the Review Conference that a deadlock ensued about agreement on a Final Declaration.

Threshold Test Ban Treaty (1974)

Bilateral agreement between the United States and Soviet Union prohibiting the underground testing of nuclear weapons exceeding 150kt. Includes provision for exchange of information on technical data for verification of testing. Not ratified by United States; however, both countries have observed terms.

Treaty of Tlatelolco (1967)

A regional non-proliferation treaty that bans the testing, use, manufacture, production and acquisition of nuclear weapons by Latin American countries. As well, the receipt, storage, installation or deployment of nuclear weapons is prohibited. The treaty is also applicable to all states that have possessions in the region (that is, the United States, the United Kingdom, France). Cuba has refused to sign the treaty, and there are questions about interpretations of the treaty by Brazil, Argentina and Chile.

Treaty on the Non-Proliferation of Nuclear Weapons (NPT) (1968)

Regarded as the most significant international agreement controlling nuclear arms because the treaty attempts to control horizontal proliferation (Article III), vertical proliferation (Article VI) and, at the same time, gives non-nuclear countries a guarantee of complete and safeguarded access to nuclear materials and technology for peaceful purposes (Article IV). It entered into force in 1970. Review Conferences take place every five years. At the First Review Conference in 1975, there were 96 parties to the treaty; at the Second Review Conference in 1980 there were 114 parties; and at the Third Review Conference in 1985 there were 130 parties to the treaty. Non-signatories include Argentina, Brazil, France, China, Israel, India, Pakistan and South Africa.

CONTRIBUTORS

Brenner, M.   Associate Professor, Graduate School of Public and International Affairs, University of Pittsburgh; author of, among others, *Nuclear Power and Non-Proliferation* and *The Politics of International Monetary Reform*.

Dewitt, D.B.   Associate Professor, Department of Political Science; Co-ordinator, Regional Conflict Studies, Research Programme in Strategic Studies, York University, Toronto; author or co-author of publications on international conflict and on Canadian foreign policy, including *Canada as a Principal Power*, and co-editor of *The Middle East at the Crossroads* and *Conflict Management in the Middle East* (forthcoming).

Dunn, L.   Assistant Director for Nuclear and Weapons Control of the United States Arms Control and Disarmament Agency; Ambassador to the 1985 Third Review Conference of the NPT; author of *Controlling the Bomb: Nuclear Proliferation in the 1980s* and many articles on international security and arms control.

Fischer, D.A.V.   Consultant on nuclear proliferation matters, Cambridge, United Kingdom; former Assistant Director-General, IAEA; co-author of *Safeguarding the Atom* and author of articles on safeguards, the NPT and the IAEA.

Freier, S.   Department of Physics, Weizmann Institute of Science, Tel-Aviv; currently Chairman, Israel Pugwash Group and Pugwash Council member and Chairman, Presidential Council for Science Policy; former Director-General, Israel Atomic Energy Commission.

271

Ing, S.　　　　Policy Analyst, Operational Research and Analysis Establishment, Department of National Defence, Ottawa.

Jennekens, J.H.　President, Atomic Energy Control Board of Canada, Chairman of the IAEA's Standing Advisory Group on Safeguards Implementation and member of the IAEA's Scientific Advisory Committee.

Kapur, A.　　　Professor, Department of Political Science, University of Waterloo; author of *International Nuclear Proliferation* and *India's Nuclear Option* and articles on nuclear proliferation in the developing world.

Keeley, J.　　　Assistant Professor, Department of Political Science, University of Calgary; co-editor, *Nuclear Exports and World Politics*, and author of articles and chapters on nuclear proliferation and Canada-United States relations.

MacOwan, W.　Vice-Chairman, Corporate Development, Howden Group Canada Limited; Director and Past Chairman, Canadian Nuclear Association.

Marwah, O.　　Visiting Professor, Jawaharlal Nehru University, New Delhi and Professor, The Graduate Institute of International Studies, Geneva; co-author of *Nuclear Power in Developing Countries* and author of articles on nuclear proliferation and on Indian defence policy.

Marín Bosch, M.　Ambassador and Deputy Permanent Representative of Mexico to the United Nations, New York; former Chef de Cabinet of the Mexican Foreign Ministry; author of several books and articles on disarmament and Mexican foreign policy and history.

Porter, D.   Vice-President, International Affairs, Westinghouse Electric Corporation, Washington, D.C.; former United States Permanent Representative to the IAEA.

Roche, D.C.   Ambassador for Disarmament, Department of External Affairs, Ottawa; former Member of Parliament; author of many books and articles on disarmament, development and international affairs.

Shaker, M.   Ambassador, Permanent Mission of the Arab Republic of Egypt to the United Nations, New York; President, Third Review Conference of the Parties to the Treaty on the Non-Proliferation of Nuclear Weapons; author of books and articles on nuclear non-proliferation.

Thompson, S.   Special Assistant to Richard Kennedy, Ambassador at Large for Nuclear Non-Proliferation and Representative to the IAEA, Washington, D.C.

CONFERENCE PARTICIPANTS

Beckett, W.M.   Director, Nuclear and Arms Control Policy, Department of National Defence, Ottawa.

Bell, G.   President, Canadian Institute of Strategic Studies, Toronto.

Braun, A.   Associate Professor, Department of Political Science, University of Toronto.

Byers, R.B.   Director, Research Programme in Strategic Studies; Associate Professor, Department of Political Science, York University, Toronto.

Chistoff, O.A.   Deputy Director, Arms Control and Disarmament Division, Department of External Affairs, Ottawa.

Duncan, M.   Head, Office of Safeguards and Physical Security, Atomic Energy Control Board, Ottawa.

Goldman, I.   Policy Analyst, Meridian Corporation, Falls Church, Virginia.

Grinius, M.   Division of Arms Control and Disarmament, Nuclear Section, Department of External Affairs, Ottawa.

Haglund, D.   Associate Professor, Department of Political Studies; Director, Centre for International Studies, Queen's University, Kingston.

Harms, A.   Professor, Department of Engineering Physics, McMaster University, Hamilton.

Hewitt, J.   Professor, Department of Chemical Engineering, University of Toronto.

Holsti, K.J.   Professor and Chairman, Department of Political Science, University of British Columbia, Vancouver.

Ignatieff, G.   Chancellor, University of Toronto; former Canadian Permanent Representative of Canada to the United Nations.

Jiadong, Q.   Ambassador, Delegation of the People's Republic of China to the Conference on Disarmament, Geneva.

Kuramochi, T.   Division of Science and Technology, Government of Japan.

Lamb, J.   Executive Director, Canadian Centre for Arms Control and Disarmament, Ottawa.

Lanphier, M.   Professor, Institute for Social Research, York University, Toronto.

Leyton-Brown, D.   Associate Director, Research Programme in Strategic Studies and Associate Professor, Department of Political Science, York University, Toronto.

MacDonald, B.   Executive Director, Canadian Institute of Strategic Studies, Toronto.

McManus, J.G.   Director, Division of Operations C, International Atomic Energy Agency, Vienna.

Merlin, H.   Advisor, Uranium and Nuclear Energy Branch, Department of Energy, Mines and Resources, Ottawa.

Nacht, M.   Associate Professor, School of Public Affairs, University of Maryland, College Park.

Newcombe, H.   Peace Research Institute, Dundas.

Pearson, G.   Executive Director, Canadian Institute for International Peace and Security, Ottawa; former Canadian Ambassador to the USSR and Advisor on Arms Control and Disarmament.

Paul, D.   Professor, Department of Physics, University of Toronto.

Pulit, F.J.   Ambassador of Argentina, Ottawa.

Rapoport, A.   Professor of Peace Studies, University of Toronto.

Reford, R.   President, Reford-McCandless International Consultants Corporation, Toronto; Chairman, United Nations Association of Canada.

Rubin, N.   Energy Probe Research Foundation, Toronto.

Ross, D.   Research Associate, Institute of International Relations, University of British Columbia, Vancouver.

Runnalls, O.J.C.   Chairman, Centre for Nuclear Engineering, University of Toronto.

Sanders, B.   Director, Information and Studies Branch, Department for Disarmament Affairs, United Nations, New York; Secretary-General of the Third Review Conference of the Parties to the Treaty on the Non-Proliferation of Nuclear Weapons.

Smith, G.   Director, Arms Control and Disarmament Division, Department of External Affairs, Ottawa.

Spiers, J.   Atomic Energy Canada, Chalk River.

Thompson, G.   Co-ordinator, Proliferation Reform Project, Institute for Resource and Security Studies, Cambridge, Massachussetts.

Von Riekhoff, H. Professor and Chairman, Department of Political Science, Carleton University, Ottawa.

Wright, G. Vice-President, Donner Canadian Foundation, Toronto.

INDEX